- Go to **awmi.net/sg439** to download PDFs of the following resources for each lesson in this study guide:
    - Outlines
    - Discipleship Questions
    - Scriptures
- Share as many copies as you'd like.
- These documents are not for resale.

Lessons from DAVID

HOW TO BE A GIANT KILLER

STUDY GUIDE

Andrew Wommack

Unless otherwise indicated, all Scripture quotations are taken from the *King James Version* of the Bible.

The author has emphasized some words in Scripture quotations with underline.

Lessons from David Study Guide
ISBN 13: 978-1-59548-222-8
eBook ISBN 13: 978-1-68031-932-3

Copyright © 2014 by Andrew Wommack Ministries Inc.
PO Box 3333
Colorado Springs CO 80934-3333

awmi.net

All rights reserved under International Copyright Law. Contents and/or cover may not be reproduced in whole or in part in any form without the express written consent of the Publisher.

Table of Contents

HOW TO USE YOUR STUDY GUIDE • VI

INTRODUCTION • VIII

Lesson 1.1
ACCEPT RESPONSIBILITY • 1

Lesson 1.2
ACCEPT RESPONSIBILITY • 15

Lesson 2
DO YOU QUALIFY? • 31

Lesson 3.1
OBEDIENCE IS BETTER • 45

Lesson 3.2
OBEDIENCE IS BETTER • 61

Lesson 4
MOVE ON! • 73

Lesson 5
A HEART FOR GOD • 91

Lesson 6.1
SEEING THROUGH THE COVENANT • 113

Lesson 6.2
SEEING THROUGH THE COVENANT • 127

Lesson 7
OVERCOMING CRITICISM • 139

Lesson 8.1
A CONFIDENT TESTIMONY • 161

Lesson 8.2
A CONFIDENT TESTIMONY • 173

Lesson 9.1
THE POWER OF GOD • 187

Lesson 9.2
THE POWER OF GOD • 201

Lesson 10
ENCOURAGE YOURSELF IN THE LORD • 213

Lesson 11
ACTIONS & THE HEART • 233

Lesson 12
"IT'S MY FAULT!" • 253

Lesson 13
A SNARE • 275

Lesson 14
A PURPOSE BIGGER THAN YOURSELF • 293

Lesson 15.1
FOLLOW GOD'S ORDER • 309

Lesson 15.2
FOLLOW GOD'S ORDER • 325

Lesson 16
THE DANGER OF PROSPERITY • 339

Lesson 17.1
"YOU ARE THE MAN!" • 357

Lesson 17.2
"YOU ARE THE MAN!" • 377

Lesson 18
THE ROOT OF ALL SIN • 391

Lesson 19
CONSEQUENCES • 411

CONCLUSION • 431

RECEIVE JESUS AS YOUR SAVIOR • 432

RECEIVE THE HOLY SPIRIT • 433

RECOMMENDED MATERIALS • 434

How to Use Your Study Guide

Whether you are teaching a class, leading a small group, discipling an individual, or studying on your own, this study guide is designed for you! Here's how it works:

Each Lesson consists of the **Lesson** text, **Outline**, **Teacher's Guide**, **Discipleship Questions**, **Answer Key**, and **Scriptures**—some of which have been divided into sections. Some studies also have additional information.

Outline for Group Study:
I. If possible, briefly review the previous study by going over the **Answer Key/Teacher's Guide** answers for the **Discipleship Questions/Teacher's Guide** questions.

II. Read the current **Lesson** text or **Teacher's Guide** aloud (or section—e.g., 1.1, 1.2, etc.).
   A. Be sure that each student has a copy of the **Outline**.
   B. While the **Lesson** text, **Teacher's Guide**, or section is being read, students should use their **Outlines** to follow along.

III. Once the **Lesson** text, **Teacher's Guide**, or section is read, facilitate discussion and study using the **Discipleship Questions/Teacher's Guide** questions (all questions are the same).
   A. Read aloud one question at a time.
   B. The group should use their **Outlines** to assist them in answering the questions.
   C. Have them read aloud each specifically mentioned scripture before answering the question.
   D. Discuss the answer/point from the **Lesson** text, as desired.
   E. As much as possible, keep the discussion centered on the scriptures and the **Lesson** text, **Teacher's Guide**, or section points at hand.
   F. Remember, the goal is understanding (Matt. 13:19).
   G. One individual should not dominate the discussion; instead, try to draw out the quieter ones for the group conversation.
   H. Repeat the process until all of the questions are discussed/answered.

Materials Needed:
   Study guide, Bible, and enough copies of the **Outline, Discipleship Questions**, and **Scriptures** for each student. (PDFs of the **Outlines, Discipleship Questions**, and **Scriptures** can be downloaded via the URL located on the first page of this study guide.)

Outline for Personal Study:
   I. Read the current **Lesson** text, **Teacher's Guide**, or section.
      A. Read additional information, if provided.
      B. Meditate on the given scriptures, as desired.
   II. Answer the corresponding **Discipleship Questions/Teacher's Guide** questions.
   III. Check your work with the **Answer Key/Teacher's Guide** answers.

Materials Needed:
   Study guide, Bible, and a writing utensil.

Introduction

Now all these things happened unto them for examples: and they are written for our admonition, upon whom the ends of the world are come.

1 CORINTHIANS 10:11

The stories of people in the Old Testament were recorded as examples for us today. God's Word plainly reveals both the good and the bad about such highly regarded individuals as Moses, Abraham, and Elijah. We're not only told how the Lord was able to move mightily in their lives but also how and why they failed. The purpose is to benefit you and me today.

Many people believe that the only way you can really learn something is through hard knocks. They think you have to experience your own hardships, situations, and circumstances. However, God wrote all of these things down in His Word so you and I wouldn't have to learn that way. We can learn through the experience of Bible characters—their successes and mistakes—instead. Personally, I've found this to be a much better way.

David's life is full of lessons for us today. In this book, we'll be exploring the differences between David, Saul, and Absalom. We'll see the importance of David's heart attitudes and relationship with God. We'll also reflect on the decisions that led to his downfall and restoration.

It doesn't matter if you're succeeding in your calling, you're just starting out, or you've failed miserably. David's life will encourage and inspire you to avoid temptation, trust God (even after you've fallen), and keep your heart sensitive to Him. The giants in your life won't stand a chance as these **Lessons from David** become your very own!

Accept Responsibility

The early part of David's life was closely woven together with Saul's. Therefore, we can't really look into the life of David without first understanding some things about Saul.

Saul was…

…a choice young man, and a goodly: and there was not among the children of Israel a goodlier person than he: from his shoulders and upward he was higher than any of the people.

1 SAMUEL 9:2

The tallest man in Israel only came up to his shoulders. So, for an Israelite, Saul was like a giant. However, he was also a very humble man. He started off being very little in his own eyes (1 Sam. 9:21), so the Lord chose him and put him over the nation of Israel as king.

During those first two or three years, Saul really did seek God. The Lord wrought some major deliverances through him and solidified the kingdom under him. The people rallied to Saul, and he was established as king.

STRANGE FIRE

In 1 Samuel 13, Saul had assembled the troops in preparation for battle with the Philistines. Samuel, the prophet, had instructed Saul to wait seven days until he came. When he arrived, Samuel was to offer a sacrifice so the army of Israel would go into battle with God's blessing.

And he [Saul] tarried seven days, according to the set time that Samuel had appointed: but Samuel came not to Gilgal; and the people were scattered from him. [9] And Saul said, Bring hither a burnt offering to me, and peace offerings. And he offered the burnt offering. [10] And it came to pass, that as soon as he had made an end of offering the burnt offering, behold, Samuel came; and Saul went out to meet him, that he might salute him.

1 SAMUEL 13:8-10, BRACKETS MINE

Saul offered this sacrifice contrary to the instructions of God. The Law prescribed that only priests could offer these sacrifices and petition the Lord like this. As a king, Saul stepped out of his position. He was a secular government official, not a priest.

However, even a priest had to do it correctly. Here is an example that shows this:

And Nadab and Abihu, the sons of Aaron [priests], took either of them his censer, and put fire therein, and put incense thereon, and offered strange fire before the LORD, which he commanded them not. [2] And there went out fire from the LORD, and devoured them, and they died before the LORD.

LEVITICUS 10:1-2, BRACKETS MINE

As priests, Nadab and Abihu were qualified to offer a sacrifice, but they didn't follow the proper order. Since they didn't do it the way the Lord had prescribed, fire came out and God struck them dead. It was very strict under the Old Testament Law. Even if you were a priest, you had to do it exactly the right way. Therefore, this example from Leviticus shows why this was a major sin on Saul's part.

EXCUSES, EXCUSES

As soon as Saul finished offering the sacrifice, Samuel showed up (1 Sam. 13:10).

And Samuel said, What hast thou done? And Saul said, Because I saw that the people were scattered from me, and that thou camest not within the days appointed, and that the Philistines gathered themselves together at Michmash; [12] Therefore said I, The Philistines will come down now upon me to Gilgal, and I have not made supplication unto the LORD: I forced myself therefore, and offered a burnt offering.

1 SAMUEL 13:11-12

Samuel reproved Saul for what he had done, and asked, "Why did you do it?" Instead of humbling himself and saying, "I was wrong. Please forgive me," Saul immediately answered, "The people were beginning to leave me." Saul was ever a people pleaser. Saul was insecure and dependent on people's approval. However, he tried to spiritualize it by saying, "I had to offer this sacrifice. I just couldn't go into battle without offering my sacrifice!" That may have been the custom, and to some degree it may have been valid, but Saul was just using this as an excuse.

Saul wasn't seeking God with all his heart. We can see this very clearly by the Lord's reaction. If this had been just a mistake—a miscalculation—God wouldn't have responded to Saul the way He did. But the Lord became very upset with Saul and brought a severe punishment upon him. The Lord knew his heart (1 Sam. 16:7). This shows that Saul knew exactly what he was doing. Yet here he was, trying to justify himself.

This is a common practice. Instead of just admitting, "I blew it. Please forgive me," most people try to excuse themselves and shift the blame.

"IT'S MY FAULT, LORD"

In stark contrast to Saul, David didn't do that. He never blamed anyone else for his failures. He always took responsibility and admitted, "It's my fault, Lord."

When David numbered the people, God became very angry (2 Sam. 24). After 70,000 Israelites died, the angel executing this judgment was about to enter Jerusalem. David fell on his face before the Lord and cried out, saying:

> *Lo, I have sinned, and I have done wickedly: but these sheep, what have they done? let thine hand, I pray thee, be against me, and against my father's house.*
> **2 SAMUEL 24:17**

David didn't try to place the blame on other people, saying, "It's their fault. They made me do it!" No, he took responsibility and shouldered the blame himself. This is one of the character traits that made David a man after God's own heart (1 Sam. 13:14).

VICTIM OR VICTOR?

David made some serious mistakes. When the Bible talks about having a pure heart—a perfect heart—it doesn't mean you never sin. But when you do sin, how do you respond? When you make a mistake, do you blame other people? Are you someone who refuses to accept the truth that it's your fault that you're in the mess you're in? Do you always blame things on the past, your dysfunctional family, etc.? Are you a victim or a victor?

This victim attitude is very common in our society. It's an attempt to dodge responsibility and blame other people. However, this was Saul's attitude. People with this attitude won't survive, be blessed, or reach their full potential. *If you want to be a person after God's own heart, take a lesson from David and start accepting responsibility when you're wrong. Stop making excuses and blaming others.* Be a victor, not a victim!

I pray that the Holy Spirit will quicken this truth to you and help you apply it to your situation. If you haven't accepted your fault and you're still blaming everything and everyone else, you need to get out of that. You need to accept responsibility. Why is this so important? It's only when you accept your responsibility that you're put in control and can change things. *If other people and circumstances are what have made you the mess that you are, then you can never change.*

There are many things you can't change. You can't change whom you were born to, the color of your skin, where you grew up, other people, etc. There are many circumstances and aspects of your environment that you have absolutely no control over. However, if you will accept responsibility and say, "Regardless of what's been done to me, it's the way I have responded to it that has made me the way I am. It's my fault, Lord. Please forgive me," then you can change you. *You are the only one you can change.* And in order to stop being a victim and start being a victor, you must accept responsibility for your own messes!

Outline

I. We can't really look into the life of David without first understanding some things about Saul.
   A. Saul was a very humble man who started off being little in his own eyes (1 Sam. 9:2 and 21), so the Lord chose him over the nation of Israel as king.
      i. During those first two or three years of his kingship, Saul really did seek God.
      ii. The Lord wrought some major deliverances through him and solidified the kingdom under him.
   B. In 1 Samuel 13, Saul offered a sacrifice contrary to the instructions of God:

   And he [Saul] tarried seven days, according to the set time that Samuel had appointed: but Samuel came not to Gilgal; and the people were scattered from him. [9] And Saul said, Bring hither a burnt offering to me, and peace offerings. And he offered the burnt offering. [10] And it came to pass, that as soon as he had made an end of offering the burnt offering, behold, Samuel came; and Saul went out to meet him, that he might salute him.
   1 SAMUEL 13:8-10, BRACKETS MINE

   C. The Law prescribed that only priests could offer these sacrifices and petition the Lord like this (Lev. 10:1-2); therefore, as a secular government official, this was a major sin on Saul's part.
   D. When Samuel reproved him for what he had done, Saul, ever a people pleaser, tried to justify himself (1 Sam. 13:11-12).
   E. This is a common practice today—most people try to excuse themselves and shift the blame.

II. In stark contrast to Saul, David didn't do that—he never blamed anyone else for his failures.
   A. He always took responsibility, saying:

   Lo, I have sinned, and I have done wickedly: but these sheep, what have they done? let thine hand, I pray thee, be against me, and against my father's house.
   2 SAMUEL 24:17

   B. This character trait made David a man after God's own heart (1 Sam. 13:14).
      i. When the Bible talks about having a pure heart—a perfect heart—it doesn't mean you never sin.
   C. Are you someone who refuses to accept the truth that it's your fault that you're in the mess you're in?
      i. A victim's attitude is a common attempt to dodge responsibility and blame others, like Saul did.

ii. People with this attitude won't survive, be blessed, or reach their full potential.
iii. However, if you will accept responsibility, then you can change you.

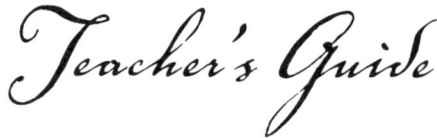

1. We can't really look into the life of David without first understanding some things about Saul. Saul was a very humble man who started off being little in his own eyes (1 Sam. 9:2 and 21), so the Lord chose him over the nation of Israel as king. During those first two or three years of his kingship, Saul really did seek God. The Lord wrought some major deliverances through him and solidified the kingdom under him. However, in 1 Samuel 13, Saul offered a sacrifice contrary to the instructions of God:

> *And he [Saul] tarried seven days, according to the set time that Samuel had appointed: but Samuel came not to Gilgal; and the people were scattered from him. [9] And Saul said, Bring hither a burnt offering to me, and peace offerings. And he offered the burnt offering. [10] And it came to pass, that as soon as he had made an end of offering the burnt offering, behold, Samuel came; and Saul went out to meet him, that he might salute him.*
>
> **1 SAMUEL 13:8-10, BRACKETS MINE**

The Law prescribed that only priests could offer these sacrifices and petition the Lord like this (Lev. 10:1-2); therefore, as a secular government official, this was a major sin on Saul's part. When Samuel reproved him for what he had done, Saul, ever a people pleaser, tried to justify himself (1 Sam. 13:11-12). This is a common practice today—most people try to excuse themselves and shift the blame.

1a. True or false: It is important to understand the life of Saul before you look into the life of David.
   True
1b. Why did the Lord choose Saul to be king over the national of Israel?
   Saul was a humble man who started off being little in his own eyes
1c. What was God able to do through him when Saul was humble?
   Wrought [achieved] some major deliverances through him and He solidified the kingdom under him
1d. By Law, why could Saul *not* offer a sacrifice to the Lord?
   A. Saul was a government official
   B. Saul was a king
   C. The Law prescribed that only priests could
   D. All of the above
   E. None of the above
   D. All of the above
1e. When Samuel reproved Saul, Saul tried to _____ himself.
   Justify
1f. *Discussion question:* How was Saul's response to Samuel's reproof typical of people today?
   Discussion question

2. In stark contrast to Saul, David didn't do that—he never blamed anyone else for his failures. He always took responsibility, saying:

> *Lo, I have sinned, and I have done wickedly: but these sheep, what have they done? let thine hand, I pray thee, be against me, and against my father's house.*
>
> 2 SAMUEL 24:17

This character trait made David a man after God's own heart (1 Sam. 13:14). When the Bible talks about having a pure heart—a perfect heart—it doesn't mean we never sin. Do we refuse to accept the truth that it's our fault that we're in the mess we're in? A victim's attitude is a common attempt to dodge responsibility and blame others, like Saul did. People with this attitude won't survive, be blessed, or reach their full potential. However, if we will accept responsibility, then we can change us.

2a. True or false: David and Saul behaved in the same way when they were confronted with their mistakes.
False

2b. What character trait made David a man after God's own heart?
He always took responsibility

2c. Having a pure heart doesn't mean you _____ sin.
Never

2d. What kind of attitude do you have if you dodge responsibility and blame others?
   A. A sinner's attitude
   B. A victim's attitude
   C. A Los Angeles Dodgers' attitude
   D. An excellent attitude
   E. A normal attitude
B. A victim's attitude

2e. *Discussion question:* Why do you think people who dodge responsibility and blame others are never blessed and never reach their full potential?
Discussion question

Discipleship Questions

1. True or false: It is important to understand the life of Saul before you look into the life of David.

2. Why did the Lord choose Saul to be king over the national of Israel?
   _____
   _____
   _____

3. What was God able to do through him when Saul was humble?
   _____
   _____
   _____

4. By Law, why could Saul *not* offer a sacrifice to the Lord?
   A. Saul was a government official
   B. Saul was a king
   C. The Law prescribed that only priests could
   D. All of the above
   E. None of the above

5. When Samuel reproved Saul, Saul tried to _____ himself.

6. *Discussion question:* How was Saul's response to Samuel's reproof typical of people today?
   _____
   _____
   _____

7. True or false: David and Saul behaved in the same way when they were confronted with their mistakes.

8. What character trait made David a man after God's own heart?
   _____
   _____
   _____

9. Having a pure heart doesn't mean you _____ sin.

LESSONS FROM DAVID

10. What kind of attitude do you have if you dodge responsibility and blame others?
    A. A sinner's attitude
    B. A victim's attitude
    C. A Los Angeles Dodgers' attitude
    D. An excellent attitude
    E. A normal attitude

11. *Discussion question:* Why do you think people who dodge responsibility and blame others are never blessed and never reach their full potential?
_____
_____
_____

Answer Key

1. True
2. Saul was a humble man who started off being little in his own eyes
3. Wrought [achieved] some major deliverance through him and He solidified the kingdom under him
4. D. All of the above
5. Justify
6. *Discussion question*
7. False
8. He always took responsibility
9. Never
10. B. A victim's attitude
11. *Discussion question*

Scriptures

1 SAMUEL 9:2
And he had a son, whose name was Saul, a choice young man, and a goodly: and there was not among the children of Israel a goodlier person than he: from his shoulders and upward he was higher than any of the people.

1 SAMUEL 9:21
And Saul answered and said, Am not I a Benjamite, of the smallest of the tribes of Israel? and my family the least of all the families of the tribe of Benjamin? wherefore then speakest thou so to me?

1 SAMUEL 13:8-12
And he tarried seven days, according to the set time that Samuel had appointed: but Samuel came not to Gilgal; and the people were scattered from him. [9] And Saul said, Bring hither a burnt offering to me, and peace offerings. And he offered the burnt offering. [10] And it came to pass, that as soon as he had made an end of offering the burnt offering, behold, Samuel came; and Saul went out to meet him, that he might salute him [11] And Samuel said, What hast thou done? And Saul said, Because I saw that the people were scattered from me, and that thou camest not within the days appointed, and that the Philistines gathered themselves together at Michmash; [12] Therefore said I, The Philistines will come down now upon me to Gilgal, and I have not made supplication unto the Lord: I forced myself therefore, and offered a burnt offering.

LEVITICUS 10:1-2
And Nadab and Abihu, the sons of Aaron, took either of them his censer, and put fire therein, and put incense thereon, and offered strange fire before the Lord, which he commanded them not. [2] And there went out fire from the Lord, and devoured them, and they died before the Lord.

1 SAMUEL 16:7
But the Lord said unto Samuel, Look not on his countenance, or on the height of his stature; because I have refused him: for the Lord seeth not as man seeth; for man looketh on the outward appearance, but the Lord looketh on the heart.

2 SAMUEL 24:17
And David spake unto the Lord when he saw the angel that smote the people, and said, Lo, I have sinned, and I have done wickedly: but these sheep, what have they done? let thine hand, I pray thee, be against me, and against my father's house.

ACCEPT RESPONSIBILITY

1 SAMUEL 13:14

But now thy kingdom shall not continue: the Lord hath sought him a man after his own heart, and the Lord hath commanded him to be captain over his people, because thou hast not kept that which the Lord commanded thee.

Accept Responsibility

And Samuel said to Saul, Thou hast done foolishly.

1 SAMUEL 13:13A

Saul had disobeyed God. He tried to rationalize and explain it away saying, "The people made me do it. I had to offer this sacrifice because I didn't want to go to war without asking God's favor." Saul had a million excuses!

You can try to make it look good, but if you disobey God, you're foolish! It doesn't matter what you say, how you justify it, or what the extenuating circumstances are—it's wrong! There is no such thing as "situational ethics." There is right and wrong. You need to quit blaming somebody else and accept the fact that if you disobey God, you're foolish!

Thou hast done foolishly: thou hast not kept the commandment of the LORD thy God, which he commanded thee: for now would the LORD have established thy kingdom upon Israel for ever.

1 SAMUEL 13:13

This statement conflicts with many people's theology. Many folks think that since God knows the end from the beginning, He also controls everything that happens in between. Since God is all-knowing and all-powerful, they believe that only what He wills comes to pass on the earth.

GOD'S ORIGINAL PLAN

Applying these faulty assumptions to Saul, people would have to say, "God knew exactly who Saul was and what he would do. He knew that Saul was going to fail. Therefore, Saul was just a temporary pick in God's true plan. All along, the Lord planned for Saul to fail so He could then raise David up. This was God's 'sovereign' plan."

However in 1 Samuel 13:13, God—speaking through the prophet Samuel—clearly told Saul, "If you would have obeyed Me and not done your own thing, trusted Me and waited just one more hour until Samuel showed up, I would have established your kingdom upon Israel forever." This means that David was not God's first choice!

The Lord didn't choose Saul as a mere interim, temporary king over Israel until the real person He wanted—David—could come of age and take over. No! God's Word plainly reveals that His first choice was Saul. If Saul would have cooperated with the Lord, He would have established his kingdom over the nation of Israel forever. This means we would have never heard of David.

Now, that's just a little hard for people who really know the Bible to comprehend. Why? David is everywhere throughout God's Word! He was blessed! As a matter of fact, the southern kingdom of the nation of Israel was preserved and lasted longer than the northern ten tribes because the Lord was honoring David. He spared his descendants because of David!

We speak today of the "sure mercies of David." God made an oath and a covenant that He would never take away a person to rule on David's throne. This was ultimately fulfilled in the Messiah—Jesus Christ—who was called "the Son of David." Prophecies spoke of the Messiah coming out of the tribe of Judah—David's tribe.

However, this verse makes it very clear that David wasn't God's first choice. If Saul would have obeyed the Lord, then we would be talking about the "sure mercies of Saul" today. The Messiah would have come out of the tribe of Benjamin—Saul's tribe. We never would have heard of David. There would never have been a Solomon. There might have been others who would have done equal or even greater things, but David wasn't God's original plan!

"AN EXPECTED END"

This is one of the most important lessons we can learn from the life of David. God chose David as a result of Saul's disobedience.

> *For now would the LORD have established thy kingdom upon Israel for ever. [14] But now thy kingdom shall not continue: the LORD hath sought him a man after his own heart, and the LORD hath commanded him to be captain over his people, because thou hast not kept that which the LORD commanded thee.*
> 1 SAMUEL 13:13C-14

The Lord sought out David AFTER Saul had rejected Him. This instance took place in the second year of Saul's reign (1 Sam. 13:1). At the end of Saul's forty-year reign (Acts 13:21), David became king when he was thirty (2 Sam. 5:4). This means David wasn't even born at that time. It would be eight years after this when David would be born.

David wasn't God's first choice—Saul was!

ACCEPT RESPONSIBILITY

Even if you have stumbled upon God's will for your life and have begun to fulfill it, that doesn't mean you'll automatically finish the course. Just because you can see His calling, anointing, and blessing on your life, it doesn't mean you can't thwart it. As far as God is concerned, He's willing and planning for you to prosper.

> *For I know the thoughts that I think toward you, saith the Lord, thoughts of peace, and not of evil, to give you an expected end.*
> JEREMIAH 29:11

God has a good plan for every individual. It's a plan that will give you an *"expected end"*—a predicted future of success. The Lord has a plan and purpose for everyone. He desires for every person to fulfill their individual destiny, but it doesn't automatically—"sovereignly"—come to pass. You can thwart God's plan for your life, as evidenced here by Saul.

Nobody who truly believes that the Bible is the Word of God can say, "Well, God knew Saul was going to do all of these things. He was just a fill-in until David came along—God's true plan." No! Saul was the one that God really planned on. That's exactly what the Word says!

GRACE CAN BE VOIDED

This is a warning to all of us. The Lord has a plan for each of us that is by grace—it's not based on our performance—but we do have to cooperate with that plan. Even though we don't deserve our God-given destiny, there are things we can do that will hinder and stop it.

So, take heed and beware! You can't just take the grace of God, His blessing, and His calling on your life for granted. You need to persevere.

Paul understood and cooperated with this truth.

> *For I am the least of the apostles…but by the grace of God I am what I am.*
> 1 CORINTHIANS 15:9-10A

His calling was by God's grace. He didn't deserve it. But then Paul went on to say…

> *And his grace which was bestowed upon me was not in vain.*
> 1 CORINTHIANS 15:10

In other words, God can give grace to you, but you can void it. The Lord has a plan for your life, but you can invalidate it.

> *His grace...was not in vain; but I laboured more abundantly than they all: yet not I, but the grace of God which was with me.*
>
> 1 CORINTHIANS 15:10

Paul was saying that the Lord—by grace—chose him. Paul wasn't really seeking God at that time; he was hunting down, persecuting, and killing Christians. According to the Lord Himself, he was kicking *"against the pricks"* (Acts 9:5). Paul wasn't chosen because of any great virtue on his part. It was a grace decision. Yet Paul was saying that he could have made it vain and voided the grace of God, but he didn't because he responded by faith to God's grace and *"laboured more abundantly."*

A SOBERING THOUGHT

Just like Saul, God has a purpose and a plan for each and every one of us. Even after Saul sinned here in 1 Samuel 13, God didn't just immediately take him out of the kingship.

> *For the gifts and calling of God are without repentance.*
>
> ROMANS 11:29

Saul remained king until the day of his death. His reign, however, instead of being a blessing, turned into a burden for the nation of Israel. Saul oppressed and took advantage of the people. He was tormented, did terrible things, and basically went crazy. He destroyed his son Jonathan's life. Saul certainly did not realize—manifest—his full potential.

God's plan for your life is by grace, but you must cooperate with that grace by faith. Like Saul, you can stop God's plan and blessing from fully materializing (1 Sam. 13:13-14). Now, that's a sobering thought!

ANDREW'S RECOMMENDATIONS FOR FURTHER STUDY

This false teaching, popularly called "the sovereignty of God," is wrong because it makes the Lord responsible for all the evil in the world. I confront and refute this wrong doctrine head on in my teaching by the same name ("The Sovereignty of God").

Outline

III. Saul had a million excuses!
    A. But Samuel told him,

Thou hast done foolishly: thou hast not kept the commandment of the LORD thy God, which he commanded thee: for now would the LORD have established thy kingdom upon Israel for ever.
1 SAMUEL 13:13

    B. You can try to make it look good, but if you disobey God, you're foolish!
    C. There is no such thing as "situational ethics"; there is right and wrong.
    D. Many folks think that since God knows the end from the beginning, He also controls everything that happens in between.
        i. They believe that only what He wills comes to pass on the earth.
    E. Applying these faulty assumptions to Saul, people would have to say then that the Lord planned for Saul to fail so He could then raise David up.

IV. David was not God's first choice!
    A. God—through the prophet Samuel—clearly told Saul that if Saul would have trusted Him, God would have established Saul's kingdom upon Israel forever (1 Sam. 13:13).
    B. The Lord didn't choose Saul as a mere interim king over Israel until the real person He wanted—David—could come of age and take over.
    C. Now, that's just a little hard for people who really know the Bible to comprehend.
        i. David is everywhere throughout God's Word!
        ii. God made an oath and a covenant that He would never take away a person to rule on David' throne, which was ultimately fulfilled in Jesus Christ—"the Son of David."
    D. If Saul would have obeyed the Lord, then we would be talking about the "sure mercies of Saul" today.
        i. The Messiah would have come out of the tribe of Benjamin—Saul's tribe.
        ii. We never would have heard of David, and there would never have been a Solomon.
    E. One of the most important lessons we can learn from the life of David is that God chose David as a result of Saul's disobedience (1 Sam. 13:13c-14).

V. The Lord sought out David AFTER Saul had rejected Him.
    A. David was born eight years after Saul's disobedience in 1 Samuel 13.
        i. This instance of Saul's disobedience took place in the second year of Saul's reign (1 Sam. 13:1).

ii. David became king when he was thirty (2 Sam. 5:4), which was at the end of Saul's forty-year reign (Acts 13:21).
B. So, just because you can see His calling, anointing, and blessing on your life, it doesn't mean you can't thwart it, as evidenced here by Saul.
C. God has an original, good plan for every individual to give them an *"expected end"* (Jer. 29:11)—a predicted future of success.
D. He desires for every person to fulfill their individual destiny, but it doesn't automatically—"sovereignly"—come to pass.
E. That's exactly what the Word says!

VI. This is a warning to all of us.
A. The Lord has a plan for each of us that is by grace—it's not based on our performance—but we do have to cooperate with that plan.
B. Paul understood and cooperated with this truth.

For I am the least of the apostles…but by the grace of God I am what I am.
1 CORINTHIANS 15:9-10A

C. Paul wasn't chosen because of any great virtue on his part; it was a grace decision.
D. Yet Paul was saying that he could have made it vain and voided the grace of God, but he didn't because he responded by faith to God's grace and *"labored more abundantly"* (1 Cor. 15:10).

VII. It's a sobering thought that Saul certainly did not realize—manifest—his full potential (1 Sam. 13:13-14).
A. Saul remained king until the day of his death.

For the gifts and calling of God are without repentance.
ROMANS 11:29

B. His reign, instead of being a blessing, turned into a burden for the nation of Israel.
C. God's plan for your life is by grace, but you must cooperate with that grace by faith.

ANDREW'S RECOMMENDATIONS FOR FURTHER STUDY

This false teaching, popularly called "the sovereignty of God," is wrong because it makes the Lord responsible for all the evil in the world. I confront and refute this wrong doctrine head on in my teaching by the same name ("The Sovereignty of God").

Teacher's Guide

3. Saul had a million excuses! But Samuel told him,

> *Thou hast done foolishly: thou hast not kept the commandment of the L*ORD *thy God, which he commanded thee: for now would the L*ORD *have established thy kingdom upon Israel for ever.*
>
> 1 SAMUEL 13:13

We can try to make it look good, but if we disobey God, we're foolish! There is no such thing as "situational ethics"; there is right and wrong. Many folks think that since God knows the end from the beginning, He also controls everything that happens in between. They believe that only what He wills comes to pass on the earth. Applying these faulty assumptions to Saul, people would have to say then that the Lord planned for Saul to fail so He could then raise David up.

3a. Samuel told Saul that he was _____ because he had disobeyed God (1 Sam. 13:13).
    Foolish
3b. True or false: A person's ethics depend upon the situation they find themselves in.
    False
3c. Which statement is true of God?
    A. He doesn't know the end from the beginning
    B. He controls everything that happens on earth
    C. Only His will comes to pass on the earth
    D. Although He knew Saul would, God did not plan for Saul to fail
    E. He can be tempted with evil
    D. Although He knew Saul would, God did not plan for Saul to fail

---

LESSONS FROM DAVID

4. David was not God's first choice! God—through the prophet Samuel—clearly told Saul that if Saul would have trusted Him, God would have established Saul's kingdom upon Israel forever (1 Sam. 13:13). The Lord didn't choose Saul as a mere interim king over Israel until the real person He wanted—David—could come of age and take over. Now, that's just a little hard for people who really know the Bible to comprehend. David is everywhere throughout God's Word! God made an oath and a covenant that He would never take away a person to rule on David' throne, which was ultimately fulfilled in Jesus Christ—"the Son of David." If Saul would have obeyed the Lord, then we would be talking about the "sure mercies of Saul" today. The Messiah would have come out of the tribe of Benjamin—Saul's tribe. We never would have heard of David, and there would never have been a Solomon. One of the most important lessons we can learn from the life of David is that God chose David as a result of Saul's disobedience (1 Sam. 13:13c-14).

4a. True or false: If Saul would have trusted God, he would not have lost his kingdom.
   True
4b. The Lord did not choose Saul as an _____ king over Israel.
   Interim
4c. David was not God's _____ choice.
   First
4d. Why is it hard for people who know the Bible to comprehend that David was not God's first choice?
   David is everywhere throughout God's Word
4e. True or false: Because of Saul's disobedience, the Messiah did not come out of the tribe of Benjamin.
   True
4f. *Discussion question:* How did Saul's disobedience change the course of history for his life, his family, and his tribe?
   Discussion question

5. The Lord sought out David AFTER Saul had rejected Him. David was born eight years after Saul's disobedience in 1 Samuel 13. This instance of Saul's disobedience took place in the second year of Saul's reign (1 Sam. 13:1). David became king when he was thirty (2 Sam. 5:4), which was at the end of Saul's forty-year reign (Acts 13:21). So, just because we can see His calling, anointing, and blessing on our lives, it doesn't mean we can't thwart it, as evidenced here by Saul. God has an original, good plan for every individual to give them an *"expected end"* (Jer. 29:11)—a predicted future of success. He desires for every person to fulfill their individual destiny, but it doesn't automatically—"sovereignly"—come to pass. That's exactly what the Word says!

5a. Saul's disobedience took place _____ David was even born.
Before

5b. At what age did David become king?
   A. At the beginning of Saul's forty-year reign
   B. When Saul was thirty
   C. When he was thirty
   D. All of the above
   E. None of the above
   C. When David was thirty

5c. True or false: Saul's life is evidence that someone can thwart God's original plan.
True

5d. *Discussion question:* God desires for every person to fulfill their individual destiny, but why doesn't it automatically come to pass?
Discussion question

6. This is a warning to all of us. The Lord has a plan for each of us that is by grace—it's not based on our performance—but we do have to cooperate with that plan. Paul understood and cooperated with this truth.

> *For I am the least of the apostles…but by the grace of God I am what I am.*
>
> 1 CORINTHIANS 15:9-10A

Paul wasn't chosen because of any great virtue on his part; it was a grace decision. Yet Paul was saying that he could have made it vain and voided the grace of God, but he didn't because he responded by faith to God's grace and *"labored more abundantly"* (1 Cor. 15:10).

6a. True or false: The Lord's plan for you is based on both grace and performance.
   False
6b. True or false: The Lord's plan for you is based on grace, but you must cooperate with it.
   True
6c. Paul wasn't chosen because of any great _____ on his part.
   Virtue
6d. How did Paul not make vain or void the grace of God?
   Because he responded to God's grace by faith
6e. *Discussion question:* Andrew says, "This is a warning to all of us." What do you think he means by this?
   Discussion question

ACCEPT RESPONSIBILITY

7. It's a sobering thought that Saul certainly did not realize—manifest—his full potential (1 Sam. 13:13-14). Saul remained king until the day of his death.

   For the gifts and calling of God are without repentance.

   ROMANS 11:29

   His reign, instead of being a blessing, turned into a burden for the nation of Israel. God's plan for our lives is by grace, but we must cooperate with that grace by faith.

7a. What reality about Saul's life does Andrew saying is a sobering thought?
   Saul did not manifest his full potential during his life

7b. Read Romans 11:29. Why did Saul remain king until his death although God had already taken away his kingdom?
   The gifts and calling of God are without repentance

7c. Saul's reign, instead of being a blessing, turned into what?
   A. A disaster for God
   B. A benefit for Israel
   C. A burden for Israel
   D. A Hebrew soap opera
   E. A spectacle for other nations
   C. A burden for Israel

7d. God's plan for your life is by _____, but you must _____ with that grace by _____.
   Grace / cooperate / faith

Discipleship Questions

12. Samuel told Saul that he was _____ because he had disobeyed God (1 Sam. 13:13).

13. True or false: A person's ethics depend upon the situation they find themselves in.

14. Which statement is true of God?
    A. God doesn't know the end from the beginning
    B. He controls everything that happens on earth
    C. Only God's will always comes to pass on the earth
    D. Although He knew Saul would, God did not plan for Saul to fail
    E. God can be tempted with evil

15. True or false: If Saul would have trusted God, he would not have lost his kingdom.

16. The Lord did not choose Saul as an _____ king over Israel.

17. David was not God's _____ choice.

18. Why is it hard for people who know the Bible to comprehend that David was not God's first choice?
    _____
    _____
    _____

19. True or false: Because of Saul's disobedience, the Messiah did not come out of the tribe of Benjamin.

20. *Discussion question:* How did Saul's disobedience change the course of history for his life, his family, and his tribe?
    _____
    _____
    _____

21. Saul's disobedience took place _____ David was even born.

ACCEPT RESPONSIBILITY

22. David became king when?
    A. At the beginning of Saul's forty-year reign
    B. When Saul was thirty
    C. When David was thirty
    D. All of the above
    E. None of the above

23. True or false: Saul's life is evidence that someone can thwart God's original plan.

24. *Discussion question:* God desires for every person to fulfill their individual destiny, but why doesn't it automatically come to pass?

25. True or false: The Lord's plan for you is based on both grace and performance.

26. True or false: The Lord's plan for you is based on grace, but you must cooperate with it.

27. Paul wasn't chosen because of any great _____ on his part.

28. How did Paul not make vain or void the grace of God?

29. *Discussion question:* Andrew says, "This is a warning to all of us." What do you think he means by this?

30. What reality about Saul's life does Andrew say is a sobering thought?

31. Read Romans 11:29. Why did Saul remain king until his death although God had already taken away his kingdom?
_____
_____
_____

32. Saul's reign, instead of being a blessing, turned into what?
    A. A disaster for God
    B. A benefit for Israel
    C. A burden for Israel
    D. A Hebrew soap opera
    E. A spectacle for other nations

33. God's plan for your life is by _____, but you must _____ with that grace by _____.

Answer Key

12. Foolish
13. False
14. D. Although He knew Saul would, God did not plan for Saul to fail
15. True
16. Interim
17. First
18. David is everywhere throughout God's Word
19. True
20. *Discussion question*
21. Before
22. C. When David was 30
23. True
24. *Discussion question*
25. False
26. True
27. Virtue
28. Because he responded to God's grace by faith
29. *Discussion question*
30. Saul did not manifest his full potential during his life
31. The gifts and calling of God are without repentance
32. C. A burden for Israel
33. Grace / cooperate / faith

1 SAMUEL 13:13-14
And Samuel said to Saul, Thou hast done foolishly: thou hast not kept the commandment of the Lord thy God, which he commanded thee: for now would the Lord have established thy kingdom upon Israel for ever. [14] But now thy kingdom shall not continue: the Lord hath sought him a man after his own heart, and the Lord hath commanded him to be captain over his people, because thou hast not kept that which the Lord commanded thee.

1 SAMUEL 13:1
Saul reigned one year; and when he had reigned two years over Israel.

ACTS 13:21
And afterward they desired a king: and God gave unto them Saul the son of Cis, a man of the tribe of Benjamin, by the space of forty years.

2 SAMUEL 5:4
David was thirty years old when he began to reign, and he reigned forty years.

JEREMIAH 29:11
For I know the thoughts that I think toward you, saith the Lord, thoughts of peace, and not of evil, to give you an expected end.

1 CORINTHIANS 15:9-10
For I am the least of the apostles, that am not meet to be called an apostle, because I persecuted the church of God. [10] But by the grace of God I am what I am: and his grace which was bestowed upon me was not in vain; but I laboured more abundantly than they all: yet not I, but the grace of God which was with me.

ACTS 9:5
And he said, Who art thou, Lord? And the Lord said, I am Jesus whom thou persecutest: it is hard for thee to kick against the pricks.

ROMANS 11:29
For the gifts and calling of God are without repentance.

Do You Qualify?

Saul's failure gave David a chance, and so he never would have even come to the surface if Saul hadn't botched it up. David, then, was God's second choice. This speaks volumes to me! Even though the Lord has used me in a mighty way, I certainly don't feel like I was His first choice.

Kathryn Kuhlman had a powerful, world-renowned ministry of healing. I used to serve as an usher in Kathryn's meetings. I saw some of the most astounding miracles that I've ever seen in my life at her meetings. She made a huge impact for the kingdom of God. Yet I heard Kathryn say on more than one occasion that she wasn't God's first, second, or even third choice. In her own dramatic way, she continued right on down the line saying that she wasn't even God's fourth or fifth choice. Kathryn would openly admit that she wasn't the best person to do the job that she was doing. And then, she'd turn right around to the preachers in the audience and chastise them, saying, "God called some of you to do what I'm doing, but you wouldn't bear up under the criticism and persecution." She would just let them have it!

That has always encouraged me because I never felt like I was the best qualified or most suited person to do what I'm doing. But one of the things I've learned from the life of David is that God doesn't necessarily choose the silver vessel—He chooses the surrendered one. The Lord is more interested in our *availability* than our *ability*.

GOD'S QUALIFICATIONS

You may feel like you have it all together, but I'm a hick from Texas. I've often had people make fun of me. They've talked about my "hick" voice and how I sound like that old television character named Gomer Pyle. I don't get upset with that. In fact, I don't particularly like my voice either. If I were God, I wouldn't have chosen me. When He did choose me and started putting in my heart the things He's told me to do, I just felt like, "God, I'm not qualified. I'm not good enough!" But then I read His list of qualifications over in 1 Corinthians:

> *For ye see your calling, brethren, how that not many wise men after the flesh, not many mighty, not many noble, are called: [27] But God hath chosen the foolish things of the world to confound the wise; and God hath chosen the weak things of the world to confound the things which are mighty.*
>
> 1 CORINTHIANS 1:26-27

LESSONS FROM DAVID

When I saw this, I thought, *Hey, I qualify! That's me!*

And base things of the world, and things which are despised, hath God chosen, yea, and things which are not, to bring to nought things that are: [29] That no flesh should glory in his presence.
1 CORINTHIANS 1:28-29

God doesn't choose the way man does. He looks on the heart. Saul started out with a tender heart, so God gave him the opportunity. He chose him. But when his heart changed, God forsook and turned away from him.

A YIELDED HEART

Now as New Testament believers, God will never leave us nor forsake us (Heb. 13:5). However, He won't continue to promote us if we get an evil heart. The Lord will still love and accept us, but He won't open doors for us. God will not promote a rotten attitude. We can stop the blessing and promotion of God from coming in our lives. He won't leave or forsake us the way He did with Saul, but we can certainly hinder, stop, and thwart His blessing in our lives.

Therefore, you need to recognize that God is looking for a humble heart. He's looking at the attitude of your heart. Just like with David, the Lord is seeking people after His own heart. This encourages me!

God didn't choose David because he was the tallest. Saul was the tallest in the entire nation, but David was the runt of the litter. Saul was a tough-looking, masculine man. He was probably weathered from being out in the sun and wind. David was ruddy and had a beautiful complexion (1 Sam. 16:12). He had a countenance that was enjoyable to look at. In other words, he was a "mama's boy." David was nice looking, but not the kind of guy you would pick to go out and fight a battle. People look on the outward appearance, but God looks on the heart (1 Sam. 16:7)!

Through David, I've learned that the Lord isn't concerned with my external qualities. It's not my skills, my abilities, or whether I have charisma or not. He's looking at my heart, whether I will trust Him. Once I saw this, I thought, *God, I may not have the education, the polish, the talent, or the looks. I may not have the strength or natural ability that other people do, but I have a heart. And I choose to commit my heart to seeking You as much as anybody ever has!* That's been my pursuit. I'm not saying that I have fully attained it, but I have consistently and honestly sought to love God in spirit and in truth with my whole heart. The Lord has honored that, blessed me, and opened up doors in my life and ministry.

I've seen many people's lives changed by the power of God's Word and the Holy Spirit. I've seen blind eyes and deaf ears opened, terminal diseases healed, and people raised from the dead—including my own son! What a blessing! Why did those things come to pass? It was because I started seeking God with my whole heart and He has shown me some things. I don't have the ability in my hands to heal or raise anyone from the dead. But I can yield my heart to Him and He can use me. God wants to use you too! It's all about your heart!

SEEK HIM WHOLEHEARTEDLY!

Even though David wasn't God's first choice, look at what the Lord was able to do with him. He had an impact! Nearly 4,000 years later, we're still learning from and talking about what a great man David was. Many people's lives were transformed. God used him to take the Israelites from being a ragtag bunch of tribal groups to a nation. They gained prominence and were established as a nation that still exists today. Great things happened!

David wasn't God's first choice. He didn't have all the qualifications. But he yielded his whole heart to God. The Lord chose him, and God's "Plan B" was better than any of us could have ever imagined His "Plan A" could've been.

The good news is that God can do the same for you. You may not have it all together. In fact, you may consider yourself weak, base, and despised. Well, according to 1 Corinthians 1:26-29, you qualify! All you have to do is yield your heart to Him.

I probably wasn't the Lord's best choice. But I've chosen God, and because of that, He's chosen to use me. Maybe someone else was better qualified, but nonetheless He's using me. I just praise Him for the opportunity. God is awesome!

You don't have to be perfect for the Lord to use you. You just have to be seeking Him with your whole heart. If you hunger and thirst for God, you will be filled (Matt. 5:6)!

Outline

I. Saul's failure gave David a chance, and so he never would have even come to the surface if Saul hadn't botched it up.
   A. David, then, was God's second choice.
   B. This speaks volumes to me because even though the Lord has used me in a might way, I don't feel like I was His first choice.
      i. I never felt like I was the best qualified or most suited person to do what I'm doing.
   C. But one of the things I've learned from the life of David is that God doesn't necessarily choose the silver vessel; He chooses the surrendered one—the Lord is more interested in our *availability* than our *ability*.

II. If I were God, I wouldn't have chosen me.
   A. But then I read His list of qualifications over in 1 Corinthians:

For ye see your calling, brethren, how that not many wise men after the flesh, not many mighty, not many noble, are called: [27] But God hath chosen the foolish things of the world to confound the wise; and God hath chosen the weak things of the world to confound the things which are mighty; [28] And base things of the world, and things which are despised, hath God chosen, yea, and things which are not, to bring to nought things that are: [29] That no flesh should glory in his presence.

1 CORINTHIANS 1:26-29

   i. I thought, *Hey, I qualify!*
   B. God doesn't choose the way man does.
   C. Saul started out with a tender heart, so God chose him.
   D. But when Saul's heart changed, God forsook him and turned away from him.

III. God will not continue to promote us if we get an evil heart.
   A. The Lord will still love us and accept us, but He won't open doors for us.
   B. He won't leave or forsake us (Heb. 13:5) the way He did with Saul, but we can certainly hinder, stop, and thwart His blessing in our lives.
   C. Therefore, we need to recognize that just like with David, the Lord is seeking people after His own heart.

IV. It's all about a yielded heart!
   A. I've seen many people's lives changed by the power of God's Word and the Holy Spirit.
      i. I've seen blind eyes and deaf ears opened.
      ii. I've seen terminal diseases healed and people, including my son, raised from the dead!
   B. I don't have the ability in my hands to heal or raise anyone from the dead.
   C. But I can yield my heart to Him and He can use me.
   D. God wants to use you too!

V. Even though David wasn't God's first choice, we should look at what the Lord was able to do with him.
   A. Nearly 4,000 years later, we're still learning from and talking about what a great man David was.
   B. Many people's lives were transformed.
   C. God's "Plan B" is better than we can ever imagine.
   D. We don't have to be perfect for the Lord to use us; we just have to be seeking Him with our whole heart.
   E. If we hunger and thirst for God, we will be filled (Matt. 5:6)!

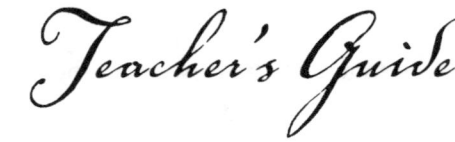

1. Saul's failure gave David a chance, and so he never would have even come to the surface if Saul hadn't botched it up. David, then, was God's second choice. This speaks volumes to Andrew because even though the Lord has used him in a mighty way, he doesn't feel like he was His first choice. He never felt like he was the best qualified or most suited person to do what he's doing. But one of the things Andrew has learned from the life of David is that God doesn't necessarily choose the silver vessel; He chooses the surrendered one—the Lord is more interested in our *availability* than our *ability*.

1a. What situation gave David the chance to be king?
   Saul's failure
1b. True or false: David was God's second choice.
   True
1c. Andrew doesn't feel like he was God's first _____.
   Choice
1d. Why doesn't Andrew feel like he was God's first choice to do what he is doing?
   He never felt best qualified or most suited
1e. *Discussion question:* What do you think it means when Andrew says, "The Lord is more interested in our availability than our ability"?
   Discussion question

2. If Andrew was God, he wouldn't have chosen Andrew. But then Andrew read His list of qualifications over in 1 Corinthians:

> *For ye see your calling, brethren, how that not many wise men after the flesh, not many mighty, not many noble, are called: [27] But God hath chosen the foolish things of the world to confound the wise; and God hath chosen the weak things of the world to confound the things which are mighty; [28] And base things of the world, and things which are despised, hath God chosen, yea, and things which are not, to bring to nought things that are: [29] That no flesh should glory in his presence.*
>
> 1 CORINTHIANS 1:26-29

Andrew thought, *Hey, I qualify!* God doesn't choose the way man does. Saul started out with a tender heart, so God chose him. But when Saul's heart changed, God forsook him and turned away from him.

2a. True or false: According to 1 Corinthians 1:26, God chooses the wise, mighty, and noble to serve Him and do His work.
False

2b. According to 1 Corinthians 1:27-28, which does He not choose?
   A. The foolish things of the world
   B. The weak things of the world
   C. The mighty things of the world
   D. The base things of the world
   E. The despised things of the world
C. The mighty things of this world

2c. When did God choose Saul?
When he was tenderhearted

2d. When did He forsake Saul and turn from him?
When his heart changed

2e. *Discussion question:* Can you give another example (from contemporary life or from the Bible) of a person whom God used but who seemed unqualified by man's standards?
Discussion question

3. God will not continue to promote us if we get an evil heart. The Lord will still love us and accept us, but He won't open doors for us. He won't leave or forsake us (Heb. 13:5) the way He did with Saul, but we can certainly hinder, stop, and thwart His blessing in our lives. Therefore, we need to recognize that just like with David, the Lord is seeking people after His own heart.

3a. When will the Lord stop promoting you?
If you get an evil heart
3b. True or false: The Lord can love you but not open doors for you.
True
3c. Although the Lord will never leave or forsake you, you can stop His _____ in your life.
Blessing
3d. From studying the life of David, you learn that the Lord is seeking what kind of people?
People after His own heart

4. It's all about a yielded heart! Andrew has seen many people's lives changed by the power of God's Word and the Holy Spirit. He's seen blind eyes and deaf ears opened. He's seen terminal diseases healed and people, including his own son, raised from the dead! He doesn't have the ability in his hand to heal or raise anyone from the dead. But he can yield his heart to Him and He can use him. God wants to use us too!

4a. What two things can change people's lives?
The power of God's Word and the Holy Spirit
4b. The main key to being used by God is what?
    A. Having a yielded heart
    B. Being obedient to the Ten Commandments
    C. Knowing the Bible better than others
    D. All of the above
    E. None of the above
A. Having a yielded heart

5. Even though David wasn't God's first choice, we should look at what the Lord was able to do with him. Nearly 4,000 years later, we're still learning from and talking about what a great man David was. Many people's lives were transformed. God's "Plan B" is better than we can ever imagine. We don't have to be perfect for the Lord to use us; we just have to be seeking Him with our whole heart. If we hunger and thirst for God, we will be filled (Matt. 5:6)!

5a. True or false: David was a great man because he wasn't God's first choice.
False

5b. You are still learning and talking about David because through him many people's lives were _____.
Transformed

5c. God's _____ is better than you can ever imagine.
Plan B

5d. What do you have to do to be used by God?
Seek Him with your whole heart

Discipleship Questions

1. What situation gave David the chance to be king?

2. True or false: David was God's second choice.

3. Andrew doesn't feel like he was God's first _____.

4. Why doesn't Andrew feel like he was God's first choice to do what he is doing?

5. *Discussion question:* What do you think it means when Andrew says, "The Lord is more interested in our availability than our ability"?

6. True or false: According to 1 Corinthians 1:26, God chooses the wise, mighty, and noble to serve Him and do His work.

7. According to 1 Corinthians 1:27-28, which does He not choose?
    A. The foolish things of the world
    B. The weak things of the world
    C. The mighty things of the world
    D. The base things of the world
    E. The despised things of the world

8. When did God choose Saul?

9. When did He forsake Saul and turn from him?

10. *Discussion question:* Can you give another example (from contemporary life or from the Bible) of a person whom God used but who seemed unqualified by man's standards?

11. When will the Lord stop promoting you?

12. True or false: The Lord can love you but not open doors for you.

13. Although the Lord will never leave or forsake you, you can stop His _____ in your life.

14. From studying the life of David, you learn that the Lord is seeking what kind of people?

15. What two things can change people's lives?

16. The main key to being used by God is what?
    A. Having a yielded heart
    B. Being obedient to the Ten Commandments
    C. Knowing the Bible better than others
    D. All of the above
    E. None of the above

17. True or false: David was a great man because he wasn't God's first choice.

18. You are still learning and talking about David because through him, many people's lives were _____.

19. God's _____ is better than you can ever imagine.

20. What do you have to do to be used by God?
_____
_____
_____

Answer Key

1. Saul's failure
2. True
3. Choice
4. He never felt best qualified or most suited
5. *Discussion question*
6. False
7. C. The mighty things of this world
8. When he was tenderhearted
9. When his heart changed
10. *Discussion question*
11. If you get an evil heart
12. True
13. Blessing
14. People after His own heart
15. The power of God's Word and the Holy Spirit
16. A. Having a yielded heart
17. False
18. Transformed
19. Plan B
20. Seek Him with your whole heart

1 CORINTHIANS 1:26-29

For ye see your calling, brethren, how that not many wise men after the flesh, not many mighty, not many noble, are called: [27] But God hath chosen the foolish things of the world to confound the wise; and God hath chosen the weak things of the world to confound the things which are mighty; [28] And base things of the world, and things which are despised, hath God chosen, yea, and things which are not, to bring to nought things that are: [29] That no flesh should glory in his presence.

HEBREWS 13:5

Let your conversation be without covetousness; and be content with such things as ye have: for he hath said, I will never leave thee, nor forsake thee.

1 SAMUEL 16:12

And he sent, and brought him in. Now he was ruddy, and withal of a beautiful countenance, and goodly to look to. And the Lord said, Arise, anoint him: for this is he.

1 SAMUEL 16:7

But the Lord said unto Samuel, Look not on his countenance, or on the height of his stature; because I have refused him: for the Lord seeth not as man seeth; for man looketh on the outward appearance, but the Lord looketh on the heart.

MATTHEW 5:6

Blessed are they which do hunger and thirst after righteousness: for they shall be filled.

Obedience Is Better

Thus saith the LORD of hosts, I remember that which Amalek did to Israel, how he laid wait for him in the way, when he came up from Egypt. [3] Now go and smite Amalek, and utterly destroy all that they have, and spare them not; but slay both man and woman, infant and suckling, ox and sheep, camel and ass.

1 SAMUEL 15:2-3

This was God's commission through Samuel to Saul. Amalek had come out and fought against the Israelites when they were vulnerable on their way out of Egypt (Ex. 17:8-14). Since Israel had become a kingdom and had a king, God wanted vengeance on the Amalekites.

This may seem harsh to us today because, truthfully speaking, this isn't acceptable New Covenant behavior. In the Old Testament, groups of people who had given themselves over to idolatry and immorality were like cancers in the body of humankind. If left untreated, that sickness would spread quickly to the rest of the body. Therefore, as terrible as amputating someone's hand, arm, or leg could be, it's still superior to letting the entire person die. Sometimes the diseased part just has to be cut out in order to save the rest of the body. This was what God—in His love and mercy toward the rest of humanity—was instructing the Israelites to do. By utterly destroying these men, women, children, and animals, they were cutting out a cancer that threatened to kill humankind.

Before Jesus came—before people could be born again, transformed, and delivered of demons—there were entire societies that were so given over to the devil, they were demon possessed. Men, women, children, and even their animals were demon possessed. There is much archaeological evidence—statues, writings, etc.—that establishes this. These people's sin was gross beyond what we can even imagine in our society today, and our sin is pretty gross in many ways. But they were participating on a wide scale in bestiality, sodomy, child sacrifice, and all these kinds of things—and they couldn't be cured of it. There was no cure before Jesus came. So, although this was an act of judgment against specific individuals, it was also an act of mercy upon the world as a whole to literally cut this cancer out and destroy it.

"THE PEOPLE..."

So, Saul had been given this command to destroy all of the Amalekites—men, women, children, and animals—but he didn't do it. He saved the king and brought him back with the best of the sheep, oxen, and cattle. When Samuel arrived, Saul claimed that he had done the will of the Lord (1 Sam. 15:13). But Samuel asked,

> *What meaneth then this bleating of the sheep in mine ears, and the lowing of the oxen which I hear?*
>
> 1 SAMUEL 15:14

In other words, Samuel was asking, "If you have truly done the Lord's will, why am I hearing these animals? I told you to destroy everything—men, women, children, and animals!"

> *And Saul said, They have brought them from the Amalekites.*
>
> 1 SAMUEL 15:15

There he was again placing the blame on others and saying, "The people made me do this!"

> *For the people spared the best of the sheep and of the oxen, to sacrifice unto the LORD thy God; and the rest we have utterly destroyed. [16] Then Samuel said unto Saul, Stay, and I will tell thee what the LORD hath said to me this night. And he said unto him, Say on. [17] And Samuel said, When thou wast little in thine own sight, wast thou not made the head of the tribes of Israel, and the LORD anointed thee king over Israel?*
>
> 1 SAMUEL 15:15B-17

Samuel was exposing the root of Saul's sin. He said, "When you were little in your own eyes, God anointed and promoted you. But when you were lifted up, you became independent, started doing things your own way, and chose not to do what God had said. Instead of killing these animals—like you were instructed to do—you decided to bring them back and sacrifice them. It was when you became arrogant that God rejected you."

PRIDE & HUMILITY

> *Pride goeth before destruction, and an haughty spirit before a fall.*
>
> PROVERBS 16:18

> *God resisteth the proud, and giveth grace to the humble.*
>
> 1 PETER 5:5C

Humility is necessary to walk with God.

OBEDIENCE IS BETTER

He [God] hath shewed thee, O man, what is good; and what doth the LORD require of thee, but to…walk humbly with thy God?

MICAH 6:8, BRACKETS MINE

You must walk humbly in order to walk with God. This is a lesson we can learn from David. David was a humble man. At times, he messed up royally and did terrible sins, but he didn't try to shift the blame onto anyone else when he was reproved. He shouldered it himself, repented, and lay before the Lord. David was a humble man.

Humility doesn't mean you do everything perfectly. It doesn't mean you don't sin. But humility does mean you have a heart that is sensitive toward the Lord. Even though you might act like you've lost your mind and gone crazy sometimes, you genuinely love God.

Humility is different than arrogance. Saul got caught up in arrogance. Pride isn't only thinking that you are better than everyone else. Pride is essentially being self-reliant instead of God-reliant. It's this attitude of independence that is one of Satan's biggest inroads into your life.

Only *by pride cometh contention.*

PROVERBS 13:10A, EMPHASIS MINE

The only thing that makes people mad is their self-centeredness—their self-reliance. This is Satan's major beachhead in our lives. If we want to shut the devil out of our lives, begin to prosper, and see the blessings of God work, then we need to walk humbly with God!

You won't find God until you come to the end of yourself. At the end of yourself is where you'll meet Him!

STAY SMALL IN YOUR OWN SIGHT

Samuel told Saul, "When you were little in your own sight, you were made the head of the tribes of Israel" (1 Sam. 15:17). When Saul was humble was when God promoted him.

At one time, I was a member of a church that had started in someone's basement. In about two years' time, it grew to 300 people. They outgrew this little church facility and took over the large grocery store building next door. On opening day, there was something like 500 people in attendance. The church had nearly doubled, and it was exciting to be a part of what was going on. People were praising God, but they were also praising the pastor and themselves. They were saying "Look who we are!" and giving a tremendous amount of attention to what they had done. This just struck me wrong.

People were standing up and prophesying, "This church is going to explode! It's going to do this and that!" Then the Lord spoke to me this exact passage of Scripture—1 Samuel 15:17. So, I went against the flow that day by standing up and saying, "It's wonderful what *GOD* has done, but all this started when we were 'little in our own eyes' and humble before the Lord. If we get into pride and arrogance, all this can leave just as quickly as it came." I wasn't real popular after that. But it's exactly what happened. The pastor actually wound up getting into some things. Now he's divorced and out of the ministry. The church fell apart. Since then, it did resurrect under another pastor, and it's doing better than ever before. But it went through a really terrible time there. So, this principle applies both to individuals and churches.

Years ago there was a major media minister who fell into sexual sin. It was made very public and finally the minister had to deal with it on his Sunday program. I watched and listened to what he had to say, trying to figure out how something like this could happen. As he confessed, he spoke of how he had fallen into pride and taken God's goodness as his own accomplishments. He said he had over $8 million coming in per month. He was on more television stations than any other person in history had been. He even said, "I'm reaching more people than Jesus ever did." He went on to say, "I thought I could do anything."

At that moment, I saw very clearly why this man fell. He was no longer humble and dependent on God. He thought he was the one causing all this prosperity in his ministry.

From the life of David, we learn that we must walk humbly with God. Saul—David's predecessor—was the Lord's first choice. But he didn't continue walking with God because he became lifted up in pride, did his own thing, and disobeyed.

ANDREW'S RECOMMENDATIONS FOR FURTHER STUDY

Now that Jesus has come, He's made a huge difference. In my teaching, *The True Nature of God*, I contrast and harmonize the difference between how God acted in the Old Testament as compared to the New. It really shines light on how the Lord can be *"the same yesterday, and to day, and for ever,"* yet appear so different (Heb. 13:8). It'll really set you free!

Also, my teachings entitled "Selfishness, the Beachhead of Satan" (Part 3 of *How to Deal with Temptation*), "The End of Self Is the Beginning of God" (Part 4 of *Faith Builders*), and "Ungodly Anger's Source" (Part 2 of *Anger Management*) will all explain this in more detail. I also have a booklet entitled *Self-Centeredness: The Source of All Grief* that brings all these teachings together into one message.

Outline

I. God gave Saul a commission through Samuel.

Thus saith the LORD of hosts, I remember that which Amalek did to Israel, how he laid wait for him in the way, when he came up from Egypt. [3] Now go and smite Amalek, and utterly destroy all that they have, and spare them not; but slay both man and woman, infant and suckling, ox and sheep, camel and ass.

1 SAMUEL 15:2-3

  A. Since Israel had become a kingdom and had a king, God wanted vengeance on the Amalekites.
  B. This may seem harsh to us today because, truthfully speaking, this isn't acceptable New Covenant behavior.
  C. In the Old Testament, groups of people who had given themselves over to idolatry and immorality were like cancers in the body of humankind.
  D. Sometimes the diseased part just has to be cut out in order to save the rest of the body.
  E. God, in His love and mercy toward the rest of humanity, told the Israelites to utterly destroy these men, women, children, and animals.
  F. There is much archaeological evidence that before Jesus came, there were entire societies that were so given over to the devil, they were demon possessed.
  G. They were participating on a wide scale in bestiality, sodomy, child sacrifice, and all these kinds of things—and they couldn't be cured of it.
  H. There was no cure before Jesus came.
  I. So, although this was an act of judgment against specific individuals, it was also an act of mercy upon the world as a whole to literally cut this cancer out and destroy it.

II. Saul claimed that he had done the will of the Lord, but in 1 Samuel 15:14, Samuel essentially asked, "If you have truly done the Lord's will, why am I hearing these animals—I told you to destroy everything!"
  A. Saul again placed the blame on others, saying, "The people made me do this!"
  B. But Samuel exposed the root of Saul's sin in 1 Samuel 15:17 by basically saying, "When you were little in your own eyes, God anointed and promoted you. But when you were lifted up, that was when you became arrogant and God rejected you."

III. Humility is necessary to walk with God (Prov. 16:18 and 1 Pet. 5:5)—this is a lesson we can learn from David.

> *He [God] hath shewed thee, O man, what is good; and what doth the LORD require of thee, but to…walk humbly with thy God?*
>
> MICAH 6:8, BRACKETS MINE

    A. At times, David messed up royally and did terrible sins, but he didn't try to shift the blame onto anyone else when he was reproved.
    B. Humility doesn't mean you do everything perfectly; it doesn't mean you don't sin.
    C. Humility does mean you have a heart that is sensitive toward the Lord.

IV. Humility is different than arrogance.
    A. Pride isn't only thinking that you are better than everyone else.
    B. Pride is essentially being self-reliant instead of God-reliant.
    C. It's this attitude of independence that is one of Satan's biggest inroads into your life.
    D. If you want to shut the devil out of your life, begin to prosper, and see the blessings of God work, then you need to walk humbly with God!
    E. You won't find God until you come to the end of yourself.

V. When Saul was humble was when God promoted him.
    A. From the life of David, we learn that we must walk humbly with God.
    B. Saul—David's predecessor—was the Lord's first choice.
    C. But Saul didn't continue walking with God because he became lifted up in pride, did his own thing, and disobeyed.

ANDREW'S RECOMMENDATIONS FOR FURTHER STUDY

Now that Jesus has come, He's made a huge difference. In my teaching, *The True Nature of God*, I contrast and harmonize the difference between how God acted in the Old Testament as compared to the New. It really shines light on how the Lord can be *"the same yesterday, and to day, and for ever,"* yet appear so different (Heb. 13:8). It'll really set you free!

Also, my teachings entitled "Selfishness, the Beachhead of Satan" (Part 3 of *How to Deal with Temptation*), "The End of Self Is the Beginning of God" (Part 4 of *Faith Builders*), and "Ungodly Anger's Source" (Part 2 of *Anger Management*) will all explain this in more detail. I also have a booklet entitled *Self-Centeredness: The Source of All Grief* that brings all these teachings together into one message.

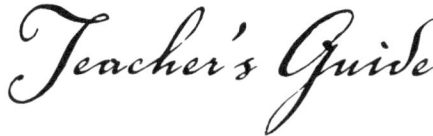

1. God gave Saul a commission through Samuel.

   Thus saith the LORD of hosts, I remember that which Amalek did to Israel, how he laid wait for him in the way, when he came up from Egypt. [3] Now go and smite Amalek, and utterly destroy all that they have, and spare them not; but slay both man and woman, infant and suckling, ox and sheep, camel and ass.

   1 SAMUEL 15:2-3

Since Israel had become a kingdom and had a king, God wanted vengeance on the Amalekites. This may seem harsh to us today because, truthfully speaking, this isn't acceptable New Covenant behavior. In the Old Testament, groups of people who had given themselves over to idolatry and immorality were like cancers in the body of humankind. Sometimes the diseased part just has to be cut out in order to save the rest of the body. God, in His love and mercy toward the rest of humanity, told the Israelites to utterly destroy these men, women, children, and animals. There is much archaeological evidence that before Jesus came, there were entire societies that were so given over to the devil, they were demon possessed. They were participating on a wide scale in bestiality, sodomy, child sacrifice, and all these kinds of things—and they couldn't be cured of it. There was no cure before Jesus came. So, although this was an act of judgment against specific individuals, it was also an act of mercy upon the world as a whole to literally cut this cancer out and destroy it.

1a. What was the commission God gave to Saul?
   A. To cause the Amalekites to remember the Lord God of Israel and to serve Him only
   B. To anoint David as king of Israel
   C. To utterly destroy and avenge the Amalekites for what they did to Israel as they were leaving Egypt
   D. To take the Amalekites' land back and make them Israel's slaves
   E. To rule his people with an iron fist
   C. To utterly destroy and avenge the Amalekites for what they did to Israel as they were leaving Egypt

1b. God was waiting until Israel was a _____ and had a _____ before He ordered vengeance on the Amalekites.
   Kingdom / king

1c. Why does this "commission" that God gave Saul seem harsh today?
   It isn't acceptable New Covenant behavior

(continued on next page)

1d. What were some of the types of immorality and idolatry that were being practiced by groups of people in the Old Testament that made them "like cancers in the body of humankind"?
   A. Sodomy
   B. Child sacrifice
   C. Bestiality
   D. All of the above
   E. None of the above
   D. All of the above

1e. *Discussion question:* Can an act of judgment against specific individuals also be an act of mercy upon the world? Why or why not?
   Discussion question

1f. True or false: There was no cure for man's immorality or idolatry before Jesus came.
   True

2. Saul claimed that he had done the will of the Lord, but in 1 Samuel 15:14, Samuel essentially asked, "If you have truly done the Lord's will, why am I hearing these animals—I told you to destroy everything!" Saul again placed the blame on others, saying, "The people made me do this!" But Samuel exposed the root of Saul's sin in 1 Samuel 15:17 by basically saying, "When you were little in your own eyes, God anointed and promoted you. But when you were lifted up, that was when you became arrogant and God rejected you."

2a. True or false: Saul had done the will of the Lord.
   False

2b. Why did Samuel disagree with Saul's claim that he had done the will of the Lord?
   Saul did not destroy everything as he was told

2c. What did Samuel pinpoint as the root of Saul's sin?
   A. God had anointed and promoted Saul
   B. Saul was little in his own eyes
   C. Bitterness
   D. Saul became arrogant
   E. Saul became too greedy
   D. Saul became arrogant

3. Humility is necessary to walk with God (Prov. 16:18 and 1 Pet. 5:5)—this is a lesson we can learn from David.

> *He* [God] *hath shewed thee, O man, what is good; and what doth the* LORD *require of thee, but to…walk humbly with thy God?*
>
> MICAH 6:8, BRACKETS MINE

At times, David messed up royally and did terrible sins, but he didn't try to shift the blame onto anyone else when he was reproved. Humility doesn't mean we do everything perfectly; it doesn't mean we don't sin. Humility does mean we have hearts that are sensitive toward the Lord.

3a. Although David messed up royally and did terrible sins, what did he never do when he was reproved?
He didn't try to shift blame

3b. True or false: Humility is when you do things perfectly and avoid sin.
False

3c. What kind of heart do you have if you have humility?
A heart that is sensitive toward the Lord

4. Humility is different than arrogance. Pride isn't only thinking that we are better than everyone else. Pride is essentially being self-reliant instead of God-reliant. It's this attitude of independence that is one of Satan's biggest inroads into our lives. If we want to shut the devil out of our lives, begin to prosper, and see the blessings of God work, then we need to walk humbly with God! We won't find God until we come to the end of ourselves.

4a. Pride is essentially being _____ instead of _____.
Self-reliant / God-reliant

4b. True or false: An attitude of independence is one of Satan's biggest inroads into your life.
True

4c. Which of the following are benefits of walking humbly with God?
  A. Prosperity
  B. Shutting the devil out of your life
  C. Seeing the blessing of God work
  D. All of the above
  E. None of the above
D. All of the above

LESSONS FROM DAVID

5. When Saul was humble was when God promoted him. From the life of David, we learn that we must walk humbly with God. Saul—David's predecessor—was the Lord's first choice. But Saul didn't continue walking with God because he became lifted up in pride, did his own thing, and disobeyed.

5a. What lesson can be learned from David's life?
   You must walk humbly with God
5b. True or false: Saul was the Lord's first choice.
   True
5c. List three things Saul did that showed he didn't continue walking with God after he became king.
   He became proud, did his own thing, and disobeyed

Discipleship Questions

1. What was the commission God gave Saul?
   A. To cause the Amalekites to remember the Lord God of Israel and to serve Him only
   B. To anoint David as king of Israel
   C. To utterly destroy and avenge the Amalekites for what they did to Israel as they were leaving Egypt
   D. To take the Amalekites' land back and make them Israel's slaves
   E. To rule his people with an iron fist

2. God was waiting until Israel was a _____ and had a _____ before He ordered vengeance on the Amalekites.

3. Why does this "commission" that God gave Saul seem harsh today?
   _____
   _____
   _____

4. What were some of the types of immorality and idolatry that were being practiced by groups of people in the Old Testament that made them "like cancers in the body of humankind"?
   A. Sodomy
   B. Child sacrifice
   C. Bestiality
   D. All of the above
   E. None of the above

5. *Discussion question:* Can an act of judgment against specific individuals also be an act of mercy upon the world? Why or why not?
   _____
   _____
   _____

6. True or false: There was no cure for man's immorality or idolatry before Jesus came.

7. True or false: Saul had done the will of the Lord.

LESSONS FROM DAVID

8. Why did Samuel disagree with Saul's claim that he had done the will of the Lord?
   _____
   _____
   _____

9. What did Samuel pinpoint as the root of Saul's sin?
   A. God had anointed and promoted Saul
   B. Saul was little in his own eyes
   C. Bitterness
   D. Saul became arrogant
   E. Saul became too greedy

10. Although David messed up royally and did terrible sins, what did he never do when he was reproved?
    _____
    _____
    _____

11. True or false: Humility is when you do things perfectly and avoid sin.

12. What kind of heart do you have if you have humility?
    _____
    _____
    _____

13. Pride is essentially being _____ instead of _____.

14. True or false: An attitude of independence is one of Satan's biggest inroads into your life.

15. Which of the following are benefits of walking humbly with God?
    A. Prosperity
    B. Shutting the devil out of your life
    C. Seeing the blessing of God work
    D. All of the above
    E. None of the above

OBEDIENCE IS BETTER

16. What lesson can be learned from David's life?
___
___
___

17. True or false: Saul was the Lord's first choice.

18. List three things Saul did that showed he didn't continue walking with God after he became king.
___
___
___

1. C. To utterly destroy and avenge the Amalekites for what they did to Israel as they were leaving Egypt
2. Kingdom / king
3. It isn't acceptable New Covenant behavior
4. D. All of the above
5. *Discussion question*
6. True
7. False
8. Saul did not destroy everything as he was told
9. D. Saul became arrogant
10. He didn't try to shift blame
11. False
12. A heart that is sensitive toward the Lord
13. Self-reliant / God-reliant
14. True
15. D. All of the above
16. You must walk humbly with God
17. True
18. He became proud, did his own thing, and disobeyed

OBEDIENCE IS BETTER

1 SAMUEL 15:2-3

Thus saith the Lord of hosts, I remember that which Amalek did to Israel, how he laid wait for him in the way, when he came up from Egypt. [3] Now go and smite Amalek, and utterly destroy all that they have, and spare them not; but slay both man and woman, infant and suckling, ox and sheep, camel and ass.

EXODUS 17:8-14

Then came Amalek, and fought with Israel in Rephidim. [9] And Moses said unto Joshua, Choose us out men, and go out, fight with Amalek: to morrow I will stand on the top of the hill with the rod of God in mine hand. [10] So Joshua did as Moses had said to him, and fought with Amalek: and Moses, Aaron, and Hur went up to the top of the hill. [11] And it came to pass, when Moses held up his hand, that Israel prevailed: and when he let down his hand, Amalek prevailed. [12] But Moses' hands were heavy; and they took a stone, and put it under him, and he sat thereon; and Aaron and Hur stayed up his hands, the one on the one side, and the other on the other side; and his hands were steady until the going down of the sun. [13] And Joshua discomfited Amalek and his people with the edge of the sword. [14] And the Lord said unto Moses, Write this for a memorial in a book, and rehearse it in the ears of Joshua: for I will utterly put out the remembrance of Amalek from under heaven.

1 SAMUEL 15:13-17

And Samuel came to Saul: and Saul said unto him, Blessed be thou of the Lord: I have performed the commandment of the Lord. [14] And Samuel said, What meaneth then this bleating of the sheep in mine ears, and the lowing of the oxen which I hear? [15] And Saul said, They have brought them from the Amalekites: for the people spared the best of the sheep and of the oxen, to sacrifice unto the Lord thy God; and the rest we have utterly destroyed. [16] Then Samuel said unto Saul, Stay, and I will tell thee what the Lord hath said to me this night. And he said unto him, Say on. [17] And Samuel said, When thou wast little in thine own sight, wast thou not made the head of the tribes of Israel, and the Lord anointed thee king over Israel?

PROVERBS 16:18

Pride goeth before destruction, and an haughty spirit before a fall.

1 PETER 5:5

Likewise, ye younger, submit yourselves unto the elder. Yea, all of you be subject one to another, and be clothed with humility: for God resisteth the proud, and giveth grace to the humble.

LESSONS FROM DAVID

MICAH 6:8

He hath shewed thee, O man, what is good; and what doth the Lord require of thee, but to do justly, and to love mercy, and to walk humbly with thy God?

PROVERBS 13:10

Only by pride cometh contention: but with the well advised is wisdom.

HEBREWS 13:8

Jesus Christ the same yesterday, and to day, and for ever.

Obedience Is Better

And Samuel said, When thou wast little in thine own sight, wast thou not made the head of the tribes of Israel, and the LORD anointed thee king over Israel? [18] And the LORD sent thee on a journey, and said, Go and utterly destroy the sinners the Amalekites, and fight against them until they be consumed. [19] Wherefore then didst thou not obey the voice of the LORD, but didst fly upon the spoil, and didst evil in the sight of the LORD?

1 SAMUEL 15:17-19

Samuel reproved Saul, but Saul kept on saying, "It's not my fault! You don't understand. I did obey God!" But he didn't.

And Saul said unto Samuel, Yea, I have obeyed the voice of the LORD, and have gone the way which the LORD sent me, and have brought Agag the king of Amalek, and have utterly destroyed the Amalekites. [21] But the people took of the spoil.

1 SAMUEL 15:20-21A

"It's not my fault! The people did this. They took the spoils of sheep and oxen." But Saul was the king. He was the one responsible. He knew what they had done. He could have commanded them to obey God's directions. The Lord wouldn't have held him guilty if the people had truly done all of this. However, Saul was the one who did it, and the people had his full approval.

The people took of the spoil, sheep and oxen, the chief of the things which should have been utterly destroyed.

1 SAMUEL 15:21

This clearly reveals that Saul knew they *"should have been utterly destroyed."* He knew what they were doing. So, Saul attempted to justify himself by saying that they took them *"to sacrifice unto the LORD thy God in Gilgal"* (1 Sam. 15:21).

And Samuel said, Hath the LORD as great delight in burnt offerings and sacrifices, as in obeying the voice of the LORD? Behold, to obey is better than sacrifice, and to hearken than the fat of rams.

1 SAMUEL 15:22

When God tells you to do something, it's not open to negotiation. You don't need to "interpret" it. You just need to do what God has told you to do!

OBEY GOD

I've had people say to me, "God has told me to come to Charis Bible College. I know I'm supposed to come, and I believe I'm supposed to come now. But it's only a couple more years before I can take an early retirement. If I wait until then, I could have that much more money than if I go now. Also, it's not a good time to sell my house right now. The market should be better if I just wait a year or two." So, they rationalize things and don't obey God. They lean on their own understanding and wonder why everything starts heading south. They tell me, "I don't understand why nothing is working. I just can't figure out what's happening!"

I answer, "Well, you aren't obeying God."

"Oh, no! I am obeying God. I'm going to come, but I just have to wait until this and that happens." They try to explain it away, but it's not what God has told them to do.

The Lord told Saul to kill all of these people and animals there when he fought against them. Instead, he decided to bring them and offer them as sacrifices before God. That's not what the Lord told him to do!

> *And Samuel said, Hath the LORD as great delight in burnt offerings and sacrifices, as in obeying the voice of the LORD? Behold, to obey is better than sacrifice, and to hearken than the fat of rams.*
>
> 1 SAMUEL 15:22

You can't make deals with God and say, "Lord, I know You told me to give this money right now, but I need it. I have something I really want to spend it on. I'll tell you what. I'll just take this money and get what I want now, and then I'll double it and give You that much later." No. That's not pleasing to the Lord. He wants you to obey Him and do what He told you to do when He told you to do it!

> *To obey is better than sacrifice.*
>
> 1 SAMUEL 15:22

WHAT ARE YOU ALLOWING?

Samuel continued by saying,

> *For rebellion is as the sin of witchcraft, and stubbornness is as iniquity and idolatry.*
>
> 1 SAMUEL 15:23A

OBEDIENCE IS BETTER

Strong statements, indeed! Not doing what God has told you to do is *rebellion*. And stubbornness is as *iniquity* and *idolatry*. We just haven't placed that kind of stigma on rebellion and stubbornness!

As a matter of fact, I'm sure you wouldn't tolerate witchcraft in your home. If your children came home with a Ouija board, started putting séances together, or tried casting spells, you'd be all over them like a coat of wet paint, declaring, "Not in this house! As long as I'm breathing, I will not allow witchcraft or idolatry in this house!" You wouldn't let them make some little graven image and begin to worship it. But there are many parents who just allow their kids to go through rebellion, be stubborn, talk back to them, disrespect authority, etc., and not even think anything of it. They reason, *Well, they're just teenagers. That's normal!*

Now don't get me wrong! I'm not saying that you can—or should—completely control your children. But I am saying that if you discern rebellion, you ought to resist it. If you detect stubbornness, you should be doing something about it. Many people just don't place that kind of importance upon this. They argue, "But rebellion is normal!" No, it's not. You're allowing witchcraft into your home (1 Sam. 15:23)!

If you permitted a poisonous snake to live in your house, maybe you could go for a day, a week, a month, or a year without it biting you. But if you allow that snake to stay in your home, then sooner or later, it could take your life or the life of one of your kids.

LISTEN TO THE LORD!

No one would live like that—it's not worth the risk! Well, many people do even worse by allowing rebellion and stubbornness a place in their lives and homes. We know we aren't doing things exactly the way God has told us to. We're aware of the fact that we are often slow to obey. God has to badger us and drive us into a corner in order to get us to do something. "But that's the way that I am. I'm just not quick to obey!" Then we're rebellious and stubborn. That's witchcraft, iniquity, and idolatry!

This was why Saul was rejected and David was chosen. If you want to be a David instead of a Saul, quit disobeying God! Stop being rebellious and stubborn! Listen to the Lord and obey Him from your heart quickly and fully!

Outline

VI. Saul kept on saying "It's not my fault! You don't understand. I did obey God!" but he didn't.

And Saul said unto Samuel, Yea, I have obeyed the voice of the L ORD, and have gone the way which the L ORD sent me, and have brought Agag the king of Amalek, and have utterly destroyed the Amalekites. [21] But the people took of the spoil.
1 SAMUEL 15:20-21A

  A. The Lord wouldn't have held him guilty if the people had truly done all of this.
  B. So, Saul attempted to justify himself by saying that the people took them *"to sacrifice unto the L ORD thy God in Gilgal"* (1 Sam. 15:21).

VII. When God tells you to do something, it's not open to negotiation.
  A. You don't need to "interpret" it—just do what God has told you to do!
    i. I've had people say to me, "God has told me to come to Charis Bible College. I know I'm supposed to come, and I believe I'm supposed to come now. But it's only a couple more years before I can take an early retirement."
    ii. I answer, "Well, you aren't obeying God."
    iii. They try to explain it away, but it's not what God has told them to do.
  B. The Lord told Saul to kill all of these people and animals there when he fought against them.
  C. Instead, he decided to bring them and offer them as sacrifices before God.
  D. That's not what the Lord told him to do!
  E. You can't make deals with God.
  F. He wants you to obey Him and do what He told you to do when He told you to do it (1 Sam. 15:22)!

VIII. Not doing what God has told you to do is *rebellion*; and stubbornness is as *iniquity* and *idolatry*.

For rebellion is as the sin of witchcraft, and stubbornness is as iniquity and idolatry.
1 SAMUEL 15:23A

    A. Most just haven't placed that kind of stigma on rebellion and stubbornness!
    B. But I'm sure you wouldn't tolerate witchcraft in your home.
        i. If your children came home with a Ouija board, started putting séances together, or tried casting spells, you'd be all over them like a coat of wet paint, declaring, "Not in this house!"
        ii. You wouldn't let them make some little graven image and begin to worship it.
    C. But there are many parents who just allow their kids to go through rebellion, be stubborn, talk back to them, disrespect authority, etc., and not even think anything of it.
    D. They argue, "But rebellion is normal!"
    E. No, it's not—you're allowing witchcraft into your home (1 Sam. 15:23)!

IX. We know we aren't doing things exactly the way God has told us to.
    A. We're aware of the fact that we are often slow to obey.
    B. God has to badger us and drive us into a corner in order to get us to do something.
    C. "But that's the way that I am. I'm just not quick to obey!"
    D. Then we're rebellious and stubborn.
    E. This was why Saul was rejected and David was chosen.
    F. If we want to be a David instead of a Saul, we need to quit disobeying God!
    G. Let's listen to the Lord and obey Him from our hearts quickly and fully!

6. Saul kept on saying "It's not my fault! You don't understand. I did obey God!" but he didn't.

   *And Saul said unto Samuel, Yea, I have obeyed the voice of the L*ORD*, and have gone the way which the L*ORD *sent me, and have brought Agag the king of Amalek, and have utterly destroyed the Amalekites. [21] But the people took of the spoil.*

   1 SAMUEL 15:20-21A

   The Lord wouldn't have held him guilty if the people had truly done all of this. So, Saul attempted to justify himself by saying that the people took them *"to sacrifice unto the L*ORD *thy God in Gilgal"* (1 Sam. 15:21).

   6a. True or false: Saul obeyed the voice of the Lord.
   False
   6b. Whom did Saul blame for his partial obedience?
   The people
   6c. When Saul gave his excuse, he was attempting to _____ himself.
   Justify

7. When God tells us to do something, it's not open to negotiation. We don't need to "interpret" it—we need to just do what God has told us to do! Andrew has had people say to him, "God has told me to come to Charis Bible College. I know I'm supposed to come, and I believe I'm supposed to come now. But it's only a couple more years before I can take an early retirement." Andrew answers, "Well, you aren't obeying God." They try to explain it away, but it's not what God has told them to do. The Lord told Saul to kill all of these people and animals there when he fought against them. Instead, he decided to bring them and offer them as sacrifices before God. That's not what the Lord told him to do! We can't make deals with God. He wants us to obey Him and do what He told us to do when He told us to do it (1 Sam. 15:22)!

   7a. True or false: You can negotiate with God when He tells you to do something you are unsure of.
   False
   7b. You don't need to _____ it—just do what God has told you to do!
   Interpret
   7c. Instead of killing all of the people and animals that Israel had fought against, Saul decided to do what?
   Bring them and offer them as sacrifices before God
   7d. *Discussion question:* Why do you think people sometimes try to negotiate, interpret, or make deals with God instead of just obeying Him? (Guideline: You can use Saul's choices as examples or think of a time in your own life when you found it hard to obey God completely.)
   Discussion question

OBEDIENCE IS BETTER

8. Not doing what God has told us to do is *rebellion*; and stubbornness is as *iniquity* and *idolatry*.

   For rebellion is as the sin of witchcraft, and stubbornness is as iniquity and idolatry.
   1 SAMUEL 15:23A

We just haven't placed that kind of stigma on rebellion and stubbornness! We wouldn't tolerate witchcraft in our homes. If our children came home with Ouija boards, started putting séances together, or tried casting spells, we'd be all over them like a coat of wet paint, declaring, "Not in this house!" We wouldn't let them make some little graven image and begin to worship it. But there are many parents who just allow their kids to go through rebellion, be stubborn, talk back to them, disrespect authority, etc. and not even think anything of it. They argue, "But rebellion is normal!" No, it's not—we're allowing witchcraft into our homes (1 Sam. 15:23)!

8a. Not doing what God has told you to do is _____.
   A. Idolatry
   B. Rebellion
   C. Wise
   D. Dependent on the circumstance
   E. Negotiable
   B. Rebellion

8b. Stubbornness is compared to what?
   A. Iniquity and idolatry
   B. Being like a mule
   C. Rebellion and witchcraft
   D. All of the above
   E. None of the above
   A. Iniquity and idolatry

8c. What do parents argue is the reason that they tolerate their teenagers' rebellion and stubbornness?
   Because they believe it's "normal"

8d. When you allow children to disrespect authority, you are allowing _____ into your home!
   Witchcraft

8e. *Discussion question:* What situations or influences do you think make parents tolerate rebellion and stubbornness from their children?
   Discussion question

9. We know we aren't doing things exactly the way God has told us to. We're aware of the fact that we are often slow to obey. God has to badger us and drive us into a corner in order to get us to do something. "But that's the way that I am. I'm just not quick to obey!" Then we're rebellious and stubborn. This was why Saul was rejected and David was chosen. If we want to be a David instead of a Saul, we need to quit disobeying God! Let's listen to the Lord and obey Him from our hearts quickly and fully!

9a. Saying "But that's the way that I am. I'm just not quick to obey" makes you what?
   A. Normal and human
   B. Wicked and evil
   C. Rebellious and stubborn
   D. All of the above
   E. None of the above
   C. Rebellious and stubborn

9b. To obey the Lord, you must obey Him from your heart _____ and _____.
   Quickly / fully

OBEDIENCE IS BETTER

Discipleship Questions

19. True or false: Saul obeyed the voice of the Lord.

20. Whom did Saul blame for his partial obedience?

21. When Saul gave his excuse, he was attempting to _____ himself.

22. True or false: You can negotiate with God when He tells you to do something you are unsure of.

23. You don't need to _____ it—just do what God has told you to do!

24. Instead of killing all of the people and animals that Israel had fought against, Saul decided to do what?

25. *Discussion question:* Why do you think that people sometimes try to negotiate, interpret, or make deals with God instead of just obeying Him? (You can use Saul's example or think of a time in your own life, you found it hard to obey God completely.)

26. Not doing what God has told you to do is?
    A. Idolatry
    B. Rebellion
    C. Wise
    D. Dependent on the circumstances
    E. Negotiable

LESSONS FROM DAVID

27. Stubbornness is compared to what?
    A. Iniquity and idolatry
    B. Being like a mule
    C. Rebellion and witchcraft
    D. All of the above
    E. None of the above

28. What do parents argue is the reason that they tolerate their teenagers' rebellion and stubbornness?
    _____
    _____
    _____

29. When you allow children to disrespect authority, you are allowing _____ into your home!

30. *Discussion question:* What situations or influences do you think make parents tolerate rebellion and stubbornness from their children?
    _____
    _____
    _____

31. Saying "But that's the way that I am. I'm just not quick to obey" makes you what?
    A. Normal and human
    B. Wicked and evil
    C. Rebellious and stubborn
    D. All of the above
    E. None of the above

32. To obey the Lord, you must obey Him from your heart _____ and _____.

Answer Key

19. False
20. The people
21. Justify
22. False
23. Interpret
24. Bring them and offer them as sacrifices before God
25. *Discussion question*
26. B. Rebellion
27. A. Iniquity and idolatry
28. Because they believe it's "normal"
29. Witchcraft
30. *Discussion question*
31. C. Rebellious and stubborn
32. Quickly / fully

Scripture

1 SAMUEL 15:17-23

And Samuel said, When thou wast little in thine own sight, wast thou not made the head of the tribes of Israel, and the Lord anointed thee king over Israel? [18] And the Lord sent thee on a journey, and said, Go and utterly destroy the sinners the Amalekites, and fight against them until they be consumed. [19] Wherefore then didst thou not obey the voice of the Lord, but didst fly upon the spoil, and didst evil in the sight of the Lord? [20] And Saul said unto Samuel, Yea, I have obeyed the voice of the Lord, and have gone the way which the Lord sent me, and have brought Agag the king of Amalek, and have utterly destroyed the Amalekites. [21] But the people took of the spoil, sheep and oxen, the chief of the things which should have been utterly destroyed to sacrifice unto the Lord thy God in Gilgal. [22] And Samuel said, Hath the Lord as great delight in burnt offerings and sacrifices, as in obeying the voice of the Lord? Behold, to obey is better than sacrifice, and to hearken than the fat of rams. [23] For rebellion is as the sin of witchcraft, and stubbornness is as iniquity and idolatry. Because thou hast rejected the word of the Lord, he hath also rejected thee from being king.

OBEDIENCE IS BETTER

Move On!

> *For rebellion is as the sin of witchcraft, and stubbornness is as iniquity and idolatry. Because thou hast rejected the word of the LORD, he hath also rejected thee from being king. [24] And Saul said unto Samuel, I have sinned: for I have transgressed the commandment of the LORD, and thy words: because I feared the people, and obeyed their voice.*
>
> 1 SAMUEL 15:23-24

Saul finally admitted, "All right, I'm wrong. But I'm wrong because I feared the people and they forced me into it!" He still didn't take direct responsibility.

If you want to be a Saul, then dodge responsibility. "I'm this way because of my dysfunctional family, the color of my skin, my lack of education, this bad thing that happened to me, etc. You don't understand. I was abused as a child!" Saul's mentality was a victim's mentality, and it leads to destruction. If you want to be a David—someone after God's own heart—then start accepting responsibility for your own wrongs and quit blaming everybody else.

In addition, quit fearing the people! Saul said, "I was afraid of the people. They coerced me into it!" He was the king. He was God's appointed leader. He had the authority. But instead of doing the right thing, he let the tail wag the dog.

"HONOR ME, PLEASE!"

Saul went on to say,

> *Now therefore, I pray thee, pardon my sin, and turn again with me, that I may worship the LORD. [26] And Samuel said unto Saul, I will not return with thee: for thou hast rejected the word of the LORD, and the LORD hath rejected thee from being king over Israel. [27] And as Samuel turned about to go away, he laid hold upon the skirt of his mantle, and it rent. [28] And Samuel said unto him, The LORD hath rent the kingdom of Israel from thee this day, and hath given it to a neighbour of thine, that is better than thou. [29] And also the Strength of Israel will not lie nor repent: for he is not a man, that he should repent. [30] Then he [Saul] said, I have sinned: yet honour me now, I pray thee, before the elders of my people, and before Israel, and turn again with me, that I may worship the LORD thy God.*
>
> 1 SAMUEL 15:25-30, BRACKETS MINE

Samuel told Saul that the Lord had rejected him. Saul would ultimately lose the kingdom. His children and family would no longer be royalty. Saul had lost everything. Yet he wanted Samuel to offer a sacrifice to the Lord with him so the people would stay with him. He wasn't as concerned about losing the Lord's approval as he was about what the people thought. Pride and insecurity were distinguishing flaws of Saul's character. The fear of man is a snare (Prov. 29:25).

"HOW LONG?"

And Samuel came no more to see Saul until the day of his death: nevertheless Samuel mourned for Saul: and the LORD repented that he had made Saul king over Israel. [16:1] And the LORD said unto Samuel, How long wilt thou mourn for Saul, seeing I have rejected him from reigning over Israel? fill thine horn with oil, and go, I will send thee to Jesse the Bethlehemite: for I have provided me a king among his sons.

1 SAMUEL 15:35-16:1

Saul was God's first choice to run the kingdom. It repented God that He had made Saul king and then had to reject him. But once that was done—once Saul made his choice—God moved on. He wasn't living in the past—sitting there sulking, pouting, and brooding over all these things. God said, "I have provided Myself another king from among the sons of Jesse." The Lord got up and went on with Plan B!

God is more concerned about getting His plan done than He is about mourning what could have and should have been. On the other hand, Samuel mourned for Saul constantly. Finally, the Lord asked him, "How long are you going to mourn for Saul?"

This can be a major problem today. People see a "move of God," and they just want to build three tabernacles and camp there (Matt. 17:4). Yet, it's time to move on. In the wilderness, there was a cloud that hovered over the tabernacle. When the cloud moved, the people had to get up and move (Ex. 40:36-38). They couldn't stay there. They had to move on and follow God. He had a place for them to go.

Likewise, God has a purpose for your life. Along the way, you'll encounter individuals who fail and fall away from Him. They may be people you've loved and respected. A church leader you idolized may fall into sexual sin, misappropriate money, or otherwise fail. I can't tell you how many people I've seen just fall apart when the person they were leaning on failed. You need to move on and continue with your life in Christ. Don't let this stop you!

MOVE ON!

WHEN IT'S TIME TO GO

Samuel was beginning to fall into this trap until God spoke to him. "How long are you going to mourn? I've rejected Saul. Now you reject him too!" That may sound harsh—and in the New Testament, God will never totally forsake you—but He can move on to Plan B. In other words, God can say, "All right, I'll use you to the degree that you're usable—that you allow Me—but I'm not going to let My kingdom suffer. I'll raise up somebody else to get the job done." and He'll move on. If God moves on, then He takes that anointing and puts it on another person. He takes that anointing from one church and puts it on another. Don't just sit there and die along with that church! If the glory cloud has lifted, move on! You do what God has told you to do!

So, He told Samuel,

Fill thine horn with oil, and go.

1 SAMUEL 16:1

In the Old Testament, oil symbolized the Holy Spirit. When they anointed priests and kings with oil, the power of the Holy Spirit came upon them and energized them to be used of God. So, basically, the Lord was telling Samuel to quit mourning over Saul. "Forget the things that are behind, and look forward to what's next! Be full of the Holy Ghost and go do what I've told you to do." That's a powerful word for you and me today!

There have been times in my life where I was just devastated. Sometimes it's been a tragedy; other times it's just been negative things that have happened. But my natural tendency was to lose my motivation. I just wanted to sit there and cry, "O God, how could this have happened?" During those times, the Lord has told me, "Get up, fill your horn with oil, and go. Move forward with the vision and mission I've given you!" The message God has given me to share is more important than my sitting down and grieving over something bad that's happened.

On other occasions, something has been so wonderful that I've just wanted to stay there. When I first started in ministry, I pastored some small groups of people. I laid my life down for them because I truly loved them. Even though I struggled because my calling and anointing is to be a teacher—not a pastor—I was doing it at the time because the Lord had led me to. When the time came and God was moving me on, I didn't want to leave those people. I was willing to just put the rest of the plans and goals for my life on hold so I could just stay there and be a blessing to those people. But God told me, "Fill your horn with oil, and go!"

So, it's not always something negative that's holding you back. Sometimes it could be a wonderful experience that you're afraid to leave. Either way, when the cloud of God starts moving, fill your horn with oil and go!

MORE HANDS IN HEAVEN

I had some friends who started out in a Presbyterian church. They began ministering to a group of college-aged kids in their home, and that group eventually grew up into a church. However, when it was time to transition from being part of the Presbyterian church to pastoring that new church, it was challenging. Although they loved the people in their other church, they knew God was guiding them to step out and lead the new one. The husband was pretty much ready to go for it, but the wife was really struggling with leaving the old church and the people they'd grown to love so much.

As they were praying about it and holding hands with friends around a kitchen table, the Lord gave the wife a word. He said, "Sometimes you have to let go of the hands you're holding onto so that there will be more hands around My table in heaven." In other words, sometimes we have to sacrifice certain relationships in order to go on and fulfill what God has called us to do. We need to be willing to do this.

Whether it's something negative that's causing us to grieve or something positive that we'd rather not leave, when God is leading us to move on, we need to fill our horn with oil and go!

Outline

I. Saul finally admitted "All right, I'm wrong," but he still didn't take direct responsibility.

For rebellion is as the sin of witchcraft, and stubbornness is as iniquity and idolatry. Because thou hast rejected the word of the LORD, he hath also rejected thee from being king. [24] And Saul said unto Samuel, I have sinned: for I have transgressed the commandment of the LORD, and thy words: because I feared the people, and obeyed their voice.

1 SAMUEL 15:23-24

    A. If you want to be a Saul, then dodge responsibility.
    B. Saul's mentality was a victim's mentality, and it leads to destruction.
    C. If you want to be a David—someone after God's own heart—then start accepting responsibility for your own wrongs and quit blaming everybody else.
    D. In addition, quit fearing the people!
    E. Saul was the king, God's appointed leader, who had the authority.
    F. Instead of doing the right thing, Saul *"feared the people, and obeyed their voice"* (1 Sam. 15:24).

II. Saul went on to say,

Now therefore, I pray thee, pardon my sin, and turn again with me, that I may worship the LORD. [26] And Samuel said unto Saul, I will not return with thee: for thou hast rejected the word of the LORD, and the LORD hath rejected thee from being king over Israel. [27] And as Samuel turned about to go away, he laid hold upon the skirt of his mantle, and it rent. [28] And Samuel said unto him, The LORD hath rent the kingdom of Israel from thee this day, and hath given it to a neighbour of thine, that is better than thou. [29] And also the Strength of Israel will not lie nor repent: for he is not a man, that he should repent. [30] Then he [Saul] said, I have sinned: yet honour me now, I pray thee, before the elders of my people, and before Israel, and turn again with me, that I may worship the LORD thy God.

1 SAMUEL 15:26-30, BRACKETS MINE

    A. Samuel told Saul that the Lord had rejected him and that Saul would ultimately lose the kingdom.
        i. His children and family would no longer be royalty.
        ii. Saul had lost everything.
    B. Yet he wanted Samuel to offer a sacrifice to the Lord with him so the people would stay with him.

C. He wasn't as concerned about losing the Lord's approval as he was about what the people thought.
D. Pride and insecurity were distinguishing flaws of Saul's character—the fear of man is a snare (Prov. 29:25).

And Samuel came no more to see Saul until the day of his death: nevertheless Samuel mourned for Saul: and the LORD repented that he had made Saul king over Israel.
1 SAMUEL 15:35

E. Saul's character didn't just affect him but Samuel also.

III. It repented God that He had made Saul king and then had to reject him.
A. But once that was done—once Saul made his choice—God moved on.

And the LORD said unto Samuel, How long wilt thou mourn for Saul, seeing I have rejected him from reigning over Israel? fill thine horn with oil, and go, I will send thee to Jesse the Bethlehemite: for I have provided me a king among his sons.
1 SAMUEL 16:1

B. God is more concerned about getting His plan done than He is about mourning what could have and should have been.
C. This can also be a major problem if people see a "move of God" and they just want to build three tabernacles and camp there (Matt. 17:4), yet it's time to move on.
D. In the wilderness, there was a cloud that hovered over the tabernacle.
   i. When the cloud moved, the people had to get up and move (Ex. 40:36-38).
   ii. They had to move on and follow God because He had a place for them to go.
E. Likewise, God has a purpose for your life.
   i. Along the way, you'll encounter individuals who fail and fall away from Him.
   ii. You need to move on and continue with your life in Christ—don't let their failure stop you!

IV. Samuel was beginning to fall into this trap until God spoke to him.
A. "How long are you going to mourn? I've rejected Saul. Now you reject him too!"
B. That may sound harsh—and in the New Testament, God will never totally forsake you—but He can move on to Plan B.
   i. In other words, God can say "All right, I'll use you to the degree that you're usable—that you allow Me—but I'm not going to let My kingdom suffer, so I'll raise up somebody else to get the job done" and He'll move on.
C. If God moves on, then He takes that anointing and puts it on another person or on another church.

D. Don't just sit there if the glory cloud has lifted—move on and do what God has told you to do!

V. So, God told Samuel,

> *Fill thine horn with oil, and go.*
>
> 1 SAMUEL 16:1

A. In the Old Testament, when they anointed priests and kings with oil, which symbolized the Holy Spirit, power came upon them and energized them to be used of God.
B. The Lord was telling Samuel to quit mourning over Saul.
C. There have been times in my life when I was just devastated, but the Lord has told me, "Get up, fill your horn with oil, and go. Move forward with the vision and mission I've given you!"
D. On other occasions, something has been so wonderful that I've just wanted to stay there.
E. So, it's not always something negative that's holding you back; sometimes it could be a wonderful experience that you're afraid to leave.
F. Either way, when the cloud of God starts moving, fill your horn with oil and go!

VI. I had some friends, a married couple, who started out in the Presbyterian church.
A. When it was time to transition from being part of the Presbyterian church to pastoring a new church, it was challenging.
B. The wife was really struggling with leaving the old church and the people there they had grown to love so much.
C. As they were praying about it with friends, the Lord gave the wife a word, saying, "Sometimes you have to let go of the hands you're holding onto so that there will be more hands around My table in heaven."
D. When God is leading you to move on, you need to fill your horn with oil and go!

Teacher's Guide

1. Saul finally admitted "All right, I'm wrong," but he still didn't take direct responsibility.

   For rebellion is as the sin of witchcraft, and stubbornness is as iniquity and idolatry. Because thou hast rejected the word of the Lord, he hath also rejected thee from being king. [24] And Saul said unto Samuel, I have sinned: for I have transgressed the commandment of the Lord, and thy words: because I feared the people, and obeyed their voice.

   1 SAMUEL 15:23-24

   If we want to be a Saul, then we should dodge responsibility. Saul's mentality was a victim's mentality, and it leads to destruction. If we want to be a David—someone after God's own heart—then we should start accepting responsibility for our own wrongs and quit blaming everybody else. In addition, we need to quit fearing the people! Saul was the king, God's appointed leader, who had the authority. Instead of doing the right thing, Saul *"feared the people, and obeyed their voice"* (1 Sam. 15:24).

   1a. True or false: Saul finally took responsibility and admitted his mistakes.
   False
   1b. If you want to be like Saul, you can do what?
   A. Accept responsibility
   B. Repent
   C. Dodge responsibility
   D. All of the above
   E. None of the above
   C. Dodge responsibility
   1c. If you want to be like David, you can do what?
   A. Accept responsibility
   B. Repent
   C. Quit blaming others
   D. A and C
   E. B and C
   D. A and C
   1d. *Discussion question:* What prevented Saul from obeying God?
   Discussion question

MOVE ON!

2. Saul went on to say,

> *Now therefore, I pray thee, pardon my sin, and turn again with me, that I may worship the LORD. [26] And Samuel said unto Saul, I will not return with thee: for thou hast rejected the word of the LORD, and the LORD hath rejected thee from being king over Israel. [27] And as Samuel turned about to go away, he laid hold upon the skirt of his mantle, and it rent. [28] And Samuel said unto him, The LORD hath rent the kingdom of Israel from thee this day, and hath given it to a neighbour of thine, that is better than thou. [29] And also the Strength of Israel will not lie nor repent: for he is not a man, that he should repent. [30] Then he [Saul] said, I have sinned: yet honour me now, I pray thee, before the elders of my people, and before Israel, and turn again with me, that I may worship the LORD thy God.*
>
> 1 SAMUEL 15:25-30, BRACKETS MINE

Samuel told Saul that the Lord had rejected him and that Saul would ultimately lose the kingdom. His children and family would no longer be royalty. Saul had lost everything. Yet he wanted Samuel to offer a sacrifice to the Lord with him so the people would stay with him. He wasn't as concerned about losing the Lord's approval as he was about what the people thought. Pride and insecurity were distinguishing flaws of Saul's character—the fear of man is a snare (Prov. 29:25).

> *And Samuel came no more to see Saul until the day of his death: nevertheless Samuel mourned for Saul: and the LORD repented that he had made Saul king over Israel.*
>
> 1 SAMUEL 15:35

Saul's character didn't just affect him but Samuel also.

2a. According to 1 Samuel 15:26, the Lord rejected Saul from being King over Israel because he did what?
Rejected the word of the Lord

2b. The ripping of Samuel's "skirt of his mantle" was a sign that what?
   A. Saul's sin was serious to God
   B. God had ripped the kingdom of Israel away from Saul
   C. God was giving the kingdom of Israel away to a foreign king
   D. All of the above
   E. None of the above
   B. God had ripped the kingdom of Israel away from Saul

2c. Which character flaws caused Saul to lose his position of king of Israel?
Pride and insecurity

3. It repented God that He had made Saul king and then had to reject him. But once that was done—once Saul made his choice—God moved on.

> *And the Lord said unto Samuel, How long wilt thou mourn for Saul, seeing I have rejected him from reigning over Israel? fill thine horn with oil, and go, I will send thee to Jesse the Bethlehemite: for I have provided me a king among his sons.*
>
> 1 SAMUEL 16:1

God is more concerned about getting His plan done than He is about mourning what could have and should have been. This can also be a major problem if people see a "move of God" and they just want to build three tabernacles and camp there (Matt. 17:4), yet it's time to move on. In the wilderness, there was a cloud that hovered over the tabernacle. When the cloud moved, the people had to get up and move (Ex. 40:36-38). They had to move on and follow God because He had a place for them to go. Likewise, God has a purpose for our lives. Along the way, we'll encounter individuals who fail and fall away from Him. We need to move on and continue with our lives in Christ—we can't let their failure stop us!

3a. Once Saul made his choice, what did God do?
   He moved on
3b. Why did God tell Samuel to fill his horn with oil?
   A. So that he could go and anoint a new king over Israel
   B. Because Samuel needed a new anointing
   C. So that he could heal Saul of his wounds of rejection
   D. All of the above
   E. None of the above
   A. So that he could go and anoint a new king over Israel
3c. God is more concerned about getting His _____ done than He is about mourning what could have and should have been.
   Plan
3d. *Discussion question:* Why do you think seeing someone you love or respect fail might cause you to stop or not go on with God's plan for your life?
   Discussion question

MOVE ON!

4. Samuel was beginning to fall into this trap until God spoke to him. "How long are you going to mourn? I've rejected Saul. Now you reject him too!" That may sound harsh—and in the New Testament, God will never totally forsake us—but He can move on to Plan B. In other words, God can say "All right, I'll use you to the degree that you're usable—that you allow Me—but I'm not going to let My kingdom suffer, so I'll raise up somebody else to get the job done" and He'll move on. If God moves on, then He takes that anointing and puts it on another person or on another church. We can't just sit there if the glory cloud has lifted—we need to move on and do what God has told us to do!

4a. What trap was Samuel beginning to fall into?
Mourning for Saul

4b. True or false: In the New Testament, God will never totally forsake you.
True

4c. What might God do if you refuse to obey Him?
He can move on to Plan B

4d. God will use you to the degree you are _____.
Usable

4e. *Discussion question:* How does God not allow His kingdom to suffer while at the same time He permits you to disobey Him?
Discussion question

5. So, God told Samuel,

> *Fill thine horn with oil, and go.*
>
> 1 SAMUEL 16:1

In the Old Testament, when priest and kings were anointed with oil, which symbolized the Holy Spirit, power came upon them and energized them to be used of God. The Lord was telling Samuel to quit mourning over Saul. There have been times in Andrew's life when he was just devastated, but the Lord has told him, "Get up, fill your horn with oil, and go. Move forward with the vision and mission I've given you!" On other occasions, something has been so wonderful that he's just wanted to stay there. So, it's not always something negative that's holding us back; sometimes it could be a wonderful experience that we're afraid to leave. Either way, when the cloud of God starts moving, we must fill our horns with oil and go!

5a. What did oil symbolize in the Old Testament?
The Holy Spirit

5b. After times when he was _____, God has told Andrew to "Get up, fill your horn with oil, and go."
Devastated

5c. True or false: God tells you to get up and go only after something negative has happened that could hold you back.
False

5d. Why would God have to tell you to get up and go after something wonderful has happened?
It's so wonderful that you are afraid to leave

6. Andrew had some friends, a married couple, who started in the Presbyterian church. When it was time to transition from being part of the Presbyterian church to pastoring a new church, it was challenging. The wife was really struggling with leaving the old church and the people there they had grown to love so much. As they were praying about it with friends, the Lord gave the wife a word, saying, "Sometimes you have to let go of the hands you're holding onto so that there will be more hands around My table in heaven." When God is leading us to move on, we need to fill our horns with oil and go!

6a. *Discussion question:* Have you ever had something that you had trouble letting go of, like the wife in this story? How does letting go of someone's hand represent moving on?
Discussion question

MOVE ON!

Discipleship Questions

1. True or false: Saul finally took responsibility and admitted his mistakes.

2. If you want to be like Saul, you can do what?
   A. Accept responsibility
   B. Repent
   C. Dodge responsibility
   D. All of the above
   E. None of the above

3. If you want to be like David, you can do what?
   A. Accept responsibility
   B. Repent
   C. Quit blaming others
   D. A and C
   E. B and C

4. *Discussion question:* What prevented Saul from obeying God?
   _____
   _____
   _____

5. According to 1 Samuel 15:26, the Lord rejected Saul from being king over Israel because he did what?
   _____
   _____
   _____

6. The ripping of Samuel's "skirt of his mantle" was a sign that what?
   A. Saul's sin was serious to God
   B. God had ripped the kingdom of Israel away from Saul
   C. God was giving the kingdom of Israel away to a foreign king
   D. All of the above
   E. None of the above

7. Which character flaws caused Saul to lose his position of king of Israel?
   _____
   _____
   _____

8. Once Saul made his choice, what did God do?
   _____
   _____
   _____

9. Why did God tell Samuel to fill his horn with oil?
   A. So that he could go and anoint a new king over Israel
   B. Because Samuel needed a new anointing
   C. So that he could heal Saul of his wounds of rejection
   D. All of the above
   E. None of the above

10. God is more concerned about getting His _____ done than He is about mourning what could have and should have been.

11. *Discussion question:* Why do you think seeing someone you love or respect fail might cause you to stop or not go on with God's plan for your life?
    _____
    _____
    _____

12. What trap was Samuel beginning to fall into?
    _____
    _____
    _____

13. True or false: In the New Testament, God will never totally forsake you.

14. What might God do if you refuse to obey Him?
    _____
    _____
    _____

15. God will use you to the degree you are _____.

MOVE ON!

16. *Discussion question:* How does God not allow His kingdom to suffer while at the same time He permits you to disobey Him?
_____
_____
_____

17. What did oil symbolize in the Old Testament?
_____
_____
_____

18. After times when he was _____, God has told Andrew to "Get up, fill your horn with oil, and go."

19. True or false: God tells you to get up and go only after something negative has happened that could hold you back.

20. Why would God have to tell you to get up and go after something wonderful has happened?
_____
_____
_____

21. *Discussion question:* Have you ever had something that you had trouble letting go of, like the wife in this story? How does letting go of someone's hand represent moving on?
_____
_____
_____

Answer Key

1. False
2. C. Dodge responsibility
3. D. A and C
4. *Discussion question*
5. Rejected the word of the Lord
6. B. God had ripped the kingdom of Israel away from Saul
7. Pride and insecurity
8. God moved on
9. A. So that he could go and anoint a new king over Israel
10. Plan
11. *Discussion question*
12. Mourning for Saul
13. True
14. He can move on to Plan B
15. Usable
16. *Discussion question*
17. The Holy Spirit
18. Devastated
19. False
20. It's so wonderful that you are afraid to leave
21. *Discussion question*

MOVE ON!

1 SAMUEL 15:23-30

For rebellion is as the sin of witchcraft, and stubbornness is as iniquity and idolatry. Because thou hast rejected the word of the Lord, he hath also rejected thee from being king. [24] And Saul said unto Samuel, I have sinned: for I have transgressed the commandment of the Lord, and thy words: because I feared the people, and obeyed their voice. [25] Now therefore, I pray thee, pardon my sin, and turn again with me, that I may worship the Lord. [26] And Samuel said unto Saul, I will not return with thee: for thou hast rejected the word of the Lord, and the Lord hath rejected thee from being king over Israel. [27] And as Samuel turned about to go away, he laid hold upon the skirt of his mantle, and it rent. [28] And Samuel said unto him, The Lord hath rent the kingdom of Israel from thee this day, and hath given it to a neighbour of thine, that is better than thou. [29] And also the Strength of Israel will not lie nor repent: for he is not a man, that he should repent. [30] Then he said, I have sinned: yet honour me now, I pray thee, before the elders of my people, and before Israel, and turn again with me, that I may worship the Lord thy God.

PROVERBS 29:25

The fear of man bringeth a snare: but whoso putteth his trust in the Lord shall be safe.

1 SAMUEL 15:35

And Samuel came no more to see Saul until the day of his death: nevertheless Samuel mourned for Saul: and the Lord repented that he had made Saul king over Israel.

1 SAMUEL 16:1

And the Lord said unto Samuel, How long wilt thou mourn for Saul, seeing I have rejected him from reigning over Israel? fill thine horn with oil, and go, I will send thee to Jesse the Bethlehemite: for I have provided me a king among his sons.

MATTHEW 17:4

Then answered Peter, and said unto Jesus, Lord, it is good for us to be here: if thou wilt, let us make here three tabernacles; one for thee, and one for Moses, and one for Elias.

EXODUS 40:36-38

And when the cloud was taken up from over the tabernacle, the children of Israel went onward in all their journeys: [37] But if the cloud were not taken up, then they journeyed not till the day that it was taken up. [38] For the cloud of the Lord was upon the tabernacle by day, and fire was on it by night, in the sight of all the house of Israel, throughout all their journeys.

A Heart for God

When Samuel went to Bethlehem and found Jesse, he told him that God had sent him to anoint a king from among his sons. "Therefore, call your house together immediately!" So, Jesse's sons came before the prophet.

> *And it came to pass, when they were come, that he looked on Eliab, and said, Surely the LORD's anointed is before him.*
>
> 1 SAMUEL 16:6

Eliab was David's oldest brother. He was the biggest, the strongest, and probably the meanest and toughest too. As a result, Samuel was looking at him and remembering Saul. Saul had been taller than anyone else in Israel from the shoulders up. He had been the oldest son of his father. The first person whom God had chosen to be king was a hunk of a man. So, Samuel was just supposing that this was the way it was going to be. When he saw Eliab—the oldest, strongest, tallest, toughest-looking son—Samuel commented, "Surely the Lord's anointed is before me!"

> *But the LORD said unto Samuel, Look not on his countenance, or on the height of his stature; because I have refused him: for the LORD seeth not as man seeth; for man looketh on the outward appearance, but the LORD looketh on the heart.*
>
> 1 SAMUEL 16:7

What an awesome truth! God doesn't look at us the way man does.

David was the runt of the litter. As a matter of fact, his father didn't even think that David had a chance, so he didn't even put David's name in the hat. Jesse had eight sons, but he only brought the eldest seven as candidates for this job of being king over Israel. He thought, *David doesn't stand a chance. Never in a million years would he be picked!* David was the youngest. He didn't look like king material. But God doesn't see the way man does!

HOW DO YOU EVALUATE?

When you are evaluating people or physical things, you can't just evaluate them on the way they look on the outside. Neither can you read a book by simply looking at its cover! (If you could, you wouldn't be reading this right now.) God looks on the inside, and He sees differently than man sees. So, you need to keep this in mind when you're evaluating other people.

This is also true for when other people evaluate you. You don't need to buy into their evaluation because they may be merely looking on your outward appearance. If you're born again, then you are a brand-new person on the inside. You are a king and priest on the inside! You are a son of God! You're anointed. You're powerful. One third of you is wall-to-wall Holy Ghost! Don't let other people's opinions and evaluations of who you are in the natural realm—your education, looks, talents, voice, abilities, etc.—limit you!

Society puts so much emphasis on outward appearance. People are starving themselves to death because they believe that skinny is beautiful and fat is ugly. I'm not saying that I think chubby is beautiful (although some cultures do), but I am saying that we put too much attention on that. Just because you're overweight, not too good looking, and don't have the greatest education doesn't mean that God can't use you. Do you remember 1 Corinthians 1:26-29? God chooses the base, weak, despised, and foolish things to confound the wise. God sees things differently than man does.

So, don't let yourself or others evaluate you on just external things. If you have a relationship with God, that qualifies you! The Lord has put all kinds of good things inside you. You just need to start seeing yourself the way God sees you!

IS YOUR NAME IN THE HAT?

Then Jesse called Abinadab, and made him pass before Samuel. And he said, Neither hath the LORD *chosen this. [9] Then Jesse made Shammah to pass by. And he said, Neither hath the* LORD *chosen this.*

1 SAMUEL 16:8-9

Finally, all seven of the sons present had passed before the prophet. Samuel said, "Nope! None of these are him!" As far as Samuel knew, Jesse had no other sons. Yet, Samuel was sensitive enough to God to know that none of them were the right one. Since he knew that God had said one of Jesse's sons would be the next king—and none of these were him—he asked, "Are these all the sons you have?"

Jesse answered,

There remaineth yet the youngest, and, behold, he keepeth the sheep. And Samuel said unto Jesse, Send and fetch him: for we will not sit down till he come hither.

1 SAMUEL 16:11B

Jesse didn't think enough of David to even put his name in the hat!

At one time, my brother owned a small mechanic shop. He was behind on some bills, and his creditors would call him to ask for money. One fellow in particular just got mean and vicious, and tried to intimidate him. Basically, my brother told him, "Look, here's the way I do it. I put everybody's name in a hat. Then I just draw names out and pay bills until I run out of money. I just haven't picked your name out of the hat yet."

The guy snarled, "Well, I want my money!"

My brother responded, "If you keep bothering me, I'm going to take your name out of the hat!" The guy stopped calling.

Jesse didn't even put David's name in the hat. He didn't think enough of his youngest son to bring him before the prophet. But Samuel said, "He must be the one! Therefore, none of us are going to sit down until David comes."

GOD IS LOOKING

Back then, they couldn't just call David on his cell phone. There were no cars to drive out to the pasture to get him. David may have been quite a ways off in the wilderness somewhere keeping those sheep. It must have taken someone—on foot, roundtrip—at least an hour to bring David back. So, Samuel saying "None of us will sit down until he comes" put a real urgency upon the situation. It was a pain for all of them to just stand there until David came.

This also showed a tremendous amount of honor and respect that the Lord was paying David. By this time, Samuel had recognized that David was the chosen one regardless of what he looked like. The prophet was going by the word of the Lord and honoring David!

Out in the wilderness, David knew what was happening. He knew that the prophet was there to anoint a king. He knew that his seven older brothers were brought as candidates and he was left out in the field with the sheep. A lesser, more insecure person would have been crying and belly-aching, "God, I didn't even get a chance!" We don't know exactly what David was doing, but there's no indication in the Word that he was whining, griping, or complaining. In fact, someone like that wouldn't have been the one that God would select. So, even though he was initially excluded, God passed by all the others and kept them standing until he arrived. The one whom no one else considered, God considered, chose, and honored. He looked on David's heart. The Lord passed over everyone else to find David!

For the eyes of the LORD run to and fro throughout the whole earth, to shew himself strong in the behalf of them whose heart is perfect toward him.

2 CHRONICLES 16:9A

"Perfect" doesn't mean sinless or problem free. Rather, it means someone whose heart is fully committed—belonging completely—to the Lord. It's someone who is seeking God with their whole heart.

God passed over an entire nation, seven older brothers—everybody—to find David. Then He made them stand until he came. The Lord put honor, favor, and blessing upon David because David had put honor, favor, and blessing upon the Lord.

"HERE I AM!"

God wants to do the same for you! You don't have to be a silver vessel—just a surrendered one. It's not your ability; it's your availability. God is looking for someone who will make Him first in their life. Your response to the Lord right now ought to be, "Look no further! Here I am! I'm turning my life over to You with my whole heart." If you will genuinely do that, you'll be promoted. You'll see God's blessing come to pass in your life.

God chose David despite the fact that in the natural, he didn't have the height, build, or looks. God chose him because of his heart. When David arrived, the Bible describes his appearance as *"ruddy"* (1 Sam. 16:12). This word literally means "reddish" (*Strong's Concordance*). Scholars aren't sure whether this means he was redheaded or had a red complexion. Either way would certainly be unusual for a Jew. This word also has the connotation that he was pampered; it's what we would call a "mama's boy" today. He was also…

…withal of a beautiful countenance, and goodly to look to.

1 SAMUEL 16:12

Now these aren't necessarily bad things, but they aren't what you would expect in a warrior-king! It certainly wasn't what Samuel was expecting in the beginning. But God told him, "Don't look on the outward appearance. Look on his heart."

Whatever your limitations are in the natural, God looks at your heart. Even if your body is handicapped, God isn't looking at that. He's looking at your heart. Your heart isn't handicapped unless you choose to let it be that way. You can choose God. You can seek Him with a perfect heart. And if you do, He'll raise you up and do miracles in your life just as surely as He did for David!

*Then Samuel took the horn of oil, and anointed him in the midst of his brethren: and the Spirit of the L*ORD *came upon David from that day forward. So Samuel rose up, and went to Ramah.*

1 SAMUEL 16:13

BE LIKE DAVID

Later in that chapter, the Word goes on to say that David was chosen out of all the Israelites to come and play his harp before Saul because he was a valiant man and God was with him (1 Sam. 16:18). The one who suggested David to Saul was just one of his servants. They were looking for someone who could play the harp and alleviate the torment of the evil spirit that was plaguing Saul. In the process, David's name just happened to be brought up. Coincidence? I don't think so!

Personally, I believe Samuel did this in secret because he was afraid of what Saul might do. But either way, the principle is true: Once you've begun to seek the Lord and He releases His anointing on your life, it's like a cork. They could put you on the bottom of a lake, but you'll rise again. It doesn't matter what they do. You're like cream—always rising to the top!

If you seek God with your whole heart, the eyes of the Lord will find you (2 Chr. 16:9). He's looking for a person like that! He'll pass over everybody in your nation, state, and city just to find you. Once He locates you and releases His power into your life, He'll cause you to be drawn to the top. God will release His blessing through you into this world. It's just a matter of time. This is exactly what happened with David!

Don't be like Saul. He was a man pleaser, motivated by pride and arrogance. Since he was afraid of people, he was always trying to please them. This caused him to disobey God, saying, "I'm not going to do it Your way. My way is better!" He refused to accept responsibility but became stubborn and rebellious instead. Humble yourself and accept responsibility. Come to the end of yourself and the beginning of God.

Be like David. Prepare your heart to seek the Lord. He's not looking for people with talent, education, or natural abilities. He's not against them, but He's not for them. What God is looking for is a heart seeking after Him. God chooses people based on their hearts. If you will hunger and thirst after righteousness, you will be filled (Matt. 5:6). You won't only be satisfied and have your needs met, but you'll be filled with the power, presence, and provision of God. He will pour you out and make you a blessing to other people. Man looks on the outward appearance, but God looks on the heart.

PREPARE YOUR HEART

If you are born again, God gave you a perfect heart. Quit walking in the vanity of your own wisdom and embrace the wisdom of God. Renew your mind to His Word so you can see yourself the way He sees you. Understand the riches He placed within your born-again spirit and how you can experience them day by day.

As a brother and fellow follower of God, I haven't arrived—but I've left. God has spoken these things into my life in a powerful way. I have prepared my heart to seek Him and be fully committed to Him.

As you can tell, I'm not the most qualified person to do what I do. I'm a hick from Texas who dropped out of college after only six months. But the Lord has used me to raise up multiple Bible schools all around the world that are training ministers and equipping believers. In the natural, it doesn't make sense. But God saw my heart, not my education (or lack thereof). You can have thirty-two degrees and still be frozen!

I'm certainly not the best-sounding or best-looking person. Yet the Lord has me preaching and teaching His Word all around the world on both radio and television. He could have easily chosen someone who sounded better, looked better, or dressed nicer. I just really don't have a corner on anything in the natural. But I've sought the Lord with my whole heart and He has blessed me. He's used me, and I'm thrilled about that.

The Lord has a plan—a destiny—for you too. As you seek Him with your whole heart, you'll find yourself walking in that plan more and more. I pray that you'll let the Holy Spirit burn these truths into your heart so that you will be a man (or woman) after God's heart too!

ANDREW'S RECOMMENDATIONS FOR FURTHER STUDY

My teachings "Who You Are in the Spirit" and *Spirit, Soul & Body* will help you understand this in a greater way.

Outline

I. God sent Samuel to anoint a king from among Jesse's sons.

And it came to pass, when they were come, that he looked on Eliab, and said, Surely the LORD's anointed is before him.

1 SAMUEL 16:6

   A. Because Eliab, David's oldest brother, was the biggest, the strongest, and probably the meanest and toughest, Samuel was looking at him and supposing he would be king.
   B. Jesse had eight sons, but he only brought the eldest seven as candidates.
   C. David was the youngest and didn't look like king material, but God doesn't see the way man does!

II. When you are evaluating people or physical things, you can't just evaluate them by the way they look on the outside.

But the LORD said unto Samuel, Look not on his countenance, or on the height of his stature; because I have refused him: for the LORD seeth not as man seeth; for man looketh on the outward appearance, but the LORD looketh on the heart.

1 SAMUEL 16:7

   A. God looks on the inside, so you need to keep this in mind when you're evaluating other people.
   B. You don't need to buy into people's evaluation about you either, because they may be merely looking on your outward appearance.
   C. If you're born again, then you are a brand-new person on the inside.
      i. You are a king, priest, and son on the inside!
      ii. You're anointed and powerful because one-third of you is wall-to-wall Holy Ghost!
   D. Don't let other people's opinions and evaluations of who you are in the natural realm—your education, looks, talents, voice, abilities, etc.—limit you!
   E. If you have a relationship with God, just start seeing yourself the way God sees you!

III. All seven of the sons present had passed before the prophet, yet Samuel was sensitive enough to God to know that none of them were the right one:

Are here all thy children?

1 SAMUEL 16:11

A. Then Jesse said, *"There remaineth yet the youngest, and, behold, he keepeth the sheep"* (1 Sam. 16:11).
　　　B. Jesse didn't think enough of David to even put his name in the hat!
　　　C. Samuel said, "He must be the one, so none of us are going to sit down until David comes!"
　　　D. By this time, Samuel had recognized that David was the chosen one regardless of what he looked like, so he was going by the word of the Lord and honoring David!

IV. The Lord passed over everyone else to find David!

*For the eyes of the L*ORD *run to and fro throughout the whole earth, to shew himself strong in the behalf of them whose heart is perfect toward him.*

　　　　　　　　　　　　　　　　　　　　　　　　　　　　　　　　　　　　2 CHRONICLES 16:9A

　　　A. *"Perfect"* doesn't mean sinless or problem free; rather, it means someone whose heart is fully committed—belonging completely—to the Lord.
　　　B. God is looking for someone who will make Him first in their life.
　　　C. If you will genuinely do that, you'll be promoted, and you'll see God's blessing come to pass in your life.

V. God chose David despite the fact that in the natural, he didn't have the height, build, or looks—God chose him because of his heart.
　　　A. When David arrived, the Bible describes his appearance as *"ruddy"* (1 Sam. 16:12), which literally means "reddish" (Strong's Concordance).
　　　　　i. Scholars aren't sure whether this means he was redheaded or had a red complexion, but either way would certainly be unusual for a Jew.
　　　　　ii. This word also has the connotation that he was pampered; it's what we would call a "mama's boy" today.
　　　B. Whatever your limitations are in the natural, God looks at your heart.
　　　　　i. Even if your body is handicapped, God isn't looking at that.
　　　　　ii. Your heart isn't handicapped unless you choose to let it be that way.
　　　C. And if you seek Him with a perfect heart, He'll raise you up and do miracles in your life just as surely as He did for David!

*Then Samuel took the horn of oil, and anointed him in the midst of his brethren: and the Spirit of the L*ORD *came upon David from that day forward. So Samuel rose up, and went to Ramah.*

　　　　　　　　　　　　　　　　　　　　　　　　　　　　　　　　　　　　　1 SAMUEL 16:13

VI. Later in that chapter, the Word goes on to say one of Saul's servants suggested David play his harp before Saul to alleviate the torment of the evil spirit that was plaguing Saul.
    A. It is no coincidence that David's name just happened to be brought up.
    B. I believe Samuel did this in secret because he was afraid of what Saul might do.
    C. This principle is true: Once you've begun to seek the Lord and He releases His anointing on your life, you're like a cork—they could put you on the bottom of a lake, but you'll rise again.

VII. Don't be like Saul—a man pleaser, motivated by pride and arrogance.
    A. Be like David and prepare your heart to seek the Lord.
        i. If you are born again, God gave you a perfect heart, so quit walking in the vanity of your own wisdom and embrace the wisdom of God.
        ii. Renew your mind to His Word so you can understand the riches He placed within your born-again spirit and how you can experience them day by day.
        iii. I'm not the most qualified person to do what I do, but God saw my heart, not my education (or lack thereof).
        iv. The Lord has a plan—a destiny—for you too, and as you seek Him with your whole heart, you'll find yourself walking in that plan more and more.
        v. Let the Holy Spirit burn these truths into your heart so that you will be a man (or woman) after God's heart too!

ANDREW'S RECOMMENDATIONS FOR FURTHER STUDY

My teachings "Who You Are in the Spirit" and *Spirit, Soul & Body* will help you understand this in a greater way.

Teacher's Guide

1. God sent Samuel to anoint a king from among Jesse's sons.

   And it came to pass, when they were come, that he looked on Eliab, and said, Surely the Lord's anointed is before him.

   1 SAMUEL 16:6

Because Eliab, David's oldest brother, was the biggest, the strongest, and probably the meanest and toughest, Samuel was looking at him and supposing he would be king. Jesse had eight sons, but he only brought the eldest seven as candidates. David was the youngest and didn't look like king material, but God doesn't see the way man does!

1a. Which brother did Samuel suppose would be king?
    Eliab
1b. Why did Samuel think that Eliab would be the next king?
    A. He was the oldest son
    B. He was tall
    C. God told him
    D. A and B
    E. B and C
    D. A and B
1c. Why did Jesse only present seven out of his eight sons?
    David didn't look like king material
1d. *Discussion question:* What does Andrew's statement "God doesn't see the way man does" mean?
    Discussion question

A HEART FOR GOD

2. When we are evaluating people or physical things, we can't just evaluate them by the way they look on the outside.

> *But the L*ORD *said unto Samuel, Look not on his countenance, or on the height of his stature; because I have refused him: for the L*ORD *seeth not as man seeth; for man looketh on the outward appearance, but the L*ORD *looketh on the heart.*
>
> 1 SAMUEL 16:7

God looks on the inside, so we need to keep this in mind when we're evaluating other people. We don't need to buy into people's evaluation about us either, because they may be merely looking on our outward appearance. If we're born again, then we are brand-new on the inside. We are kings, priests, and sons on the inside! We're anointed and powerful because one-third of us is wall-to-wall Holy Ghost! We can't let other people's opinions and evaluations of who we are in the natural realm—our education, looks, talents, voices, abilities, etc.—limit us! If we have a relationship with God, we need to just start seeing ourselves the way God sees us!

2a. What do you need to keep in mind when you are evaluating people?
God looks on the inside

2b. If you are born again, what are you?
   A. A brand-new creature
   B. A king and priest
   C. One-third wall-to-wall Holy Ghost
   D. All of the above
   E. None of the above
D. All of the above

2c. Which of the following is not part of the natural realm?
   A. Your spirit
   B. Your looks
   C. Your education
   D. Your voice
   E. Your car
A. Your spirit

2d. How should you see and evaluate yourself and others?
The way God does

3. All seven of the sons present had passed before the prophet, yet Samuel was sensitive enough to God to know that none of them were the right one:

> *Are here all thy children?*
>
> 1 SAMUEL 16:11

Then Jesse said, *"There remaineth yet the youngest, and, behold, he keepeth the sheep"* (1 Sam. 16:11). Jesse didn't think enough of David to even put his name in the hat! Samuel said, "He must be the one, so none of us are going to sit down until David comes!" By this time, Samuel had recognized that David was the chosen one regardless of what he looked like, so he was going by the word of the Lord and honoring David!

3a. True or false: Samuel refused to look at the first seven sons of Jesse.
   False
3b. How did Samuel know that none of the first seven sons of Jesse were going to be king?
   He was sensitive to God
3c. What did Jesse finally admit to the prophet?
   A. He didn't want any of his sons to be king
   B. He had a youngest son who was not there
   C. Jesse himself secretly wanted to be king
   D. All of the above
   E. None of the above
   B. He had a youngest son who was not there
3d. What had Samuel realized by that time?
   That David was the chosen one regardless of what he looked like

4. The Lord passed over everyone else to find David!

   For the eyes of the LORD run to and fro throughout the whole earth, to shew himself strong in the behalf of them whose heart is perfect toward him.

   2 CHRONICLES 16:9A

"Perfect" doesn't mean sinless or problem free; rather, it means someone whose heart is fully committed—belonging completely—to the Lord. God is looking for someone who will make Him first in their life. If we will genuinely do that, we'll be promoted, and we'll see God's blessing come to pass in our lives.

4a. True or false: The Lord passed over everyone else to find David.
   True
4b. Perfect, to God, means what?
   A. Sinless
   B. Healthy
   C. Fully committed
   D. All of the above
   E. None of the above
   C. Fully committed
4c. What will happen if you genuinely put God first in your life?
   You'll be promoted, and you'll see God's blessing come to pass in your life

5. God chose David despite the fact that in the natural, he didn't have the height, stature, build, or looks—God chose him because of his heart. When David arrived, the Bible describes his appearance as *"ruddy"* (1 Sam. 16:12), which literally means "reddish" (*Strong's Concordance*). Scholars aren't sure whether this means he was redheaded or had a red complexion, but either way would certainly be unusual for a Jew. This word also has the connotation that he was pampered; it's what we would call a "mama's boy" today. Whatever our limitations are in the natural, God looks at our hearts. Even if our bodies are handicapped, God isn't looking at that. Our hearts aren't handicapped unless we choose to let them be that way. And if we seek Him with a perfect heart, He'll raise us up and do miracles in our lives just as surely as He did for David!

> *Then Samuel took the horn of oil, and anointed him in the midst of his brethren: and the Spirit of the LORD came upon David from that day forward. So Samuel rose up, and went to Ramah.*
>
> 1 SAMUEL 16:13

5a. Which quality or qualities did David lack to be king in the natural?
   A. Height
   B. Build
   C. Looks
   D. All of the above
   E. None of the above
   D. All of the above

5b. True or false: It was common for a Jew to be ruddy.
   False

5c. Even if your body is limited, God is looking at your _____.
   Heart

5d. According to 1 Samuel 16:13, what happened to David from the time that Samuel anointed him with oil?
   The Spirit of the Lord came on him from that day forward

6. Later in that chapter, the Word goes on to say one of Saul's servants suggested David play his harp before Saul to alleviate the torment of the evil spirit that was plaguing Saul. It is no coincidence that David's name just happened to be brought up. I believe Samuel did this in secret because he was afraid of what Saul might do. This principle is true: Once we've begun to seek the Lord and He releases His anointing on our lives, we're like corks—they could put us on the bottom of a lake, but we'll rise again.

6a. Why did David play the harp for Saul?
To alleviate the torment of an evil spirit that was plaguing Saul

6b. True or false: It is just a coincidence that David ended up in the palace after he had been anointed as king.
False

6c. *Discussion question*: Explain this principle that Andrew says is true: Once you've begun to seek the Lord and He releases His anointing on your life, you're like a cork.
Discussion question

7. We shouldn't be like Saul—man pleasers, motivated by pride and arrogance. We should be like David and prepare our hearts to seek the Lord. If we are born again, God gave us perfect hearts, so let's quit walking in the vanity of our own wisdom and embrace the wisdom of God. We must renew our minds to His Word so we can understand the riches He placed within our born-again spirits and how we can experience them day by day. Andrew's not the most qualified person to do what he does, but God saw his heart, not his education (or lack thereof). The Lord has a plan—a destiny—for us too, and as we seek Him with our whole hearts, we'll find ourselves walking in that plan more and more. Let's let the Holy Spirit burn these truths into our hearts so that we will be men (or women) after God's heart too!

7a. True or false: Pride and arrogance caused Saul to please man instead of God.
True

7b. To walk in the wisdom of God, what do you have to quit walking in?
The vanity of your own wisdom

7c. *Discussion question*: Did God choose Andrew because he lacked the qualifications or in spite of the fact that he wasn't qualified? Explain.
Discussion question

Discipleship Questions

1. Which brother did Samuel suppose would be king?

2. Why did Samuel think that Eliab would be the next king?
   A. He was the oldest son
   B. He was tall
   C. God told him
   D. A and B
   E. B and C

3. Why did Jesse only present seven out of his eight sons?

4. *Discussion question:* What does Andrew's statement "God doesn't see the way man does" mean?

5. What do you need to keep in mind when you are evaluating people?

6. If you are born again, what are you?
   A. A brand-new creature
   B. A king and priest
   C. One-third wall-to-wall Holy Ghost
   D. All of the above
   E. None of the above

7. Which of the following is not part of the natural realm?
   A. Your spirit
   B. Your looks
   C. Your education
   D. Your voice
   E. Your car

8. How should you see and evaluate yourself and others?
   _____
   _____
   _____

9. True or false: Samuel refused to look at the first seven sons of Jesse.

10. How did Samuel know that none of the first seven sons of Jesse were going to be king?
    _____
    _____
    _____

11. What did Jesse finally admit to the prophet?
    A. He didn't want any of his sons to be king
    B. He had a youngest son who was not there
    C. Jesse himself secretly wanted to be king
    D. All of the above
    E. None of the above

12. What had Samuel realized by that time?
    _____
    _____
    _____

13. True or false: The Lord passed over everyone else to find David.

14. Perfect to God means what?
    A. Sinless
    B. Healthy
    C. Fully committed
    D. All of the above
    E. None of the above

15. What will happen if you genuinely put God first in your life?
_____
_____
_____

16. Which quality or qualities did David lack to be king in the natural?
    A. Height
    B. Build
    C. Looks
    D. All of the above
    E. None of the above

17. True or false: It was common for a Jew to be ruddy.

18. Even if your body is limited, God is looking at your _____.

19. According to 1 Samuel 16:13, what happened to David from the time that Samuel anointed him with oil?
_____
_____
_____

20. Why did David play the harp for Saul?
_____
_____
_____

21. True or false: It is just a coincidence that David ended up in the palace after he had been anointed as king.

22. *Discussion question:* Explain this principle that Andrew says is true: Once you've begun to seek the Lord and He releases His anointing on your life, you're like a cork.
_____
_____
_____

23. True or false: Pride and arrogance caused Saul to please man instead of God.

24. To walk in the wisdom of God, what do you have to quit walking in?

25. *Discussion question:* Did God choose Andrew because he lacked the qualifications or in spite of the fact that he wasn't qualified? Explain.

1. Eliab
2. D. A and B
3. David didn't look like king material
4. *Discussion question*
5. God looks on the inside
6. D. All of the above
7. A. Your spirit
8. The way God does
9. False
10. He was sensitive to God
11. B. He had a youngest son who was not there
12. That David was the chosen one regardless of what he looked like
13. True
14. C. Fully committed
15. You'll be promoted, and you'll see God's blessing come to pass in your life
16. D. All of the above
17. False
18. Heart
19. The Spirit of the Lord came on him from that day forward
20. To alleviate the torment of an evil spirit that was plaguing Saul
21. False
22. *Discussion question*
23. True
24. The vanity of your own wisdom
25. *Discussion question*

1 SAMUEL 16:6-9
And it came to pass, when they were come, that he looked on Eliab, and said, Surely the Lord's anointed is before him. [7] But the Lord said unto Samuel, Look not on his countenance, or on the height of his stature; because I have refused him: for the Lord seeth not as man seeth; for man looketh on the outward appearance, but the Lord looketh on the heart. [8] Then Jesse called Abinadab, and made him pass before Samuel. And he said, Neither hath the Lord chosen this. [9] Then Jesse made Shammah to pass by. And he said, Neither hath the Lord chosen this.

1 CORINTHIANS 1:26-29
For ye see your calling, brethren, how that not many wise men after the flesh, not many mighty, not many noble, are called: [27] But God hath chosen the foolish things of the world to confound the wise; and God hath chosen the weak things of the world to confound the things which are mighty; [28] And base things of the world, and things which are despised, hath God chosen, yea, and things which are not, to bring to nought things that are: [29] That no flesh should glory in his presence.

1 SAMUEL 16:11-13
And Samuel said unto Jesse, Are here all thy children? And he said, There remaineth yet the youngest, and, behold, he keepeth the sheep. And Samuel said unto Jesse, Send and fetch him: for we will not sit down till he come hither. [12] And he sent, and brought him in. Now he was ruddy, and withal of a beautiful countenance, and goodly to look to. And the Lord said, Arise, anoint him: for this is he. [13] Then Samuel took the horn of oil, and anointed him in the midst of his brethren: and the Spirit of the Lord came upon David from that day forward. So Samuel rose up, and went to Ramah.

2 CHRONICLES 16:9
For the eyes of the Lord run to and fro throughout the whole earth, to shew himself strong in the behalf of them whose heart is perfect toward him. Herein thou hast done foolishly: therefore from henceforth thou shalt have wars.

1 SAMUEL 16:18
Then answered one of the servants, and said, Behold, I have seen a son of Jesse the Bethlehemite, that is cunning in playing, and a mighty valiant man, and a man of war, and prudent in matters, and a comely person, and the Lord is with him.

MATTHEW 5:5
Blessed are the meek: for they shall inherit the earth.

Seeing Through the Covenant

David was anointed to be king in secret. Nobody knew he was king yet, except his family and Samuel, and they were hiding it. If the present king—Saul—had heard this news, he would have killed them all. Samuel acknowledged this in 1 Samuel 16:2.

David had actually been playing the harp in Saul's court. However, Saul didn't know yet who he was. Then the Philistines came down to fight, so he went off to battle and sent David home again. While there, David was back to keeping his father's sheep. A proud person wouldn't have been able to do this. David had become the anointed and rightful king, yet he was tending his father's sheep, just as he had done before all this happened. Another characteristic of humility is patience. Impatience is a sure sign of our own arrogance and self-reliance.

Jesse's three oldest sons—Eliab, Shammah, and Abinadab—were in the army, so they went with Saul to battle.

But as they went out to battle, a champion of the Philistines—a giant named Goliath—came out and challenged the armies of Israel.

THE PHILISTINE CHAMPION

And there went out a champion out of the camp of the Philistines, named Goliath, of Gath, whose height was six cubits and a span.

1 SAMUEL 17:4

Most scholars believe he stood at least nine feet nine inches high. (Some say he may have been as tall as thirteen feet!)

And he had an helmet of brass upon his head, and he was armed with a coat of mail; and the weight of the coat was five thousand shekels of brass.

1 SAMUEL 17:5

Scholars estimate that the coat of mail he wore weighed about 125 pounds! The giant's armor—not even counting Goliath himself—probably weighed more than David did.

And he had greaves of brass upon his legs, and a target of brass between his shoulders. [7] And the staff of his spear was like a weaver's beam; and his spear's head weighed six hundred shekels of iron: and one bearing a shield went before him.

1 SAMUEL 17:6-7

They estimate that his spearhead weighed fifteen pounds. The actual shaft of his spear must have been like a rounded off four-by-four post. It had to have quite a bit of weight in order to balance out that heavy of a head. So, if the head was fifteen pounds and the shaft was another fifteen pounds to balance it out, can you imagine trying to throw a thirty-pound spear?

This is an indication of how big and strong Goliath was. He wasn't just tall and skinny. This was a well-proportioned, muscular giant of a man. In the natural realm, nobody could compete with him. He was easily their superior!

"WHAT IS THE REWARD?"

And he stood and cried unto the armies of Israel, and said unto them, Why are ye come out to set your battle in array? am not I a Philistine, and ye servants to Saul? choose you a man for you, and let him come down to me. [9] If he be able to fight with me, and to kill me, then will we be your servants: but if I prevail against him, and kill him, then shall ye be our servants, and serve us. [10] And the Philistine said, I defy the armies of Israel this day; give me a man, that we may fight together. [11] When Saul and all Israel heard those words of the Philistine, they were dismayed, and greatly afraid.

1 SAMUEL 17:8-11

The Israelites actually hid themselves behind rocks, in dens, and in caves. Among the entire nation of Israel, there wasn't a single person willing to go up against this giant!

David's father called him in from keeping the sheep. He gave him some bread and cheese, and basically said, "Take this to your brothers and to the captain over them in the army. Find out how they're doing and bring me back word" (1 Sam. 17:17-18).

Back then they didn't have newspapers, radio, television, or internet for news broadcasts. If you wanted to find out what was happening to your children out fighting in a battle, you had to send someone to get a firsthand report. So, Jesse took his youngest son—David—and sent him to do this.

As David arrived to see his brothers, the armies had lined up and this Philistine champion issued his challenge once again. Then he cursed the Israelites and called them cowards as they fled from before him

---

SEEING THROUGH THE COVENANT

(1 Sam. 17:23-24). After David saw and heard these things, he asked, "What will be done for the man who kills this giant and takes away our reproach?" Instead of running away and being afraid like everybody else, David was saying, "This guy needs to be stopped! What are they promising the fellow who will go out and defeat this giant?"

THE RIGHT WAY TO THINK

Remember, David was still a youth at this time. Most scholars believe he was around seventeen years old when he was anointed to be king. Therefore, he was probably eighteen or nineteen here, but he certainly wasn't very old. All those seasoned men of war who were bigger, stronger, and more experienced than he was were standing all around him, full of fear. All these guys were shaking in their boots, but David challenged them, saying, "What right does this man have to say these kinds of things?"

What made David able to fight this giant, kill him, and bring this great deliverance? He wasn't bigger or stronger than anyone else. It wasn't that he'd been trained in a military school and had natural combat knowledge. It wasn't anything in the natural at all. What was different about David was his heart—specifically the attitude of his heart. His heart was sensitive to God, and because of that, he was fearless. He didn't see things the way other people did. They were looking on the outward appearance, but David knew that God looks on the heart. That's why he'd been chosen!

So, David not only looked at himself the way God saw him, but he also viewed other things—including giants—the way God saw them. Goliath's heart was not right with God. He was not sensitive at all to the Lord. So, in that sense, David already had him beat. It was an unfair fight, it really was. Goliath didn't stand a chance! Most people—considering outward appearances—would have said, "David doesn't stand a chance. It's an unfair fight!" But when you look at it from the inside, it was absolutely lopsided. David was the one who had the right heart, was anointed, and had the covenant relationship with God. Goliath had nothing. He was powerless. Now that's the right way to look at things!

What I'm saying here is different than the way most people think. That's why most people run and hide behind rocks, in holes, and in caves from their Enemy. They don't think this way. But this is how the Bible will teach you to think. It's the right way to think!

I. David was anointed to be king in secret.
   A. If the present king—Saul—had heard this news, he would have killed them all (1 Sam. 16:2).
   B. David had actually been playing the harp in Saul's court; however, Saul didn't know yet who he was.
   C. Then the Philistines came down to fight, so Saul went off to battle and sent David home again.
   D. While there, David went back to keeping his father's sheep.
   E. A proud person wouldn't have been able to do this.
   F. Another characteristic of humility is patience.
   G. Impatience is a sure sign of our own arrogance and self-reliance.

II. Jesse's three oldest sons were in the army, so they went with Saul to battle.
   A. But as they went out to battle, a champion of the Philistines—a giant named Goliath—came out and challenged the armies of Israel.

And there went out a champion out of the camp of the Philistines, named Goliath, of Gath, whose height was six cubits and a span.

1 SAMUEL 17:4

   B. Most scholars believe he stood at least nine feet nine inches high (some say he may have been as tall as thirteen feet!).

And he had an helmet of brass upon his head, and he was armed with a coat of mail; and the weight of the coat was five thousand shekels of brass.

1 SAMUEL 17:5

   C. The giant's armor—not even counting Goliath himself—probably weighed more than David did.

And he had greaves of brass upon his legs, and a target of brass between his shoulders. [7] And the staff of his spear was like a weaver's beam; and his spear's head weighed six hundred shekels of iron: and one bearing a shield went before him.

1 SAMUEL 17:6-7

D. They estimate that his spearhead weighed fifteen pounds, so if the head was fifteen pounds and the shaft was another fifteen pounds to balance it out, can you imagine trying to throw a thirty-pound spear?
E. This is an indication of how big and strong Goliath was; he was a well-proportioned, muscular giant of a man.
F. In the natural realm, nobody could compete with him.

III. Among the entire nation of Israel, there wasn't a single person willing to go up against this giant!

And he stood and cried unto the armies of Israel, and said unto them, Why are ye come out to set your battle in array? am not I a Philistine, and ye servants to Saul? choose you a man for you, and let him come down to me. [9] If he be able to fight with me, and to kill me, then will we be your servants: but if I prevail against him, and kill him, then shall ye be our servants, and serve us. [10] And the Philistine said, I defy the armies of Israel this day; give me a man, that we may fight together. [11] When Saul and all Israel heard those words of the Philistine, they were dismayed, and greatly afraid.

1 SAMUEL 17:8-11

A. David's father called him in from keeping the sheep; he gave him some bread and cheese, and said, "Take this to your brothers and to the captain over them in the army. Find out how they're doing and bring me back word" (1 Sam. 17:17-18).
B. As David arrived to see his brothers, the armies had lined up and this Philistine champion issued his challenge once again (1 Sam. 17:23-24).
C. After David saw and heard these things, he asked, "What will be done for the man who kills this giant and takes away our reproach?"
D. Instead of running away and being afraid like everybody else, David was saying, "This guy needs to be stopped! What are they promising the fellow who will go out and defeat this giant?"

IV. Remember, David was still a youth at this time.
A. All those seasoned men of war who were bigger, stronger, and more experienced than he was and were standing all around him, full of fear.
B. What made David able to fight this giant, kill him, and bring this great deliverance?
C. He wasn't bigger or stronger than anyone else, and it wasn't that he'd been trained in a military school and had natural combat knowledge—it wasn't anything in the natural at all.
D. What was different about David was his heart—specifically the attitude of his heart.
E. His heart was sensitive to God, and because of that, he was fearless.
F. David not only looked at himself the way God saw him, but he also viewed other things—including giants—the way God saw them.

G. Most people—considering outward appearances—would have said, "David doesn't stand a chance. It's an unfair fight!"
H. But when you look at it from the inside, it was absolutely lopsided.
   i. David was the one who had the right heart, was anointed, and had the covenant relationship with God.
   ii. Goliath had nothing—he was powerless.
I. What I'm saying here is different than the way most people think.
J. But this is how the Bible will teach you to think, and it's the right way to think!

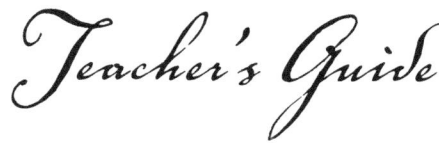

Teacher's Guide

1. David was anointed to be king in secret. If the present king—Saul—had heard this news, he would have killed them all (1 Sam. 16:2). David had actually been playing the harp in Saul's court; however, Saul didn't know yet who he was. Then the Philistines came down to fight, so Saul went off to battle and sent David home again. While there, David went back to keeping his father's sheep. A proud person wouldn't have been able to do this. Another characteristic of humility is patience. Impatience is a sure sign of our own arrogance and self-reliance.

1a. Why was David anointed to be king in secret?
   Because the present king—Saul—would've killed them all (1 Sam. 16:2)
1b. What happened to David when the Philistines came down to fight?
   He was sent home and went back to keeping his father's sheep
1c. *Discussion question:* In your opinion, why would pride and a lack of humility prevent someone from doing like David did?
   Discussion question

2. Jesse's three oldest sons were in the army, so they went with Saul to battle. But as they went out to battle, a champion of the Philistines—a giant named Goliath—came out and challenged the armies of Israel.

> *And there went out a champion out of the camp of the Philistines, named Goliath, of Gath, whose height was six cubits and a span.*
>
> 1 SAMUEL 17:4

Most scholars believe he stood at least nine feet nine inches high (some say he may have been as tall as thirteen feet!).

> *And he had an helmet of brass upon his head, and he was armed with a coat of mail; and the weight of the coat was five thousand shekels of brass.*
>
> 1 SAMUEL 17:5

The giant's armor—not even counting Goliath himself—probably weighed more than David did.

> *And he had greaves of brass upon his legs, and a target of brass between his shoulders. [7] And the staff of his spear was like a weaver's beam; and his spear's head weighed six hundred shekels of iron: and one bearing a shield went before him.*
>
> 1 SAMUEL 17:6-7

They estimate that his spearhead weighed fifteen pounds, so if the head was fifteen pounds and the shaft was another fifteen pounds to balance it out, that means he carried a thirty-pound spear. This is an indication of how big and strong Goliath was; he was a well-proportioned, muscular giant of a man. In the natural realm, nobody could compete with him.

2a. *Discussion question:* Meditate on what Goliath must've looked like in the natural. Share your thoughts.
Discussion question

3. Among the entire nation of Israel, there wasn't a single person willing to go up against this giant!

   And he stood and cried unto the armies of Israel, and said unto them, Why are ye come out to set your battle in array? am not I a Philistine, and ye servants to Saul? choose you a man for you, and let him come down to me. [9] If he be able to fight with me, and to kill me, then will we be your servants: but if I prevail against him, and kill him, then shall ye be our servants, and serve us. [10] And the Philistine said, I defy the armies of Israel this day; give me a man, that we may fight together. [11] When Saul and all Israel heard those words of the Philistine, they were dismayed, and greatly afraid.

   1 SAMUEL 17:8-11

David's father called him in from keeping the sheep; he gave him some bread and cheese, and said, "Take this to your brothers and to the captain over them in the army. Find out how they're doing and bring me back word" (1 Sam. 17:17-18). As David arrived to see his brothers, the armies had lined up and this Philistine champion issued his challenge once again (1 Sam. 17:23-24). After David saw and heard these things, he asked, "What will be done for the man who kills this giant and takes away our reproach?" Instead of running away and being afraid like everybody else, David was saying, "This guy needs to be stopped! What are they promising the fellow who will go out and defeat this giant?"

3a. Until David came along, was anyone willing to go up against this giant?
    No
3b. True or false: David ran away like everyone else did.
    False

LESSONS FROM DAVID

4. Remember, David was still a youth at this time. All those seasoned men of war who were bigger, stronger, and more experienced than he was were standing all around him, full of fear. What made David able to fight this giant, kill him, and bring this great deliverance? He wasn't bigger or stronger than anyone else, and it wasn't that he'd been trained in a military school and had natural combat knowledge—it wasn't anything in the natural at all. What was different about David was his heart—specifically the attitude of his heart. His heart was sensitive to God, and because of that, he was fearless. David not only looked at himself the way God saw him, but he also viewed other things—including giants—the way God saw them. Most people—considering outward appearances—would have said, "David doesn't stand a chance. It's an unfair fight!" But when we look at it from the inside, it was absolutely lopsided. David was the one who had the right heart, was anointed, and had the covenant relationship with God. Goliath had nothing—he was powerless. What Andrew is saying here is different than the way most people think. But this is how the Bible will teach us to think, and it's the right way to think!

4a. What made David able to fight this giant, kill him, and bring this great deliverance?
    A. He was bigger and stronger than everyone else
    B. His heart was sensitive to God
    C. He had been trained in military school and had natural combat knowledge
    D. All of the above
    E. None of the above
    B. His heart was sensitive to God

4b. *Discussion question*: Why did David's attitude and perspective make a difference in how he dealt with Goliath?
    Discussion question

4c. *Discussion question*: Do you agree with the statement "This is how the Bible will teach you to think, and it's the right way to think!"? Why or why not?
    Discussion question

Discipleship Questions

1. Why was David anointed to be king in secret?

2. What happened to David when the Philistines came down to fight?

3. *Discussion question:* In your opinion, why would pride and a lack of humility prevent someone from doing like David did?

4. *Discussion question:* Meditate on what Goliath must've looked like in the natural. Share your thoughts.

5. Until David came along, was anyone willing to go up against this giant?

6. True or false: David ran away like everyone else did.

7. What made David able to fight this giant, kill him, and bring this great deliverance?
   A. He was bigger and stronger than everyone else
   B. His heart was sensitive to God
   C. He had been trained in military school and had natural combat knowledge
   D. All of the above
   E. None of the above

8. *Discussion question:* Why did David's attitude and perspective make a difference in how he dealt with Goliath?
___
___
___

9. *Discussion question:* Do you agree with the statement "This is how the Bible will teach you to think, and it's the right way to think!"? Why or why not?
___
___
___

Answer Key

1. Because the present king—Saul—would've killed them all (1 Sam. 16:2)
2. He was sent home and went back to keeping his father's sheep
3. *Discussion question*
4. *Discussion question*
5. No
6. False
7. B. His heart was sensitive to God
8. *Discussion question*
9. *Discussion question*

1 SAMUEL 16:2
And Samuel said, How can I go? if Saul hear it, he will kill me. And the LORD said, Take an heifer with thee, and say, I am come to sacrifice to the LORD.

1 SAMUEL 17:4-11
And there went out a champion out of the camp of the Philistines, named Goliath, of Gath, whose height was six cubits and a span. [5] And he had an helmet of brass upon his head, and he was armed with a coat of mail; and the weight of the coat was five thousand shekels of brass. [6] And he had greaves of brass upon his legs, and a target of brass between his shoulders. [7] And the staff of his spear was like a weaver's beam; and his spear's head weighed six hundred shekels of iron: and one bearing a shield went before him. [8] And he stood and cried unto the armies of Israel, and said unto them, Why are ye come out to set your battle in array? am not I a Philistine, and ye servants to Saul? choose you a man for you, and let him come down to me. [9] If he be able to fight with me, and to kill me, then will we be your servants: but if I prevail against him, and kill him, then shall ye be our servants, and serve us. [10] And the Philistine said, I defy the armies of Israel this day; give me a man, that we may fight together. [11] When Saul and all Israel heard those words of the Philistine, they were dismayed, and greatly afraid.

1 SAMUEL 17:17-18
And Jesse said unto David his son, Take now for thy brethren an ephah of this parched corn, and these ten loaves, and run to the camp to thy brethren; [18] And carry these ten cheeses unto the captain of their thousand, and look how thy brethren fare, and take their pledge.

1 SAMUEL 17:23-24
And as he talked with them, behold, there came up the champion, the Philistine of Gath, Goliath by name, out of the armies of the Philistines, and spake according to the same words: and David heard them. [24] And all the men of Israel, when they saw the man, fled from him, and were sore afraid.

SEEING THROUGH THE COVENANT

Seeing Through the Covenant

And David spake to the men that stood by him, saying, What shall be done to the man that killeth this Philistine, and taketh away the reproach from Israel? for who is this uncircumcised Philistine, that he should defy the armies of the living God?
1 SAMUEL 17:26

David was expressing here an attitude that was exactly opposite the rest of the Israelites. He was saying, "This guy is nothing. He's a nobody. He's easy!" Everyone else was saying, "He's so big and powerful! I'm nothing. I'm a nobody!" David had an entirely different attitude. Where did it come from? He stated it right here:

Who is this uncircumcised Philistine, that he should defy the armies of the living God?
1 SAMUEL 17:26B

When David used this term *"uncircumcised Philistine,"* he was saying that Goliath didn't have a covenant with God. Circumcision was a sign of the covenant God had made with the nation of Israel. He was saying, "We're superior. Why are we letting somebody who doesn't even have God on their side intimidate us?" David's attitude came from the covenant, the Word, and the promises of God!

Do you want a different attitude? Do you want to stand apart from all the people who are so fearful today? They're always griping, complaining, and talking about everything that could possibly go wrong. Do you desire to go out and make your life count? If you want to do exploits like David did, you're going to have to have a different attitude. You're going to have to look at God's Word and evaluate your Enemy, circumstances, and problems based on what the Word says about them. David's confidence came from the fact that he had a covenant with God. He was dominated by what the Lord had to say, not by the physical presence of this giant or by what the army of Israel was saying. Only the Word—not other people—moved him. That's powerful!

TREMENDOUS OPPORTUNITY FOR VICTORY

Even though I've seen this and lived it to a great degree, living in this physical world is like gravity. Unbelief, doubt, and negativity pull on us constantly. We need to be so dominated by His Word that we don't let other people's opinions and what things look like in the physical realm dominate us. I've done this to a degree, but I desire to be stronger than ever before!

LESSONS FROM DAVID

That's what made David different. He wasn't the strongest, biggest, meanest, or toughest. David saw things differently than other people did. He looked at this man and said, "He's powerless. He doesn't have my covenant!" Nobody else had thought of the covenant or the promises of God. They were all just evaluating the situation based on Goliath's height, the size of his weapons, and the weight of his armor. They were looking only in the physical realm, but David was looking at the heart. Therefore, his conclusion was "This man is bankrupt! He has nothing!"

It doesn't matter how big your problems are. If you evaluated things this way, you'd recognize that you're the one with the promises. You're the one who has an edge on any enemy you could face—financial problems, physical issues, etc. Really, the bigger the problem confronting you, the greater the opportunity there is to do an exploit for God, to see Him come through, and to have a better testimony. You'll be so blessed just knowing that you're going to get to see how God will deliver you from this totally impossible situation!

We never would have heard of David had he killed a dwarf. Instead of praising him and talking about what a great battle this was, people would have criticized him and declared, "This was unfair!" The headlines in the morning paper would have read, "David Kills Dwarf: Sent to Prison for Life!" People would have criticized him had Goliath been a dwarf, but the fact remains that he was a giant. This means that David had a tremendous opportunity for the Lord to come through with an awesome victory!

Likewise, instead of seeing how big our problems are, we should think of how great a testimony it will be when the Lord gives us victory over them.

RAISED FROM THE DEAD

Even though it's a terrible thing and I wouldn't wish it on anyone, I've seen my son raised from the dead. I felt the same emotions as anyone else, but within a very short period of time, I spoke my faith. Then I started thinking, *This is wonderful! What an opportunity this will be. I believe the Lord is going to raise him from the dead!* My son had been dead for approximately five hours, had already turned black, and had already been toe tagged in the hospital cooler. Yet God raised him from the dead!

During the hour's drive into town—before I knew what the outcome would be—I was excited, rejoicing, and praising God. You might think, *Come on, Andrew, that's impossible! You couldn't have been*, but that's my testimony. I was there. I remember. That's how it was!

David was the same way. He wasn't intimidated. He knew he had a covenant with God. Due to this, David had a completely different attitude than most people. He thought, *What a great opportunity! I've*

SEEING THROUGH THE COVENANT

been anointed king. This is what the Lord has called me to do—defend His people. So, by His grace, I'm going to stand up and do it!

This was what God used to propel David into the public eye. Perhaps He could have done it some other way. We don't know. But this was how the Lord promoted David and got the entire nation to love him. After he killed Goliath, the women came out dancing and singing, *"Saul hath slain his thousands, and David his ten thousands"* (1 Sam. 18:7). David made the hit list! He was front-page news in all the papers. Beating Goliath propelled David to a place that actually paved the way for him to take over the kingdom of Israel. What an opportunity!

However, all these other men were there too. They had the same opportunity. They were Israelites—covenant people. They could have been used. But they weren't looking at this situation with Goliath through the covenant.

SPEAK FORTH YOUR FAITH!

David saw this opportunity through the covenant:

Who is this uncircumcised Philistine, that he should defy the armies of the living God?
1 SAMUEL 17:26

He declared, "I have the Lord's promises, and this guy doesn't. He's separated from God. I have him licked, no problem!"

And when the words were heard which David spake, they rehearsed them before Saul: and he sent for him.
1 SAMUEL 17:31

David had to start speaking forth his faith. If he had just stood there and not spoken his vision, it wouldn't have come to pass. It wasn't enough just to boldly stand there while everyone else was running and hiding behind rocks, in caves, and such. He had to start speaking his faith. After he spoke those words of faith, then the Lord promoted him. God took those words and passed them through the army all the way up to the king.

You have to speak forth what the Lord has put in your heart. You can't be timid. Words are powerful! God will use your words to open up doors and stop the devil in his tracks.

Outline

V. David had an entirely different attitude.

And David spake to the men that stood by him, saying, What shall be done to the man that killeth this Philistine, and taketh away the reproach from Israel? for who is this uncircumcised Philistine, that he should defy the armies of the living God?
1 SAMUEL 17:26

    A. When David used this term *"uncircumcised Philistine,"* he was saying that Goliath didn't have a covenant with God.

Who is this uncircumcised Philistine, that he should defy the armies of the living God?
1 SAMUEL 17:26B

    B. Circumcision was a sign of the covenant God had made with the nation of Israel.
    C. David's attitude came from the covenant, the Word, and the promises of God!
    D. If you want to do exploits like David did, you're going to have to have a different attitude.
    E. You're going to have to look at God's Word and evaluate your Enemy, circumstances, and problems based on what the Word says about them.

VI. Living in this physical world is like gravity—unbelief, doubt, and negativity pull on us constantly.
    A. We need to be so dominated by His Word that we don't let other people's opinions and what things look like in the physical realm dominate us.
    B. It doesn't matter how big our problems are.
    C. If we evaluated things this way, we'd recognize that we're the ones with the promises.
    D. We're the ones who have an edge on any enemy we could face—financial problems, physical issues, etc.
    E. Really, the bigger the problem confronting you, the greater the opportunity there is to do an exploit for God, to see Him come through, and to have a better testimony.
    F. We never would have heard of David had he killed a dwarf.
    G. David had a tremendous opportunity for the Lord to come through with an awesome victory!
    H. Likewise, instead of seeing how big our problems are, we should think of how great a testimony it will be when the Lord gives us victory over them.

VII. David wasn't intimidated; he knew he had a covenant with God.
   A. Due to this, David had a completely different attitude than most people.
   B. This was what God used to propel David into the public eye.
   C. After he killed Goliath, the women came out dancing and singing, *"Saul hath slain his thousands, and David his ten thousands"* (1 Sam. 18:7).
   D. Beating Goliath propelled David to a place that actually paved the way for him to take over the kingdom of Israel.
   E. However, all these other men were there too; they had the same opportunity.
   F. They were Israelites—covenant people—and they could have been used.
   G. But they weren't looking at this situation with Goliath through the covenant.

VIII. David saw this opportunity through the covenant:

Who is this uncircumcised Philistine, that he should defy the armies of the living God?
1 SAMUEL 17:26B

   A. He declared, "I have the Lord's promises, and this guy doesn't. He's separated from God. I have him licked, no problem!"

And when the words were heard which David spake, they rehearsed them before Saul: and he sent for him.
1 SAMUEL 17:31

   B. David had to start speaking forth his faith.
   C. If he had just stood there and not spoken his vision, it wouldn't have come to pass.
   D. It wasn't enough just to boldly stand there while everyone else was running and hiding behind rocks, in caves, and such.
   E. After he spoke those words of faith, then the Lord promoted him—God took those words and passed them through the army all the way up to the king.
   F. You have to speak forth what the Lord has put in your heart.
   G. Words are powerful!
   H. God will use your words to open up doors and stop the devil in his tracks.

LESSONS FROM DAVID

Teacher's Guide

5. David had an entirely different attitude.

   And David spake to the men that stood by him, saying, What shall be done to the man that killeth this Philistine, and taketh away the reproach from Israel? for who is this uncircumcised Philistine, that he should defy the armies of the living God?

   1 SAMUEL 17:26

When David used this term *"uncircumcised Philistine,"* he was saying that Goliath didn't have a covenant with God.

   Who is this uncircumcised Philistine, that he should defy the armies of the living God?

   1 SAMUEL 17:26B

Circumcision was a sign of the covenant God had made with the nation of Israel. David's attitude came from the covenant, the Word, and the promises of God! If we want to do exploits like David did, we're going to have to have a different attitude. We're going to have to look at God's Word and evaluate our Enemy, circumstances, and problems based on what the Word says about them.

5a. *Discussion question:* Using 1 Samuel 17:26, describe David's attitude toward this situation.
   Discussion question
5b. If you want to do _____ like David did, you're going to have to have a _____ attitude.
   Exploits / different
5c. You're going to have to what?
   A. Look at God's Word and evaluate your Enemy, circumstances, and problems based on what the Word says about them
   B. Pray long and hard and evaluate your Enemy, circumstances, and problems based on your feelings and past experiences
   C. Look at God's Word and evaluate your Enemy, circumstances, and problems based on what you think about them
   D. All of the above
   E. None of the above
   A. Look at God's Word and evaluate your Enemy, circumstances, and problems based on what the Word says about them

SEEING THROUGH THE COVENANT

6. Living in this physical world is like gravity—unbelief, doubt, and negativity pull on us constantly. We need to be so dominated by His Word that we don't let other people's opinions and what things look like in the physical realm dominate us. It doesn't matter how big our problems are. If we evaluated things this way, we'd recognize that we're the ones with the promises. We're the ones who have an edge on any enemy we could face—financial problems, physical issues, etc. Really, the bigger the problem confronting you, the greater the opportunity there is to do an exploit for God, to see Him come through, and to have a better testimony. We never would have heard of David had he killed a dwarf. David had a tremendous opportunity for the Lord to come through with an awesome victory! Likewise, instead of seeing how big our problems are, we should think of how great a testimony it will be when the Lord gives us victory over them.

6a. *True or false:* Unbelief, doubt, and negativity pull on you constantly.
True

6b. *Discussion question:* Why could facing a big problem be a good thing?
Discussion question

7. David wasn't intimidated; he knew he had a covenant with God. Due to this, David had a completely different attitude than most people. This was what God used to propel David into the public eye. After he killed Goliath, the women came out dancing and singing, *"Saul hath slain his thousands, and David his ten thousands"* (1 Sam. 18:7). Beating Goliath propelled David to a place that actually paved the way for him to take over the kingdom of Israel. However, all these other men were there too; they had the same opportunity. They were Israelites—covenant people—and they could have been used. But they weren't looking at this situation with Goliath through the covenant.

7a. Why was David not intimidated?
He knew he had a covenant with God

7b. What did beating Goliath accomplish for David?
It propelled him to a place that actually paved the way for him to take over the kingdom of Israel

7c. *Discussion question:* Share your thoughts about the other men who were there with David and who had the same opportunity. Discuss what you can learn from those men.
Discussion question

8. David saw this opportunity through the covenant:

   Who is this uncircumcised Philistine, that he should defy the armies of the living God?
   1 SAMUEL 17:26

He declared, "I have the Lord's promises, and this guy doesn't. He's separated from God. I have him licked, no problem!"

   And when the words were heard which David spake, they rehearsed them before Saul: and he sent for him.
   1 SAMUEL 17:31

David had to start speaking forth his faith. If he had just stood there and not spoken his vision, it wouldn't have come to pass. It wasn't enough just to boldly stand there while everyone else was running and hiding behind rocks, in caves, and such. After he spoke those words of faith, then the Lord promoted him—God took those words and passed them through the army all the way up to the king. We have to speak forth what the Lord has put in our hearts. Words are powerful! God will use our words to open up doors and stop the devil in his tracks.

8a. David had to start _____ forth his _____.
   Speaking / faith
8b. If David had just stood there and not spoken his vision, would it have come to pass?
   No
8c. *Discussion question:* What sort of words have you been speaking? Are they the kind that God can use to open doors and stop the devil in his tracks? What changes, if any, do you feel you need to make in what you say?
   Discussion question

SEEING THROUGH THE COVENANT

Discipleship Questions

10. *Discussion question:* Using 1 Samuel 17:26, describe David's attitude toward this situation.

    _____
    _____
    _____

11. If you want to do _____ like David did, you're going to have to have a _____ attitude.

12. You're going to have to what?
    A. Look at God's Word and evaluate your Enemy, circumstances, and problems based on what the Word says about them
    B. Pray long and hard and evaluate your Enemy, circumstances, and problems based on your feelings and past experiences
    C. Look at God's Word and evaluate your Enemy, circumstances, and problems based on what you think about them
    D. All of the above
    E. None of the above

13. True or false: Unbelief, doubt, and negativity pull on you constantly.

14. *Discussion question:* Why could facing a big problem be a good thing?

    _____
    _____
    _____

15. Why was David not intimidated?

    _____
    _____
    _____

16. What did beating Goliath accomplish for David?

    _____
    _____
    _____

17. *Discussion question:* Share your thoughts about the other men who were there with David and had the same opportunity. Discuss what you can learn from those men.
___
___
___

18. David had to start _____ forth his _____.

19. If David had just stood there and not spoken his vision, would it have come to pass?
___
___
___

20. *Discussion question:* What sort of words have you been speaking? Are the kind that God can use to open doors and stop the devil in his tracks? What changes, if any, do you feel you need to make in what you say?
___
___
___

Answer Key

10. *Discussion question*
11. Exploits / different
12. A. Look at God's Word and evaluate your Enemy, circumstances, and problems based on what the Word says about them
13. True
14. *Discussion question*
15. He knew he had a covenant with God
16. It propelled him to a place that actually paved the way for him to take over the kingdom of Israel
17. *Discussion question*
18. Speaking / faith
19. No
20. *Discussion question*

1 SAMUEL 17:26
And David spake to the men that stood by him, saying, What shall be done to the man that killeth this Philistine, and taketh away the reproach from Israel? for who is this uncircumcised Philistine, that he should defy the armies of the living God?

1 SAMUEL 18:2
And Saul took him that day, and would let him go no more home to his father's house.

1 SAMUEL 17:31
And when the words were heard which David spake, they rehearsed them before Saul: and he sent for him.

1 SAMUEL 18:7
And the women answered one another as they played, and said, Saul hath slain his thousands, and David his ten thousands.

Overcoming Criticism

And Eliab his [David's] eldest brother heard when he spake unto the men; and Eliab's anger was kindled against David, and he said, Why camest thou down hither? and with whom hast thou left those few sheep in the wilderness? I know thy pride, and the naughtiness of thine heart; for thou art come down that thou mightest see the battle.

1 SAMUEL 17:28, BRACKETS MINE

Here's David standing up to the enemy, operating in faith, and doing nothing but good things that should be admired and praised. Yet when his older brother heard it, he railed on him. Eliab turned on David and began to question why he came, saying, "You're irresponsible. You've left those few sheep alone in the wilderness!" The truth was that he didn't leave them alone. He left them with a keeper. Also, he didn't go down there on his own out of pride. David was submitted to his father, who had commanded him to go. Everything David was doing was exactly right.

FAITH CONDEMNS MEDIOCRITY

If you're going to be a giant killer, you need to recognize that criticism will come your way. If you get a different attitude and start operating in faith instead of fear, if you stand up to your giants instead of running from them, if you recognize your covenant rights and privileges—and start speaking forth your faith—you will be criticized. If you decide you aren't going to sit there and bow down to sickness, disease, poverty, oppression, and fear the way everyone else does, there will be people who will turn on you. They'll criticize your vision and mock you. It happens every single time!

When you believe for victory, speak forth your faith, and go for it, you condemn the average person's mediocre life. That's the number one reason they criticize and fight against you. If what you're saying about walking in health, prosperity, and joy is true, then they're wrong. If you don't have to be defeated by circumstances, then their excuses are exposed. If you're saying "It doesn't matter where you come from. All that matters is where you're going, because you can do all things through Christ," then it confronts these people who have been saying "Well, I'm a mess because of what my parents did when I was two years old. I was hated in the womb. I wasn't wanted. I'm a victim." These folks who have been moaning, bellyaching, and using these things to excuse their ineffective, defeated, and powerless lives are going to be condemned by what you say. They have to do one of two things: repent and change, or criticize.

Either they'll criticize or they'll say "You know what, I've been wrong. I believed a lie. I can be prosperous, victorious, and healthy too. I'm changing, and I'm going to believe God's Word." Very few people do this because it requires integrity and taking responsibility for their attitudes and actions. Not many people are willing to do that. Most people will just try to discredit and stop you. Instead of climbing up to your level, they'll just try to pull you down to theirs through criticism.

ANGER & JEALOUSY

This was why David's oldest brother was so vicious toward him in saying these things. Eliab was there when David was chosen as the next king. The Word says he was anointed *"in the midst of his brethren"* (1 Sam. 16:13). And if you remember, Eliab was the first one the prophet Samuel looked at.

> *He looked on Eliab, and said, Surely the LORD's anointed is before him.*
>
> 1 SAMUEL 16:6

When Samuel first saw Eliab, he became excited and thought, *Surely this must be the next king!* This must have caused Eliab's hopes to soar, thinking, *I'm the oldest and strongest. I'm the toughest and meanest. Who could be king better than me?* Then he saw Samuel hear from God and pass over him—and all the others—in favor of the runt of the family. He had to stand there and honor David—with all of his rejected brothers—for however long it took for someone to go and fetch him. Eliab was angry and jealous, thinking, *Why didn't God choose me?*

Then, they're on the battlefield with Saul's army. Eliab had been just like all the other soldiers—hiding from Goliath. He was operating in cowardice and fear. And here came his little brother saying, *"Who is this uncircumcised Philistine?"* (1 Sam. 17:26). Boy, this just got under his skin. It had to have, because it forced Eliab either to admit "My youngest brother here is the one who's right. He's a powerful man of God and I'm a zero—a nothing" or contend "I'm right and he's not" and then impute some kind of wrong to David.

LAWYERS & FAMILY

This happens all the time in court! When a person testifies and gives condemning witness against someone else, nine out of ten times this is what the lawyer's tactic will be. They won't try to disprove what they're saying or defend their client. Instead, they'll turn on this witness and try to discredit them. They'll say, "This guy is a loser. He's been convicted of perjury. He's done this and that. He doesn't have any character." If they're successful in their effort, then the court just throws his testimony out, and all of the damage it could have done is reversed.

This is done on an individual basis too. When you start talking victory—"God wants me well. I will prosper and succeed. No weapon formed against me will prosper!"—the person who's living a defeated life has to either repent or condemn you. A lot of people will condemn you, which is why criticism comes. If you get the attitude of David, start basing your evaluation of things on the covenant, and get bold enough to speak it, you will be criticized. I guarantee it!

Many times this criticism comes through the people who know you the best—your family. After Jesus' own brothers mocked him, He said,

> *A prophet is not without honour, but in his own country, and among his own kin, and in his own house.*
>
> MARK 6:4

The people who know you the best have a hard time believing that there's really anything special about you, because they know you. They know where you've been and what you've done, your mistakes and immaturity—everything about you. Since they're basing their judgment on outward appearance, it's hard for them to really see what God has done in you.

YOU'LL BE CHALLENGED

When I first became turned on to the Lord, some of my family were the very people who said negative things toward me. They didn't do it maliciously. I've always loved my mother, brother, sister, and in-laws, and enjoyed a pretty good relationship with them. But when I first became turned on to the Lord, I just went fanatical! I started believing for miracles and confessing that I could receive the power of God. Some of them were critical of this, not because they hated me, but because they didn't understand it. When they looked at me, I was exactly the same as before. I was telling them that I'd had this special encounter with the Lord and He had spoken to me, but they weren't there. They didn't know what was going on because they were looking on the outward appearance.

I'm not saying that all the criticism is mean and malicious or that you can't overcome it. I'm just saying it's natural. The people who know you the best are still going to consider you as their little brother, neighbor, coworker, or whatever: "He's just off in la-la land somewhere!" They don't know what God said, and they can't see what's happened on the inside of you.

But after a period of time, they can. My family now basically embraces me and approves of what has happened. They know that something happened because it changed my life. Now they see me differently. However, prior to this, it was just my word. They didn't know—because they couldn't yet see—what had happened on the inside of me.

I'm not trying to throw stones at anyone, but if you're going to become a giant killer, criticism will come. When you start trying to overcome your problems instead of just sitting down and being overcome by them, when you begin to believe and speak forth your faith instead of just running and hiding like everyone else, you'll be challenged. Criticism will come—and sometimes it'll be from within your own family. However, you just have to get on with it. You can't let criticism stop you. If criticism could kill a person, I'd be dead!

GRASSHOPPER OR GIANT KILLER?

It doesn't matter what other people say about you. It's what you say about yourself that counts! This truth is clearly illustrated when Moses sent twelve men to spy out the Promised Land. Ten of them came back saying, "It's a good land, but we can't take it because there are giants there!"

We were in our own sight as grasshoppers, and so we were in their sight.

NUMBERS 13:33B

Other people may criticize you because they don't see you the way God does. They aren't going to recognize your true power and potential. But it doesn't really matter what other people say. It might be a factor, but it's not the determining factor. What really counts is how you see yourself. Do you see yourself as a grasshopper or a giant killer?

People have mocked, criticized, and railed on me over all kinds of things. They hadn't seen the power of God in my life, and they didn't know what the Lord had spoken to me. But by the grace of God, I've been able to see differently than what people say. I know God has touched my life. I know He's done something on the inside of me. So, it doesn't really matter what other people say about me. What matters is what I say about myself based on what God has spoken to me.

This is a tremendous lesson from the life of David! You need to find out who you are. You need to discover what God has called you to do. Then—no matter what criticism you might face—go on in His power and do it!

STAY ON TRACK!

My good friend Joe Nay has made a huge impact on my life. He's the one who actually helped stir me up to seek the Lord. Immediately after I became turned on to Jesus, I started receiving criticism from both my family and my church. The leaders in my church would just rail on me. Due to my fanaticism, one of them wanted to excommunicate me—kick me out of the church! Even though I was still going on with God, all this criticism was beginning to wear on me. So, I went to one of Joe Nay's meetings.

Joe called me out in front of everyone and started prophesying, "Andrew, I see you like a runner on a track. You're running a race and doing good. In fact, you're out there leading the pack. But the people in the grandstands are criticizing you. They're yelling at you and telling you that you're doing it all wrong. I see you getting off of the track and going up into the grandstands to argue with these spectators. But even if you win the argument, you're going to lose the race. Don't worry about what other people say. Get back on track and finish the race! Do what God has told you to do!"

That was a powerful word that really ministered to me. I've even given it to other people in the form of a prophecy. If it works for me, I believe it'll work for them. That's a powerful truth! God really spoke to me through that.

When you start going for it, Satan raises up people to criticize you. His purpose is to divert you from what you're supposed to do. The devil wants you off track, arguing with spectators in the grandstands, justifying yourself to other people, and trying to gain the approval of man. However, even if you win the argument, you'll still lose the race. You need to get to the place where you don't let criticism change you. Stay on track, and don't let it change your message!

WHO CARES?

That is exactly what David did. After his brother said all of these things, he responded,

What have I now done? Is there not a cause?

1 SAMUEL 17:29

In other words, David said, "What are you on my case for? I haven't done anything wrong!"

And he turned from him toward another, and spake after the same manner.

1 SAMUEL 17:30

David just turned to the next guy and repeated the same words, "Who is this uncircumcised Philistine?" He didn't let his older brother's criticism slow him down one bit!

If you are going to be a giant killer, you're going to have to get beyond criticism. If you're going to start overcoming problems and bring deliverance to yourself and others, you're going to have to get to where you aren't so touchy. Who cares what other people have to say about you?

LESSONS FROM DAVID

David overcame this criticism and continued to speak forth his faith.

And when the words were heard which David spake, they rehearsed them before Saul: and he sent for him. [32] And David said to Saul, Let no man's heart fail because of him; thy servant will go and fight with this Philistine.

1 SAMUEL 17:31-32

Outline

I. Here's David standing up to the enemy, operating in faith, and doing nothing but good things that should be admired and praised.

And Eliab his [David's] eldest brother heard when he spake unto the men; and Eliab's anger was kindled against David, and he said, Why camest thou down hither? and with whom hast thou left those few sheep in the wilderness? I know thy pride, and the naughtiness of thine heart; for thou art come down that thou mightest see the battle.
1 SAMUEL 17:28, BRACKETS MINE

    A. Yet when his older brother heard it, he railed on him.
    B. Eliab turned on David and began to question why he came.
    C. David was submitted to his father, who had commanded him to go.
    D. Everything David was doing was exactly right.

II. If you're going to be a giant killer, you need to recognize that criticism will come your way.
    A. If you get a different attitude and start operating in faith instead of fear, if you stand up to your giants instead of running from them, if you recognize your covenant rights and privileges—and start speaking forth your faith—you will be criticized.
    B. When you believe for victory, speak forth your faith, and go for it, you condemn the average person's mediocre life.
    C. That's the number one reason they criticize and fight against you.
    D. If what you're saying about walking in health, prosperity, and joy is true, then they're wrong.
    E. These folks who have been moaning, bellyaching, and using these things to excuse their ineffective, defeated, and powerless lives are going to be condemned by what you say.
    F. They have to do one of two things: repent and change, or criticize.
    G. Very few people repent, because it requires integrity and taking responsibility for their attitudes and actions.
    H. Most people will just try to discredit and stop you.
    I. Instead of climbing up to your level, they'll just try to pull you down to theirs through criticism.

III. Eliab was there when David was chosen as the next king (1 Sam. 16:13).
    A. He saw Samuel hear from God and pass over him—and all the others—in favor of the runt of the family.
    B. Eliab was angry and jealous, thinking, *Why didn't God choose me?*

C. Then on the battlefield with Saul's army, Eliab had been just like all the other soldiers—hiding from Goliath.
D. And here came his little brother saying, *"Who is this uncircumcised Philistine?"* (1 Sam. 17:26).
E. It forced him either to admit "My youngest brother here is the one who's right. He's a powerful man of God and I'm a zero—a nothing" or contend "I'm right and he's not" and then impute some kind of wrong to David.
F. This happens all the time in court!
   i. When a person testifies and gives condemning witness against someone else, nine out of ten times this is what the lawyer's tactic will be.
   ii. They'll turn on this witness and try to discredit them.
   iii. If they're successful in their effort, then the court just throws his testimony out, and all of the damage it could have done is reversed.
   iv. This is done on an individual basis too.

IV. If you get the attitude of David, start basing your evaluation of things on the covenant, and get bold enough to speak it, you will be criticized—I guarantee it!
   A. Many times this criticism comes through the people who know you the best: your family.
   B. After Jesus' own brothers mocked him, He said,

A prophet is not without honour, but in his own country, and among his own kin, and in his own house.

MARK 6:4

   C. The people who know you the best have a hard time believing that there's really anything special about you, because they know you.
   D. Since they're basing their judgment on outward appearance, it's hard for them to really see what God has done in you.

V. I'm not saying that all the criticism is mean and malicious or that you can't overcome it.
   A. I'm just saying it's natural.
   B. The people who know you the best are still going to consider you as their little brother, neighbor, coworker, or whatever.
   C. They don't know what God said, and they can't see what's happened on the inside of you.
   D. But after a period of time, they can.
   E. If you're going to become a giant killer, criticism will come.
   F. When you start trying to overcome your problems instead of just sitting down and being overcome by them, when you begin to believe and speak forth your faith instead of just running and hiding like everyone else, you'll be challenged.
   G. However, you can't let criticism stop you.

VI. It doesn't matter what other people say about you; it's what you say about yourself that counts!
   A. This truth is clearly illustrated when Moses sent twelve men to spy out the Promised Land.
   B. Ten of them came back saying, "It's a good land, but we can't take it because there are giants there!"

We were in our own sight as grasshoppers, and so we were in their sight.

NUMBERS 13:33B

   C. What other people say might be a factor, but it's not the determining factor.
   D. What really counts is how you see yourself.
   E. Do you see yourself as a grasshopper or a giant killer?
   F. This is a tremendous lesson from the life of David!
   G. You need to find out who you are and what God has called you to do.
   H. Then—no matter what criticism you might face—go on in His power and do it!

VII. My good friend Joe Nay has made a huge impact on my life.
   A. He's the one who actually helped stir me up to seek the Lord.
   B. Immediately after I became turned on to Jesus, I started receiving criticism from both my family and my church, and all this criticism was beginning to wear on me.
   C. So, I went to one of Joe Nay's meetings.
   D. Joe called me out in front of everyone and started prophesying, "Andrew, I see you going up into the grandstands to argue with these spectators. But even if you win the argument, you're going to lose the race."
   E. That was a powerful word that really ministered to me.
   F. When you start going for it, Satan raises up people to criticize you.
   G. His purpose is to divert you from what you're supposed to do.
   H. You need to get to the place where you don't let criticism change you.
   I. Stay on track, and don't let it change your message!

VIII. That is exactly what David did.
   A. After his brother said all of these things, he responded,

What have I now done? Is there not a cause?

1 SAMUEL 17:29

   B. In other words, David said, "What are you on my case for? I haven't done anything wrong!"

And he turned from him toward another, and spake after the same manner.

1 SAMUEL 17:30

C. David just turned to the next guy and repeated the same words, *"Who is this uncircumcised Philistine?"* (1 Sam. 17:26).
D. He didn't let his older brother's criticism slow him down one bit!
E. If you are going to be a giant killer, you're going to have to get beyond criticism.
F. If you're going to start overcoming problems and bring deliverance to yourself and others, you're going to have to get to where you aren't so touchy.
G. Who cares what other people have to say about you?
H. David overcame this criticism and continued to speak forth his faith.

And when the words were heard which David spake, they rehearsed them before Saul: and he sent for him. [32] And David said to Saul, Let no man's heart fail because of him; thy servant will go and fight with this Philistine.
1 SAMUEL 17:31-32

Teacher's Guide

1. Here's David standing up to the enemy, operating in faith, and doing nothing but good things that should be admired and praised.

    And Eliab his [David's] eldest brother heard when he spake unto the men; and Eliab's anger was kindled against David, and he said, Why camest thou down hither? and with whom hast thou left those few sheep in the wilderness? I know thy pride, and the naughtiness of thine heart; for thou art come down that thou mightest see the battle.

    1 SAMUEL 17:28, BRACKETS MINE

    Yet when his older brother heard it, he railed on him. Eliab turned on David and began to question why he came. David was submitted to his father, who had commanded him to go. Everything David was doing was exactly right.

1a. Was David doing everything exactly right?
    Yes

1b. *Discussion question:* Have you ever faced a situation like David's, where someone close to you criticized your actions, even when you were doing what you were supposed to do? How did you deal with the situation?
    Discussion question

LESSONS FROM DAVID

2. If we're going to be giant killers, we need to recognize that criticism will come our way. If we get a different attitude and start operating in faith instead of fear, if we stand up to our giants instead of running from them, if we recognize our covenant rights and privileges—and start speaking forth our faith—we will be criticized. When we believe for victory, speak forth our faith, and go for it, we condemn the average person's mediocre life. That's the number one reason they criticize and fight against us. If what we're saying about walking in health, prosperity, and joy is true, then they're wrong. These folks who have been moaning, bellyaching, and using these things to excuse their ineffective, defeated, and powerless lives are going to be condemned by what we say. They have to do one of two things: repent and change, or criticize. Very few people repent, because it requires integrity and taking responsibility for their attitudes and actions. Most people will just try to discredit and stop us. Instead of climbing up to our level, they'll just try to pull us down to theirs through criticism.

2a. If you're going to be a _____ _____, you need to recognize that _____ will come your way.
Giant killer / criticism

2b. True or false: If you get a different attitude and start operating in faith instead of fear, if you stand up to your giants instead of running from them, if you recognize your covenant rights and privileges—and start speaking forth your faith—you will be wholly accepted.
False

2c. *Discussion question:* Discuss why a lot of people criticize those who begin to speak forth their faith.
Discussion question

2d. Why do very few people repent?
   A. It requires a blood sacrifice and a wave offering
   B. It requires effort and time that they can't spare from their busy schedules
   C. It requires good character and an excellent lineage
   D. All of the above
   E. None of the above
   E. None of the above

2e. What will most people do?
They will just try to discredit and stop you—instead of climbing up to your level, they'll just try to pull you down to theirs through criticism

3. Eliab was there when David was chosen as the next king (1 Sam. 16:13). He saw Samuel hear from God and pass over him—and all the others—in favor of the runt of the family. Eliab was angry and jealous, thinking, *Why didn't God choose me?* Then on the battlefield with Saul's army, Eliab had been just like all the other soldiers—hiding from Goliath. And here came his little brother saying, *"Who is this uncircumcised Philistine?"* (1 Sam. 17:26). It forced him either to admit "My youngest brother here is the one who's right. He's a powerful man of God and I'm a zero—a nothing" or contend "I'm right and he's not" and then impute some kind of wrong to David. This happens all the time in court! When a person testifies and gives condemning witness against someone else, nine out of ten times this is what the lawyer's tactic will be. They'll turn on this witness and try to discredit them. If they're successful in their effort, then the court just throws his testimony out, and all of the damage it could have done is reversed. This is done on an individual basis too.

3a. According to 1 Samuel 16:13, where was Eliab when David was chosen as the next king?
He was there

3b. *Discussion question:* What is the significance of the answer to question #3a?
Discussion question

4. If we get the attitude of David, start basing our evaluation of things on the covenant, and get bold enough to speak it, we will be criticized—Andrew guarantees it! Many times this criticism comes through the people who know us the best: our families. After Jesus' own brothers mocked him, He said,

> *A prophet is not without honour, but in his own country, and among his own kin, and in his own house.*
>
> MARK 6:4

The people who know us the best have a hard time believing that there's really anything special about us, because they know us. Since they're basing their judgment on outward appearance, it's hard for them to really see what God has done in us.

4a. Many times, where does criticism come from?
Those who know you best: your family

4b. What did Jesus say in Mark 6:4?
"A prophet is not without honour, but in his own country, and among his own kin, and in his own house"

4c. *Discussion question:* Find some examples in the Scriptures of people being criticized by those closest to them (like their families) and discuss what you can learn from their experiences.
Discussion question

5. Andrew is not saying that all the criticism is mean and malicious or that we can't overcome it. He's just saying it's natural. The people who know us the best are still going to consider us as their little brothers or sisters, neighbors, coworkers, or whatever. They don't know what God said, and they can't see what's happened on the inside of us. But after a period of time, they can. If we're going to become giant killers, criticism will come. When we start trying to overcome our problems instead of just sitting down and being overcome by them, when we begin to believe and speak forth our faith instead of just running and hiding like everyone else, we'll be challenged. However, we can't let criticism stop us.

5a. True or false: After a period of time, the people who know you best will be able to see what's happened on the inside of you.
True

5b. You can't let criticism _____ you.
Stop

6. It doesn't matter what other people say about us; it's what we say about ourselves that counts! This truth is clearly illustrated when Moses sent twelve men to spy out the Promised Land. Ten of them came back saying, "It's a good land, but we can't take it because there are giants there!"

> *We were in our own sight as grasshoppers, and so we were in their sight.*
> NUMBERS 13:33B

What other people say might be a factor, but it's not the determining factor. What really counts is how we see ourselves. Do we see ourselves as grasshoppers or giant killers? This is a tremendous lesson from the life of David! We need to find out who we are and what God has called us to do. Then—no matter what criticism we might face—we need to go on in His power and do it!

6a. *Discussion question:* Think about what you have been saying about yourself. Do you think what others have been saying has impacted what you say about yourself? Do you feel any changes need to be made in your life?
Discussion question

6b. *Discussion question:* How could things have been different if the ten spies had brought back a positive report in Numbers 13:33?
Discussion question

6c. What do you need to find out?
A. Who you are and how to become a muay thai fighter
B. Who you are and what your parents want you to do
C. Who you are and what God has called you to do
D. All of the above
E. None of the above
C. Who you are and what God has called you to do

7. Andrew's good friend Joe Nay has made a huge impact on his life. He's the one who actually helped stir Andrew up to seek the Lord. Immediately after Andrew became turned on to Jesus, he started receiving criticism from both his family and his church, and all this criticism was beginning to wear on him. So, he went to one of Joe Nay's meetings. Joe called him out in front of everyone and started prophesying, "Andrew, I see you going up into the grandstands to argue with the spectators. But even if you win the argument, you're going to lose the race." That was a powerful word that really ministered to Andrew. When we start going for it, Satan raises up people to criticize us. His purpose is to divert us from what we're supposed to do. We need to get to the place where we don't let criticism change us. We need to stay on track and not let it change our message!

7a. What is the problem with arguing with the spectators in the grandstands instead of running your race?
Even if you win the argument, you're going to lose the race

7b. *Discussion question:* How can criticism possibly change your message?
Discussion question

8. That is exactly what David did. After his brother said all of these things, he responded,

> *What have I now done? Is there not a cause?*
>
> 1 SAMUEL 17:29

In other words, David said, "What are you on my case for? I haven't done anything wrong!"

> *And he turned from him toward another, and spake after the same manner.*
>
> 1 SAMUEL 17:30

David just turned to the next guy and repeated the same words, *"Who is this uncircumcised Philistine?"* (1 Sam. 17:26). He didn't let his older brother's criticism slow him down one bit! If we are going to be giant killers, we're going to have to get beyond criticism. If we're going to start overcoming problems and bring deliverance to ourselves and others, we're going to have to get to where we aren't so touchy. Who cares what other people have to say about us? David overcame this criticism and continued to speak forth his faith.

> *And when the words were heard which David spake, they rehearsed them before Saul: and he sent for him. [32] And David said to Saul, Let no man's heart fail because of him; thy servant will go and fight with this Philistine.*
>
> 1 SAMUEL 17:31-32

8a. What did David do after his brother Eliab criticized him?
He turned to the next guy and repeated his question—he didn't let his older brother's criticism slow him down one bit

8b. Read 1 Samuel 17:31-32. What else did David do?
He overcame this criticism and continued to speak his faith

Discipleship Questions

1. Was David doing everything exactly right?

2. *Discussion question:* Have you ever faced a situation like David's, where someone close to you criticized your actions, even when you were doing what you were supposed to do? How did you deal with the situation?

3. If you're going to be a _____ _____, you need to recognize that _____ will come your way.

4. True or false: If you get a different attitude and start operating in faith instead of fear, if you stand up to your giants instead of running from them, if you recognize your covenant rights and privileges—and start speaking forth your faith—you will be wholly accepted.

5. *Discussion question:* Discuss why a lot of people criticize those who begin to speak forth their faith.

6. Why do very few people repent?
    A. It requires a blood sacrifice and a wave offering
    B. It requires effort and time that they can't spare from their busy schedules
    C. It requires good character and an excellent lineage
    D. All of the above
    E. None of the above

7. What will most people do?

8. According to 1 Samuel 16:13, where was Eliab when David was chosen as the next king?

9. *Discussion question:* What is the significance of the answer to question #8?

10. Many times, where does criticism come from?

11. What did Jesus say in Mark 6:4?

12. *Discussion question:* Find some examples in the Scriptures of people being criticized by those closest to them (like their families) and discuss what you can learn from their experiences.

13. True or false: After a period of time, the people who know you best will be able to see what's happened on the inside of you.

14. You can't let criticism _____ you.

15. *Discussion question:* Think about what you have been saying about yourself. Do you think what others have been saying has impacted what you say about yourself? Do you feel any changes need to be made in your life?

16. *Discussion question:* How could things have been different if the ten spies had brought back a positive report in Numbers 13:33?
_____
_____
_____

17. What do you need to find out?
    A. Who you are and how to become a muay thai fighter
    B. Who you are and what your parents want you to do
    C. Who you are and what God has called you to do
    D. All of the above
    E. None of the above

18. What is the problem with arguing with the spectators in the grandstands instead of running your race?
_____
_____
_____

19. *Discussion question:* How can criticism possibly change your message?
_____
_____
_____

20. What did David do after his brother Eliab criticized him?
_____
_____
_____

21. Read 1 Samuel 17:31-32. What else did David do?
_____
_____
_____

1. Yes
2. *Discussion question*
3. Giant killer / criticism
4. False
5. *Discussion question*
6. E. None of the above
7. They will just try to discredit and stop you—instead of climbing up to your level, they'll just try to pull you down to theirs through criticism
8. He was there
9. *Discussion question*
10. Those who know you best: your family
11. *"A prophet is not without honour, but in his own country, and among his own kin, and in his own house"*
12. *Discussion question*
13. True
14. Stop
15. *Discussion question*
16. *Discussion question*
17. C. Who you are and what God has called you to do
18. Even if you win the argument, you're going to lose the race
19. *Discussion question*
20. He turned to the next guy and repeated his question—he didn't let his older brother's criticism slow him down one bit
21. He overcame this criticism and continued to speak his faith

Scriptures

1 SAMUEL 17:28-32
And Eliab his eldest brother heard when he spake unto the men; and Eliab's anger was kindled against David, and he said, Why camest thou down hither? and with whom hast thou left those few sheep in the wilderness? I know thy pride, and the naughtiness of thine heart; for thou art come down that thou mightest see the battle. [29] And David said, What have I now done? Is there not a cause? [30] And he turned from him toward another, and spake after the same manner: and the people answered him again after the former manner. [31] And when the words were heard which David spake, they rehearsed them before Saul: and he sent for him. [32] And David said to Saul, Let no man's heart fail because of him; thy servant will go and fight with this Philistine.

1 SAMUEL 16:13
Then Samuel took the horn of oil, and anointed him in the midst of his brethren: and the Spirit of the LORD came upon David from that day forward. So Samuel rose up, and went to Ramah.

1 SAMUEL 16:6
And it came to pass, when they were come, that he looked on Eliab, and said, Surely the LORD's anointed is before him.

MARK 6:4
But Jesus said unto them, A prophet is not without honour, but in his own country, and among his own kin, and in his own house.

NUMBERS 13:33
And there we saw the giants, the sons of Anak, which come of the giants: and we were in our own sight as grasshoppers, and so we were in their sight.

LESSONS FROM DAVID

A Confident Testimony

And Saul said to David, Thou art not able to go against this Philistine to fight with him: for thou art but a youth, and he a man of war from his youth.

1 SAMUEL 17:33

After receiving criticism from his own family, here now was the most powerful and influential man in the entire nation—the king—telling David, "You can't fight against this Philistine giant. You're just a youth, and he's a man of war. You don't stand a chance!"

David was bold because he believed God and was aware of his covenant. He recognized that this Philistine was uncircumcised and had no relationship with God. But even though David's *faith* was in the promises contained in God's Word, what he said next reveals where his *confidence* came from.

And David said unto Saul, Thy servant kept his father's sheep, and there came a lion, and a bear, and took a lamb out of the flock: [35] And I went out after him, and smote him, and delivered it out of his mouth: and when he arose against me, I caught him by his beard, and smote him, and slew him. [36] Thy servant slew both the lion and the bear: and this uncircumcised Philistine shall be as one of them, seeing he hath defied the armies of the living God. [37a] David said moreover, The LORD that delivered me out of the paw of the lion, and out of the paw of the bear, he will deliver me out of the hand of this Philistine.

1 SAMUEL 17:34-37A

David was saying, "Look, I've already proven God to be faithful. I have a history! This isn't the first time I've ever believed God. I've trusted Him and seen Him work miracles through me before. Because of this past experience, I have confidence, hope, and belief that it's going to happen again!"

FAITHFUL IN THE LEAST

One of the reasons David was able to overcome the giant—and the others weren't—was because he had been faithful and proven God in the small things.

Jesus said,

He that is faithful in that which is least is faithful also in much: and he that is unjust in the least is unjust also in much.

LUKE 16:10

In other words, if you aren't faithful in small things, you won't be entrusted with the great things. Most people are waiting until they get into a crisis situation—until the big thing—to believe God. However, they aren't trusting Him on a daily basis. They're taking the easy way out. Either they're learning to cope with things and are not fighting for their God-given rights, or they're just sitting there and using some other method. They're taking a shortcut to get their needs met, but they aren't believing God.

In the area of health, some people plan to trust God if cancer ever knocks on their door. However, they pop a pill just as soon as they get a headache and rely on medication to treat their colds. They take something to wake them up and something else to put them to sleep. They aren't trusting God for their health in the small things, but when the big thing comes, they're going to trust Him. Right!

Don't misunderstand what I'm saying. God isn't mad at you if you take aspirin or cold medicine. I'm not saying that you have to do this, or that you're evil if you rely on those things. But I am asking, when are you going to start trusting God with your health? Are you waiting until something becomes tragic and the doctors can't do anything about it, and then—and only then—will you trust Him? If that's the way you're thinking, your faith isn't going to work.

THE GROWTH PROCESS

Your faith has to grow and increase with use. You don't go from zero to a thousand miles per hour in the spirit instantly. You have to accelerate. You have to build up momentum and speed.

Jesus said that the kingdom of God is…

> …as if a man should cast seed into the ground; [27] And should sleep, and rise night and day, and the seed should spring and grow up, he knoweth not how. [28] For the earth bringeth forth fruit of herself; first the blade, then the ear, after that the full corn in the ear.
> MARK 4:26B-28

The kingdom of heaven works like a seed. You don't just plant an acorn and then—BOOM!—instantly it becomes a full-grown oak tree. It takes time and many seasons for the seed to go through the growth process to maturity.

> First the blade, then the ear, after that the full corn in the ear.
> MARK 4:28B

A CONFIDENT TESTIMONY

This is a principle of God. It's how everything works. You don't just go from never having trusted Him to, all of a sudden, killing a giant. You must start trusting the Lord in smaller things and then you progress and increase.

A BIG VISION

I shared this truth with one of our Bible college students once. This man had some problems and had previously lived in a mental institution. He had been declared completely unable to work and so derived his total income from welfare. I really liked this guy. He was kind and had some great qualities, but he'd never really trusted the Lord before in his finances.

As I ministered God's Word on prosperity and told the students they should be givers instead of takers, this guy really became excited. He came to me some time later and shared how he had found an old hotel, a historic building that was mostly stone. It was a beautiful building, but it had burned awhile back and became derelict. It was water damaged, the roof had caved in, etc. Anyway, the building was for sale for $1.5 million. He talked to some builders and found out it would take between $2 million and $2.5 million to restore it. This would be a total of $4 million for both the purchase and restoration.

He had it all worked out: how many rooms there were, what he could charge if he filled them up, etc. He showed me on paper how he could pay for all of the loans, cover the expenses, make money, and be ahead. It was a great idea. After telling me all of this, he asked, "What do you think about it?"

At first, I complimented him for the fact that he was breaking out of the poverty mentality and trying to believe God. I encouraged him and told him, "There are some really good things here, but I can guarantee you that this is not God. The Lord will not do that through you."

You might be saying, "But Andrew, that's terrible! You discouraged him!" I admit, he was discouraged. In fact, he even became a little upset with me. "Well then, why would you tell him that?" Because according to Mark 4, the kingdom of God works like a seed.

First the blade, then the ear, after that the full corn in the ear.

MARK 4:28B

There has to be a growth process. You can't go from never believing God for a quarter to make a phone call, right into raising $1.5 million. You can't jump from never having earned a dime in your entire life to financing and pulling off a $2.5 million construction project. That's just not how the kingdom works!

INSIGNIFICANT MATTERS

Sure enough, it didn't work out that way. Things didn't come together like he thought. But he's growing and going on with God. Maybe sometime in the future, something will happen with that vision, but not right away. It's a growth process.

This battle between David and Goliath didn't happen the way some people picture it. David didn't just go out there and—BOOM!—all of a sudden this spirit of faith came upon him enabling him to rise up and kill this giant. No, David had been seeking God. He'd been faithful in smaller things.

In fact, David had been faithful in seemingly insignificant things. We don't know exactly how many sheep David kept, but according to Eliab's statement, it was just a few (1 Sam. 17:28). No matter what size the herd really was, in some ways it was insignificant. It certainly wasn't worth David's life. Even though shepherds were expected to defend the sheep by attempting to scare off wild animals, surely Jesse wouldn't have wanted David to die trying to save one lamb from a lion or a bear. He may have expected David to try to shoo them off and do things that are prudent, but certainly not go up and grab a lion or a bear by the beard, which is exactly what he did (1 Sam. 17:35). No father would want his son to risk his life to save a sheep! Sheep are important, but not that important.

So, basically, David had a very small responsibility. This wasn't a huge herd of sheep. In most people's opinion, it definitely wasn't worth his life. It was small, insignificant. But David was faithful, even to the point of laying his life on the line in a small, insignificant matter.

Outline

I. David was bold because he believed God and was aware of his covenant.

   A. But even though David's *faith* was in the promises contained in God's Word, what he said next reveals where his *confidence* came from.

   And David said unto Saul, Thy servant kept his father's sheep, and there came a lion, and a bear, and took a lamb out of the flock: [35] And I went out after him, and smote him, and delivered it out of his mouth: and when he arose against me, I caught him by his beard, and smote him, and slew him. [36] Thy servant slew both the lion and the bear: and this uncircumcised Philistine shall be as one of them, seeing he hath defied the armies of the living God. [37a] David said moreover, The LORD that delivered me out of the paw of the lion, and out of the paw of the bear, he will deliver me out of the hand of this Philistine.

   1 SAMUEL 17:34-37A

   B. David was saying, "Look, I've already proven God to be faithful. I have a history! This isn't the first time I've ever believed God. I've trusted Him and seen Him work miracles through me before. Because of this past experience, I have confidence, hope, and belief that it's going to happen again!"
   C. One of the reasons David was able to overcome the giant—and the others weren't—was because he had been faithful and proven God in the small things.
   D. Jesus said,

   He that is faithful in that which is least is faithful also in much: and he that is unjust in the least is unjust also in much.

   LUKE 16:10

   E. In other words, if you aren't faithful in a small thing, you won't be entrusted with the great things.
   F. Most people are waiting until they get into a crisis situation—until the big thing—to believe God; however, they aren't trusting Him on a daily basis.
   G. If that's the way you're thinking, your faith isn't going to work.

II. Your faith has to grow and increase with use.
   A. You have to accelerate—you have to build up momentum and speed.
   B. Jesus said that the kingdom of God is…

…as if a man should cast seed into the ground; [27] And should sleep, and rise night and day, and the seed should spring and grow up, he knoweth not how. [28] For the earth bringeth forth fruit of herself; first the blade, then the ear, after that the full corn in the ear.
MARK 4:26B-28

   C. The kingdom of heaven works like a seed.
   D. It takes time and many seasons for the seed to go through the growth process to maturity.

First the blade, then the ear, after that the full corn in the ear.
MARK 4:28B

   E. This is a principle of God; it's how everything works.
   F. You must start trusting the Lord in smaller things and then progress and increase.

III. This battle between David and Goliath didn't happen the way some people picture it.
   A. David didn't just go out there and—BOOM!—all of a sudden this spirit of faith came upon him enabling him to rise up and kill this giant.
   B. No, David had been seeking God.
   C. He'd been faithful in smaller things—in fact, David had been faithful in seemingly insignificant things.
      i. We don't know exactly how many sheep David kept, but according to Eliab's statement, it was just a few (1 Sam. 17:28).
      ii. No matter what size the herd really was, in some ways it was insignificant—it certainly wasn't worth David's life.
      iii. Even though shepherds were expected to defend the sheep by attempting to scare off wild animals, surely Jesse wouldn't have wanted David to die trying to save one lamb from a lion or a bear (1 Sam. 17:35).
      iv. Sheep are important, but not that important.
      v. In most people's opinion, it definitely wasn't worth his life—it was small, insignificant.
   D. But David was faithful, even to the point of laying his life on the line in a small, insignificant matter.

A CONFIDENT TESTIMONY

Teacher's Guide

1. David was bold because he believed God and was aware of his covenant. But even though David's *faith* was in the promises contained in God's Word, what he said next reveals where his *confidence* came from.

> *And David said unto Saul, Thy servant kept his father's sheep, and there came a lion, and a bear, and took a lamb out of the flock: [35] And I went out after him, and smote him, and delivered it out of his mouth: and when he arose against me, I caught him by his beard, and smote him, and slew him. [36] Thy servant slew both the lion and the bear: and this uncircumcised Philistine shall be as one of them, seeing he hath defied the armies of the living God. [37a] David said moreover, The LORD that delivered me out of the paw of the lion, and out of the paw of the bear, he will deliver me out of the hand of this Philistine.*
>
> 1 SAMUEL 17:34-37A

David was saying, "Look, I've already proven God to be faithful. I have a history! This isn't the first time I've ever believed God. I've trusted Him and seen Him work miracles through me before. Because of this past experience, I have confidence, hope, and belief that it's going to happen again!" One of the reasons David was able to overcome the giant—and the others weren't—was because he had been faithful and proven God in the small things. Jesus said,

> *He that is faithful in that which is least is faithful also in much: and he that is unjust in the least is unjust also in much.*
>
> LUKE 16:10

In other words, if we aren't faithful in a small thing, we won't be entrusted with the great things. Most people are waiting until they get into a crisis situation—until the big thing—to believe God; however, they aren't trusting Him on a daily basis. If that's the way we're thinking, our faith isn't going to work.

1a. Why was David bold?
   Because he believed God and was aware of his covenant
1b. *Discussion question:* Where did David's confidence come from (1 Sam. 17:34-37)?
   Discussion question
1c. What does Luke 16:10 say?
   "He that is faithful in that which is least is faithful also in much: and he that is unjust in the least is unjust also in much"
1d. *Discussion question:* How does Luke 16:10 relate to trusting God?
   Discussion question

LESSONS FROM DAVID

2. Our faith has to grow and increase with use. We have to accelerate—we have to build up momentum and speed. Jesus said that the kingdom of God is…

> …as if a man should cast seed into the ground; [27] And should sleep, and rise night and day, and the seed should spring and grow up, he knoweth not how. [28] For the earth bringeth forth fruit of herself; first the blade, then the ear, after that the full corn in the ear.
> MARK 4:26B-28

The kingdom of heaven works like a seed. It takes time and many seasons for the seed to go through the growth process to maturity.

> First the blade, then the ear, after that the full corn in the ear.
> MARK 4:28B

This is a principle of God; it's how everything works. We must start trusting the Lord in smaller things and then progress and increase.

2a. Your faith has to _____ and _____ with use.
   Grow / increase
2b. The kingdom of God works like a what?
   A. Slot machine
   B. Watch
   C. Seed
   D. All of the above
   E. None of the above
   C. Seed
2c. *Discussion question:* Explain how Mark 4:28b is how everything works.
   Discussion question

3. This battle between David and Goliath didn't happen the way some people picture it. David didn't just go out there and—BOOM!—all of a sudden this spirit of faith came upon him enabling him to rise up and kill this giant. No, David had been seeking God. He'd been faithful in smaller things—in fact, David had been faithful in seemingly insignificant things. We don't know exactly how many sheep David kept, but according to Eliab's statement, it was just a few (1 Sam. 17:28). No matter what size the herd really was, in some ways it was insignificant—it certainly wasn't worth David's life. Even though shepherds were expected to defend the sheep by attempting to scare off wild animals, surely Jesse wouldn't have wanted David to die trying to save one lamb from a lion or a bear (1 Sam. 17:35). Sheep are important, but not that important. In most people's opinion, it definitely wasn't worth his life—it was small, insignificant. But David was faithful, even to the point of laying his life on the line in a small, insignificant matter.

3a. *Discussion question:* Why do you think David was faithful in seemingly insignificant things?
   Discussion question

A CONFIDENT TESTIMONY

Discipleship Questions

1. Why was David bold?

2. *Discussion question:* Where did David's confidence come from (1 Sam. 17:34-37)?

3. What does Luke 16:10 say?

4. *Discussion question:* How does Luke 16:10 relate to trusting God?

5. Your faith has to _____ and _____ with use.

6. The kingdom of God works like a what?
   A. Slot machine
   B. Watch
   C. Seed
   D. All of the above
   E. None of the above

7. *Discussion question:* Explain how Mark 4:28b is how everything works.

LESSONS FROM DAVID

8. *Discussion question:* Why do you think David was faithful in seemingly insignificant things?

Answer Key

1. Because he believed God and was aware of his covenant
2. *Discussion question*
3. "He that is faithful in that which is least is faithful also in much: and he that is unjust in the least is unjust also in much"
4. *Discussion question*
5. Grow / increase
6. C. Seed
7. *Discussion question*
8. *Discussion question*

Scriptures

1 SAMUEL 17:33-37

And Saul said to David, Thou art not able to go against this Philistine to fight with him: for thou art but a youth, and he a man of war from his youth. [34] And David said unto Saul, Thy servant kept his father's sheep, and there came a lion, and a bear, and took a lamb out of the flock: [35] And I went out after him, and smote him, and delivered it out of his mouth: and when he arose against me, I caught him by his beard, and smote him, and slew him. [36] Thy servant slew both the lion and the bear: and this uncircumcised Philistine shall be as one of them, seeing he hath defied the armies of the living God. [37] David said moreover, The Lord that delivered me out of the paw of the lion, and out of the paw of the bear, he will deliver me out of the hand of this Philistine. And Saul said unto David, Go, and the Lord be with thee.

LUKE 16:10

He that is faithful in that which is least is faithful also in much: and he that is unjust in the least is unjust also in much.

MARK 4:26-28

And he said, So is the kingdom of God, as if a man should cast seed into the ground; [27] And should sleep, and rise night and day, and the seed should spring and grow up, he knoweth not how. [28] For the earth bringeth forth fruit of herself; first the blade, then the ear, after that the full corn in the ear.

1 SAMUEL 17:28

And Eliab his eldest brother heard when he spake unto the men; and Eliab's anger was kindled against David, and he said, Why camest thou down hither? and with whom hast thou left those few sheep in the wilderness? I know thy pride, and the naughtiness of thine heart; for thou art come down that thou mightest see the battle.

A Confident Testimony

This is how you become a giant killer. You don't wait until big things—like cancer—knock on your door. You start trusting God in the small things every day. You fight to keep your joy and peace just like you were fighting a giant out there. You stand on principle on the small things, doing what's right even when nobody else is watching.

David was on the backside of the desert. The grandstands weren't full. Nobody even knew what was going on. David may or may not have told other people what had happened. This certainly wasn't something that hit the front pages of the local newspaper. David risked his life in a relatively insignificant manner, in a way that he might never have received recognition and acclaim for. Yet he was just as faithful with that as if it were something big and important.

Many people want the great victory, but few are willing to pay the price of faithfulness. Everybody wants to kill a giant and hear the people sing their praise, but very few are willing to risk their lives on the backside of the desert when nobody's watching. If you aren't faithful in small things, you won't be ruler over much. If you haven't ever started trusting God for the ability to overcome headaches and colds, chances are you won't be able to stand when cancer comes your way.

You need to learn to trust God in the everyday things. Do you control your temper when somebody cuts you off in traffic? Or are you someone who gets upset, lays on the horn, and flashes them or—God forbid—makes an obscene sign? If you can't control yourself with something small like that, you'll never make it when the big things come. If you aren't faithfully working for your boss, you'll never become the boss.

Why should God give you a better car if you aren't even taking care of the junk heap you have now? Is your car so full of food and trash that it's hard for somebody else to get in? Why would the Lord give you a new car to mess up? "Come on, Andrew, you're straining at a gnat here. This isn't that important!" It may not be to you, but that's probably the reason you haven't seen the mighty exploits yet. That very attitude may be why God hasn't used you in a bigger way.

INCREMENTAL STEPS

One of the common traits I've noticed among people whom God is using in a mighty way is that they are faithful in the little as well as the big. Even if there are only five people in attendance, they preach their hearts out as if there were a thousand. They give it everything they've got. They're people of integrity who are faithful in the little things. They aren't just faithful when big things are on the line and someone's watching. They do the right thing even if nobody's looking.

This is one of the reasons God used David to kill Goliath. He was faithful in small things. He'd been faithfully serving his father and protecting those sheep. Because of that, he had confidence to go in and fight the big battle.

The Lord told me that I was limiting Him in some ways and that I needed to grow. So, we moved from a 15,000-square-foot building into a 110,000-square-foot building, which was a giant step of faith for me! I went from zero payments to where our monthly building payment alone was $25,000. Our utilities were up to $8,000 per month.

Then we outgrew that building and I started a 220,000-square-foot-building project for a new Charis Bible College campus that will cost $52 million. We're doing it debt free. And that's not the end. There is more to come. We couldn't have done this all at once. I've been growing in trusting the Lord for decades. I definitely couldn't have done so without trusting God through the years and taking many incremental steps of faith.

I remember when Jamie and I wrote out our first covenant. We were believing God for $300 per month. This was the total income for both the ministry and us—and it allowed us to give $100 away each month. That's 33 percent! I didn't get there overnight. It took me a while to grow up to that. When we moved to Manitou Springs and began our ministry in the Colorado Springs area, we had to believe God for something like $700 per month to run the whole ministry back then. If I hadn't taken these incremental steps through the years, there's no way I could have believed God for $500,000 a month in 2003. That paid for my staff, building, equipment, radio and television bills, etc. In 2013, we needed $3 million per month, and this will only increase in the future. I couldn't do this without being faithful and believing God for those smaller things.

This is a tremendous principle that you need to grab hold of. You can't prepare for the future any better than just by starting to be faithful today. Make the decision today that you are going to start believing God, walking in joy, choosing to do the right thing, controlling your emotions, studying the Word, and blessing other people. Choose to spend time with God, even if there's nothing pressing—just do it to be a faithful servant. Faithfully serve other people. Serve your boss today. Do things with integrity and excellence. If you do this over a period of time and prove yourself faithful, then when the giant comes knocking on your door, you'll have the ability to stand against him and overcome!

"THE KINGDOM IS IN YOUR HANDS"

Right after David testified to Saul about killing the lion and the bear, he boldly declared, "This uncircumcised Philistine will be like one of them!"

And Saul said unto David, Go, and the Lord be with thee.

1 SAMUEL 17:37B

This was nearly as big of a miracle as David killing Goliath! The terms of this contest had already been set forth. If Goliath won, all the Israelites would become the Philistines' servants. But if an Israelite won, all the Philistines would serve the Israelites. So, when Saul said, "Go," he was basically putting his entire kingdom—the whole nation of Israel—into the hands of this youth whom he had just moments before told, "You don't stand a chance!"

Apparently, David's response to Saul's previous comments persuaded him otherwise. David spoke with such conviction about God being faithful when he had killed both the lion and the bear. He testified of how the Lord had proven Himself and come through for him again and again. There was so much authority and anointing in David's words that it literally caused the king to place his entire kingdom into his hands. Now that's a miracle!

I think Saul recognized the anointing of God on David's life. Saul had experienced this in his early years. He became a new man (1 Sam. 10:9) and was able to win some impossible battles (1 Sam. 11). I believe he was putting his faith not just in David but also in the power of God that was on David's life.

BELIEVE THE WORD YOU SPEAK

As you mature, people will respond to you. As you recognize your covenant and believe God, as you stand up and speak forth your faith, as you are faithful in the small things and grow, you'll come to a place where what you say will command respect. When you have absolute faith and confidence in what you're saying, it'll inspire faith and confidence in those who hear you. When you know what you're talking about—by both revelation and experience, not just theory—people will respond to you in ways they don't respond to others.

When I minister God's Word, I speak from my heart. I'm not just rehearsing something I've heard someone else say. I share what the Lord has shown me on whatever subject it is. In fact, I've never heard anyone preach the things we've discussed thus far in this book. These are things I've lived. They're coming out of the lessons God Himself has personally taught me through the life of David.

People can perceive it when you're ministering God's Word from your heart. It rings true and gives you credibility in their sight. That's when they'll respond to you.

If God has called you to be a leader, you need to apply these truths and become totally convinced of what He's given you to share. People have come up to me and remarked, "What you say is so convincing. It sounds so strong and overwhelming." That's because I am convinced. I believe the Word I teach with all of my heart. When you believe what you speak with all of your heart, then the people who listen to you will be able to believe it with all of their heart too. That's a great lesson from the life of David!

Outline

IV. This is how you become a giant killer—you start trusting God in the small things every day.
   A. You fight to keep your joy and peace just like you were fighting a giant out there.
   B. You stand on principle on the small things, doing what's right even when nobody else is watching.
   C. David risked his life in a relatively insignificant manner, in a way that he might never have received recognition and acclaim for.
   D. Yet he was just as faithful with that as if it were something big and important.
   E. Many people want the great victory, but few are willing to pay the price of faithfulness.
   F. You need to learn to trust God in the everyday things.
   G. If you can't control yourself with something small, you'll never make it when the big things come.

V. One of the common traits I've noticed among people whom God is using in a mighty way is that they are faithful in the little as well as the big.
   A. They aren't just faithful when big things are on the line and someone's watching—they do the right thing even if nobody's looking.
   B. This is one of the reasons God used David to kill Goliath.
      i. He was faithful in small things.
      ii. He'd been faithfully serving his father and protecting those sheep.
      iii. Because of that, he had confidence to go in and fight the big battle.
   C. You can't prepare for the future any better than just by starting to be faithful today.
   D. Make the decision today that you are going to start believing God, walking in joy, choosing to do the right thing, controlling your emotions, studying the Word, and blessing other people.
   E. Choose to spend time with God, even if there's nothing pressing—just do it to be a faithful servant.
   F. Do things with integrity and excellence.
   G. If you do this over a period of time and prove yourself faithful, then when the giant comes knocking on your door, you'll have the ability to stand against him and overcome!

VI. Right after David testified to Saul about killing the lion and the bear, he boldly declared, "This uncircumcised Philistine will be like one of them!"

And Saul said unto David, Go, and the LORD be with thee.

1 SAMUEL 17:37B

      A. This was nearly as big of a miracle as David killing Goliath!
      B. The terms of this contest had already been set forth.
          i. If Goliath won, all the Israelites would become the Philistines' servants.
          ii. But if an Israelite won, all the Philistines would serve the Israelites.
      C. So, when Saul said, "Go," he was basically putting his entire kingdom—the whole nation of Israel—into the hands of this youth whom he had just moments before told, "You don't stand a chance!"
      D. Apparently, David's response to Saul's previous comments persuaded him otherwise.
      E. There was so much authority and anointing in David's words that it literally caused the king to place his entire kingdom into his hands.
      F. I think Saul recognized the anointing of God on David's life.
      G. Saul had experienced this in his early years (1 Sam. 10:9 and 11:1-15).
      H. I believe he was putting his faith not just in David but also in the power of God that was on David's life.

VII. As you mature, people will respond to you.
      A. As you recognize your covenant and believe God, as you stand up and speak forth your faith, as you are faithful in the small things and grow, you'll come to a place where what you say will command respect.
      B. When you have absolute faith and confidence in what you're saying, it'll inspire faith and confidence in those who hear you.
      C. When you know what you're talking about—by both revelation and experience, not just theory—people will respond to you in ways they don't respond to others.
      D. People can perceive it when you're ministering God's Word from your heart—it rings true and gives you credibility in their sight.
      E. If God has called you to be a leader, you need to apply these truths and become totally convinced of what He's given you to share.
      F. When you believe what you speak with all of your heart, then the people who listen to you will be able to believe it with all of their heart too.

Teacher's Guide

4. This is how we become giant killers—we start trusting God in the small things every day. We fight to keep our joy and peace just like we were fighting a giant out there. We stand on principle on the small things, doing what's right even when nobody else is watching. David risked his life in a relatively insignificant manner, in a way that he might never have received recognition and acclaim for. Yet he was just as faithful with that as if it were something big and important. Many people want the great victory, but few are willing to pay the price of faithfulness. We need to learn to trust God in the everyday things. If we can't control ourselves with something small, we'll never make it when the big things come.

4a. How do you become a giant killer?
   You start trusting God in the small things every day
4b. Many people want the great victory, but few are willing to do what?
   Pay the price of faithfulness
4c. *Discussion question:* What are some of the small things that you can trust God in?
   Discussion question

LESSONS FROM DAVID

5. One of the common traits Andrew has noticed among people whom God is using in a mighty way is that they are faithful in the little as well as the big. They aren't just faithful when big things are on the line and someone's watching—they do the right thing even if nobody's looking. This is one of the reasons God used David to kill Goliath. He was faithful in small things. He'd been faithfully serving his father and protecting those sheep. Because of that, he had confidence to go in and fight the big battle. We can't prepare for the future any better than just by starting to be faithful today. Let's make the decision today that we are going to start believing God, walking in joy, choosing to do the right thing, controlling our emotions, studying the Word, and blessing other people. Let's choose to spend time with God, even if there's nothing pressing—we should just do it to be faithful servants. We should do things with integrity and excellence. If we do this over a period of time and prove ourselves faithful, then when the giant comes knocking on our doors, we'll have the ability to stand against him and overcome!

5a. True or false: One of the common traits among people whom God is using in a mighty way is that they are faithful in only the big things.
False

5b. You can't prepare for the future any better than by what?
   A. Consulting a financial planner
   B. Starting to be faithful today
   C. Going to church at every opportunity
   D. All of the above
   E. None of the above
   B. Starting to be faithful today

5c. *Discussion question*: Why would doing things with integrity and excellence make a difference?
Discussion question

6. Right after David testified to Saul about killing the lion and the bear, he boldly declared, "This uncircumcised Philistine will be like one of them!"

And Saul said unto David, Go, and the LORD be with thee.

1 SAMUEL 17:37B

This was nearly as big of a miracle as David killing Goliath! The terms of this contest had already been set forth. If Goliath won, all the Israelites would become the Philistines' servants. But if an Israelite won, all the Philistines would serve the Israelites. So, when Saul said, "Go," he was basically putting his entire kingdom—the whole nation of Israel—into the hands of this youth whom he had just moments before told, "You don't stand a chance!" Apparently, David's response to Saul's previous comments persuaded him otherwise. There was so much authority and anointing in David's words that it literally caused the king to place his entire kingdom into his hands. Andrew thinks Saul recognized the anointing of God on David's life. Saul had experienced this in his early years (1 Sam. 10:9 and 11:1-15). Andrew believes Saul was putting his faith not just in David but also in the power of God that was on David's life.

6a. Why was Saul telling David *"Go, and the LORD be with thee"* nearly as big of a miracle as David killing Goliath?
Saul was basically putting the entire kingdom—the whole nation of Israel—in David's hands

6b. What changed Saul's mind?
David's response and the authority and anointing in his words

7. As we mature, people will respond to us. As we recognize our covenant and believe God, as we stand up and speak forth our faith, as we are faithful in the small things and grow, we'll come to a place where what we say will command respect. When we have absolute faith and confidence in what we're saying, it'll inspire faith and confidence in those who hear us. When we know what we're talking about—by both revelation and experience, not just theory—people will respond to us in ways they don't respond to others. People can perceive it when we're ministering God's Word from our hearts—it rings true and gives us credibility in their sight. If God has called us to be leaders, we need to apply these truths and become totally convinced of what He's given us to share. When we believe what we speak with all of our hearts, then the people who listen to us will be able to believe it with all of their hearts too.

7a. *Discussion question:* Discuss why people will respond to you as you mature.
Discussion question

7b. If God has called you to be a leader, what do you need to do?
Apply these truths and become totally convinced of what He's given you to share

Discipleship Questions

9. How do you become a giant killer?

10. Many people want the great victory, but few are willing to do what?

11. *Discussion question:* What are some of the small things that you can trust God in?

12. True or false: One of the common traits among people whom God is using in a mighty way is that they are faithful in only the big things.

13. You can't prepare for the future any better than by what?
    A. Consulting a financial planner
    B. Starting to be faithful today
    C. Going to church at every opportunity
    D. All of the above
    E. None of the above

14. *Discussion question:* Why would doing things with integrity and excellence make a difference?

15. Why was Saul telling David "Go, and the Lord be with thee" nearly as big of a miracle as David killing Goliath?

16. What changed Saul's mind?

17. *Discussion question:* Discuss why people will respond to you as you mature.

18. If God has called you to be a leader, what do you need to do?

9. You start trusting God in the small things every day
10. Pay the price of faithfulness
11. *Discussion question*
12. False
13. B. Starting to be faithful today
14. *Discussion question*
15. Saul was basically putting the entire kingdom—the whole nation of Israel—in David's hands
16. David's response and the authority and anointing in his words
17. *Discussion question*
18. Apply these truths and become totally convinced of what He's given you to share

Scriptures

1 SAMUEL 17:37
David said moreover, The Lord that delivered me out of the paw of the lion, and out of the paw of the bear, he will deliver me out of the hand of this Philistine. And Saul said unto David, Go, and the Lord be with thee.

1 SAMUEL 10:9
And it was so, that when he had turned his back to go from Samuel, God gave him another heart: and all those signs came to pass that day.

1 SAMUEL 11:1-15
Then Nahash the Ammonite came up, and encamped against Jabeshgilead: and all the men of Jabesh said unto Nahash, Make a covenant with us, and we will serve thee. [2] And Nahash the Ammonite answered them, On this condition will I make a covenant with you, that I may thrust out all your right eyes, and lay it for a reproach upon all Israel. [3] And the elders of Jabesh said unto him, Give us seven days' respite, that we may send messengers unto all the coasts of Israel: and then, if there be no man to save us, we will come out to thee. [4] Then came the messengers to Gibeah of Saul, and told the tidings in the ears of the people: and all the people lifted up their voices, and wept. [5] And, behold, Saul came after the herd out of the field; and Saul said, What aileth the people that they weep? And they told him the tidings of the men of Jabesh. [6] And the Spirit of God came upon Saul when he heard those tidings, and his anger was kindled greatly. [7] And he took a yoke of oxen, and hewed them in pieces, and sent them throughout all the coasts of Israel by the hands of messengers, saying, Whosoever cometh not forth after Saul and after Samuel, so shall it be done unto his oxen. And the fear of the Lord fell on the people, and they came out with one consent. [8] And when he numbered them in Bezek, the children of Israel were three hundred thousand, and the men of Judah thirty thousand. [9] And they said unto the messengers that came, Thus shall ye say unto the men of Jabeshgilead, To morrow, by that time the sun be hot, ye shall have help. And the messengers came and shewed it to the men of Jabesh; and they were glad. [10] Therefore the men of Jabesh said, To morrow we will come out unto you, and ye shall do with us all that seemeth good unto you. [11] And it was so on the morrow, that Saul put the people in three companies; and they came into the midst of the host in the morning watch, and slew the Ammonites until the heat of the day: and it came to pass, that they which remained were scattered, so that two of them were not left together. [12] And the people said unto Samuel, Who is he that said, Shall Saul reign over us? bring the men, that we may put them to death. [13] And Saul said, There shall not a man be put to death this day: for to day the Lord hath wrought salvation in Israel. [14] Then said Samuel to the people, Come, and let us go to Gilgal, and renew the kingdom there. [15] And all the people went to Gilgal; and there they made Saul king

before the Lord in Gilgal; and there they sacrificed sacrifices of peace offerings before the Lord; and there Saul and all the men of Israel rejoiced greatly.

The Power of God

And Saul armed David with his armour, and he put an helmet of brass upon his head; also he armed him with a coat of mail. [39] And David girded his sword upon his armour, and he assayed to go; for he had not proved it. And David said unto Saul, I cannot go with these; for I have not proved them. And David put them off him.

1 SAMUEL 17:38-39

At first, nobody believed in David. They judged him based on his external appearance. People stacked up his physical stature against Goliath's and didn't believe in him. Finally, he spoke with such conviction, authority, faith, and power that he won the people over—including the king. They finally said, "Well, okay. Go! We'll trust you." But they wanted to arm him with their armor.

Saul's armor wasn't doing him any good. Saul was the largest, tallest, biggest, and strongest of all the Israelites. He had all of this armor and weaponry, yet he was still hiding. He hadn't gone out and fought Goliath. If his armor wasn't going to grant him victory, what made him think it would give David victory?

Can you just imagine David putting on this armor? Here's this little runt of a guy swallowed up in the armor of the largest man in the entire nation of Israel. David could probably turn around in the armor without ever moving it! This armor was burdensome to him. David had enough wisdom to recognize that this wasn't the way it was going to work. He said, "I can't do this." It's not that the armor itself was evil. He was still trusting in the Lord. The issue was that David had never proved it. He wasn't familiar with it. It wasn't what he had used before. He wasn't trusting in some physical thing to overcome Goliath. It wasn't the protection that armor could give him. It was his faith in God that was going to put him over. So, he had enough sense not to go with something that had never worked for him before.

STICK WITH WHAT WORKS!

People will try to talk you out of serving God. They'll say, "You're fanatical. You can't do it." But if you persist, they'll finally say, "Well, okay. Do it. But at least do this." And they'll try to give you their theories about how it should be done that are not working for them. They aren't doing anything. There's no victory in their lives, yet they're quick to tell you what to do. "Here, put on my armor that isn't working for me!"

God may have spoken something to you, and you're trying to obey Him. You are taking a step of faith, but the truth is that you aren't going with what's in your heart. You aren't doing what God told you

---

LESSONS FROM DAVID

to do. You're trying to live off somebody else's revelation. They may mean well, but you can't go by what God has told them to do. You can't just attend some seminar and figure out how another person grew a church or business, and then go back and do it that way, thinking, *If it worked for one, it'll work for another.* You need to hear what God is telling you. You can't just be parroting things. You need to get in the presence of God and develop your own relationship with Him. Don't just take what He gave someone else. Hear for yourself what the Lord tells you to do, and then go with it!

Andrew Wommack Ministries has given away millions of cassette tapes—not to mention CDs, books, DVDs, and MP3 downloads (most of my teaching series are available free as MP3 files on our website). That's no gimmick! The majority—over 50 percent—of the people who contact our ministry never give us a dime. Yet, we send them CDs, DVDs, books, and other materials. How does that work? It's the blessing of God!

There was a time in my life when I couldn't buy the Word. My wife had gone two weeks without food. She was eight months' pregnant, and we were struggling. I looked at a man's tape table and knew there were truths on those cassettes that could have changed my life and brought us out of poverty. Yet I couldn't buy them! My wife had tears in her eyes, and I was about to cry myself. It was a terrible situation. As I stood there, I made a promise. "Lord, if You ever show me something from Your Word that will help another person, I'll never deny them access to it because of finances." And I try to do that.

Now if we have an entire series of messages, we suggest a donation, but we give it to people regardless of what they can send. If it's something like twenty or thirty messages in a set, we'll make the CDs available to people one at a time if they'll just get them that way. We don't want to hand out tens of thousands of CDs to people who aren't giving anything. But I do try to make my messages available as much as I can. This has worked for me. I have faith for it.

Yet I've had well-known, international ministers come to me and say, "You're wrong! You need to sell your CDs. You could make a lot more money!" I'm not against other people selling their messages. They can do whatever they want. I don't think that someone isn't trusting God or that they're a bad minister if they don't give their materials away. I'm just saying that this is what has worked for me—and I'm sticking with what works!

DAVID'S STRENGTH

You need to become secure in the Lord and hear from Him. You need to have God tell you some things. Then, when He does tell you something, don't let other people talk you out of it. Don't reason it away, saying, "Well, here's what God says, but it doesn't make sense. So, I think I'll go ahead and do it this other way." You're getting off onto thin ice when you start doing something like that. You need to follow God and do what He says! That's where your strength lies.

David's strength wasn't in armor or a sword. It was in trusting God. When Goliath saw David walk out toward him with just a slingshot, he laughed at him. The giant disdained and even cursed him for coming out against him with sticks and stones. Goliath didn't recognize the power of God.

> *And he [David] took his staff in his hand, and chose him five smooth stones out of the brook, and put them in a shepherd's bag which he had, even in a scrip; and his sling was in his hand: and he drew near to the Philistine. [41] And the Philistine came on and drew near unto David; and the man that bare the shield went before him. [42] And when the Philistine looked about, and saw David, he disdained him: for he was but a youth, and ruddy, and of a fair countenance. [43] And the Philistine said unto David, Am I a dog, that thou comest to me with staves? And the Philistine cursed David by his gods. [44] And the Philistine said to David, Come to me, and I will give thy flesh unto the fowls of the air, and to the beasts of the field. [45] Then said David to the Philistine, Thou comest to me with a sword, and with a spear, and with a shield: but I come to thee in the name of the LORD of hosts, the God of the armies of Israel, whom thou hast defied. [46] This day will the LORD deliver thee into mine hand; and I will smite thee, and take thine head from thee; and I will give the carcases of the host of the Philistines this day unto the fowls of the air, and to the wild beasts of the earth; that all the earth may know that there is a God in Israel. [47] And all this assembly shall know that the LORD saveth not with sword and spear: for the battle is the LORD's, and he will give you into our hands.*
>
> 1 SAMUEL 17:40-47, BRACKETS MINE

This is tremendous! Goliath began to rail on and ridicule David. He pointed out his physical weakness, comparatively small size, and lack of a sword. Then he cursed David by his gods. However, not Goliath nor Saul nor the rest of the army knew that David wasn't just a youth. He was an anointed king. He had the power and anointing of Almighty God on the inside of him.

YOU'RE THE WINNER!

You can't always see that power and anointing just by looking at someone. But the truth is that if you're born again, you have a covenant with God and you're the winner. You're the one who is an anointed priest and king (Rev. 1:6 and 5:10). Don't just approach your giant and listen to the railing diatribe they hurl against you. Listen instead to what God has to say about you: "You're the winner. You're the one with authority. You're an anointed king!"

LESSONS FROM DAVID

David was a king. Goliath didn't know it. Saul didn't know it. But David knew it. He knew he was anointed. So, instead of responding to this curse and being intimidated, he came right back, saying, "Your confidence is in your physical size, your sword, and your shield. But my confidence is in the name of the Lord. It's God who is going to fight for me. It's His battle today, and I'm going to take your head off you!" David didn't even have a sword, yet he prophesied that he would behead Goliath!

David had thought this thing through. He didn't just see himself going out there and killing Goliath with a sling. He saw himself using a sword to cut his head off. David declared, "I'm going to lift your head off you today and give the carcasses of all the Philistines to the fowls of the air and the beasts of the field!" Then he ran at Goliath.

> *And David put his hand in his bag, and took thence a stone, and slang it, and smote the Philistine in his forehead, that the stone sunk into his forehead; and he fell upon his face to the earth. [50] So David prevailed over the Philistine with a sling and with a stone, and smote the Philistine, and slew him; but there was no sword in the hand of David.*
>
> 1 SAMUEL 17:49-50

David may have been a perfect marksman with his sling. However, he may have just been good or even average. It's possible that he just went out there and slung that stone, and God supernaturally directed it and caused it to hit its mark.

Outline

I. First Samuel 17:38-39 says,

And Saul armed David with his armour, and he put an helmet of brass upon his head; also he armed him with a coat of mail. [39] And David girded his sword upon his armour, and he assayed to go; for he had not proved it. And David said unto Saul, I cannot go with these; for I have not proved them. And David put them off him.

 A. Saul's armor wasn't doing him any good.
 B. He had all of this armor and weaponry, yet he was still hiding—he hadn't gone out and fought Goliath.
 C. If his armor wasn't going to grant him victory, what made him think it would give David victory?
 D. This armor was burdensome to David.
 E. The issue was that David had never proved it.
 F. He wasn't familiar with it, and it wasn't what he had used before.
 G. He wasn't trusting in some physical thing to overcome Goliath—it was his faith in God that was going to put him over.

II. People will try to talk you out of serving God.
 A. But if you persist, they'll finally say "Well, okay. Do it. But at least do this"—and they'll try to give you their theories about how it should be done that are not working for them.
 B. There's no victory in their lives, yet they're quick to tell you what to do.
 C. God may have spoken something to you, and you're trying to obey Him.
 D. You are taking a step of faith, but the truth is that you aren't going with what's in your heart—you aren't doing what God told you to do.
 E. You're trying to live off somebody else's revelation.
 F. They may mean well, but you can't go by what God has told them to do.
 G. You need to get in the presence of God and develop your own relationship with Him.

III. You need to become secure in the Lord and hear from Him.
 A. Then, when He does tell you something, don't let other people talk you out of it.
 B. You need to follow God and do what He says!
 C. That's where your strength lies.
 D. David's strength wasn't in armor or a sword—it was in trusting God.
 E. When Goliath saw David walk out toward him with just a slingshot, he laughed at him.
 F. Goliath didn't recognize the power of God.

LESSONS FROM DAVID

And he [David] took his staff in his hand, and chose him five smooth stones out of the brook, and put them in a shepherd's bag which he had, even in a scrip; and his sling was in his hand: and he drew near to the Philistine. [41] And the Philistine came on and drew near unto David; and the man that bare the shield went before him. [42] And when the Philistine looked about, and saw David, he disdained him: for he was but a youth, and ruddy, and of a fair countenance. [43] And the Philistine said unto David, Am I a dog, that thou comest to me with staves? And the Philistine cursed David by his gods. [44] And the Philistine said to David, Come to me, and I will give thy flesh unto the fowls of the air, and to the beasts of the field. [45] Then said David to the Philistine, Thou comest to me with a sword, and with a spear, and with a shield: but I come to thee in the name of the LORD of hosts, the God of the armies of Israel, whom thou hast defied. [46] This day will the LORD deliver thee into mine hand; and I will smite thee, and take thine head from thee; and I will give the carcases of the host of the Philistines this day unto the fowls of the air, and to the wild beasts of the earth; that all the earth may know that there is a God in Israel. [47] And all this assembly shall know that the LORD saveth not with sword and spear: for the battle is the LORD's, and he will give you into our hands.

1 SAMUEL 17:40-47, BRACKETS MINE

    G. Goliath began to rail on and ridicule David; then he cursed David by his gods.

    H. However, David was an anointed king—he had the power and anointing of Almighty God on the inside of him.

IV. You can't always see that power and anointing just by looking at someone.
    A. But the truth is that if you're born again, you have a covenant with God and you're the winner.
    B. You're the one who is an anointed priest and king (Rev. 1:6 and 5:10).
    C. David was a king—he knew he was anointed.
    D. David had thought this thing through.
        i. He didn't just see himself going out there and killing Goliath with a sling.
        ii. He saw himself using a sword to cut his head off.
    E. Then he ran at Goliath.

And David put his hand in his bag, and took thence a stone, and slang it, and smote the Philistine in his forehead, that the stone sunk into his forehead; and he fell upon his face to the earth. [50] So David prevailed over the Philistine with a sling and with a stone, and smote the Philistine, and slew him; but there was no sword in the hand of David.

1 SAMUEL 17:49-50

1. First Samuel 17:38-39 says,

   And Saul armed David with his armour, and he put an helmet of brass upon his head; also he armed him with a coat of mail. [39] And David girded his sword upon his armour, and he assayed to go; for he had not proved it. And David said unto Saul, I cannot go with these; for I have not proved them. And David put them off him.

Saul's armor wasn't doing him any good. He had all of this armor and weaponry, yet he was still hiding—he hadn't gone out and fought Goliath. If his armor wasn't going to grant him victory, what made him think it would give David victory? This armor was burdensome to David. The issue was that David had never proved it. He wasn't familiar with it, and it wasn't what he had used before. He wasn't trusting in some physical thing to overcome Goliath—it was his faith in God that was going to put him over.

1a. *Discussion question:* What lessons do you glean from 1 Samuel 17:38-39?
   Discussion question
1b. Was Saul's armor doing him any good? Why or why not?
   No—he had all of that armor and weaponry, yet he was still hiding; he hadn't gone out and fought Goliath
1c. What was David's issue with Saul's armor?
   A. It wasn't polished enough
   B. He wanted his own armor
   C. He had never proved it
   D. All of the above
   E. None of the above
   C. He had never proved it

2. People will try to talk us out of serving God. But if we persist, they'll finally say "Well, okay. Do it. But at least do this"—and they'll try to give us their theories about how it should be done that are not working for them. There's no victory in their lives, yet they're quick to tell us what to do. God may have spoken something to us, and we're trying to obey Him. We are taking a step of faith, but the truth is that we aren't going with what's in our hearts—we aren't doing what God told us to do. We're trying to live off somebody else's revelation. They may mean well, but we can't go by what God has told them to do. We need to get in the presence of God and develop our own relationship with Him.

2a. *Discussion question:* Why do you think people will try to talk you out of serving God?
Discussion question
2b. There's no _____ in their lives, yet they're quick to tell _____ what to do.
Victory / you
2c. *Discussion question:* Why is it so important to develop your own relationship with God?
Discussion question

3. We need to become secure in the Lord and hear from Him. Then, when He does tell us something, we can't let other people talk us out of it. We need to follow God and do what He says! That's where our strength lies. David's strength wasn't in armor or a sword—it was in trusting God. When Goliath saw David walk out toward him with just a slingshot, he laughed at him. Goliath didn't recognize the power of God.

> *And he [David] took his staff in his hand, and chose him five smooth stones out of the brook, and put them in a shepherd's bag which he had, even in a scrip; and his sling was in his hand: and he drew near to the Philistine. [41] And the Philistine came on and drew near unto David; and the man that bare the shield went before him. [42] And when the Philistine looked about, and saw David, he disdained him: for he was but a youth, and ruddy, and of a fair countenance. [43] And the Philistine said unto David, Am I a dog, that thou comest to me with staves? And the Philistine cursed David by his gods. [44] And the Philistine said to David, Come to me, and I will give thy flesh unto the fowls of the air, and to the beasts of the field. [45] Then said David to the Philistine, Thou comest to me with a sword, and with a spear, and with a shield: but I come to thee in the name of the LORD of hosts, the God of the armies of Israel, whom thou hast defied. [46] This day will the LORD deliver thee into mine hand; and I will smite thee, and take thine head from thee; and I will give the carcases of the host of the Philistines this day unto the fowls of the air, and to the wild beasts of the earth; that all the earth may know that there is a God in Israel. [47] And all this assembly shall know that the LORD saveth not with sword and spear: for the battle is the LORD's, and he will give you into our hands.*
>
> 1 SAMUEL 17:40-47, BRACKETS MINE

Goliath began to rail on and ridicule David; then he cursed David by his gods. However, David was an anointed king—he had the power and anointing of Almighty God on the inside of him.

3a. Once you become secure in the Lord and hear from Him, what should you not do?
Let other people talk you out of what He's told you

3b. True or false: David's strength wasn't in armor or a sword—it was in trusting God.
True

3c. *Discussion question:* Why do you think David let Goliath berate and curse him? Do you think many people today would react the way David did? Why or why not?
Discussion question

4. We can't always see that power and anointing just by looking at someone. But the truth is that if we're born again, we have a covenant with God and we're the winners. We're the ones who are anointed priests and kings (Rev. 1:6 and 5:10). David was a king—he knew he was anointed. David had thought this thing through. He didn't just see himself going out there and killing Goliath with a sling. He saw himself using a sword to cut his head off. Then he ran at Goliath.

> *And David put his hand in his bag, and took thence a stone, and slang it, and smote the Philistine in his forehead, that the stone sunk into his forehead; and he fell upon his face to the earth. [50] So David prevailed over the Philistine with a sling and with a stone, and smote the Philistine, and slew him; but there was no sword in the hand of David.*
>
> 1 SAMUEL 17:49-50

4a. What do Revelation 1:6 and 5:10 tell you?
That you are an anointed priest and king

4b. *Discussion question:* What difference can the answer to #4a make in your life?
Discussion question

4c. What did David do when it was time to battle with Goliath?
   A. He ran at Goliath
   B. He ran from Goliath
   C. He waited for Israel's army to back him up
   D. All of the above
   E. None of the above
   A. He ran at Goliath

Discipleship Questions

1. *Discussion question:* What lessons do you glean from 1 Samuel 17:38-39?

2. Was Saul's armor doing him any good? Why or why not?

3. What was David's issue with Saul's armor?
   A. It wasn't polished enough
   B. He wanted his own armor
   C. He had never proved it
   D. All of the above
   E. None of the above

4. *Discussion question:* Why do you think people will try to talk you out of serving God?

5. There's no _____ in their lives, yet they're quick to tell _____ what to do.

6. *Discussion question:* What is it so important to develop your own relationship with God?

7. Once you become secure in the Lord and hear from Him, what should you not do?

8. True or false: David's strength wasn't in armor or a sword—it was in trusting God.

9. *Discussion question:* Why do you think David let Goliath berate and curse him? Do you think many people today would react the way David did? Why or why not?
_____
_____
_____

10. What do Revelation 1:6 and 5:10 tell you?
_____
_____
_____

11. *Discussion question:* What difference can the answer to #10 make in your life?
_____
_____
_____

12. What did David do when it was time to battle with Goliath?
    A. He ran at Goliath
    B. He ran from Goliath
    C. He waited for Israel's army to back him up
    D. All of the above
    E. None of the above

1. *Discussion question*
2. No—he had all of that armor and weaponry, yet he was still hiding; he hadn't gone out and fought Goliath
3. C. He had never proved it
4. *Discussion question*
5. Victory / you
6. *Discussion question*
7. Let other people talk you out of what He's told you
8. True
9. *Discussion question*
10. That you are an anointed priest and king
11. *Discussion question*
12. A. He ran at Goliath

LESSONS FROM DAVID

Scriptures

1 SAMUEL 17:38-47

And Saul armed David with his armour, and he put an helmet of brass upon his head; also he armed him with a coat of mail. [39] And David girded his sword upon his armour, and he assayed to go; for he had not proved it. And David said unto Saul, I cannot go with these; for I have not proved them. And David put them off him. [40] And he took his staff in his hand, and chose him five smooth stones out of the brook, and put them in a shepherd's bag which he had, even in a scrip; and his sling was in his hand: and he drew near to the Philistine. [41] And the Philistine came on and drew near unto David; and the man that bare the shield went before him. [42] And when the Philistine looked about, and saw David, he disdained him: for he was but a youth, and ruddy, and of a fair countenance. [43] And the Philistine said unto David, Am I a dog, that thou comest to me with staves? And the Philistine cursed David by his gods. [44] And the Philistine said to David, Come to me, and I will give thy flesh unto the fowls of the air, and to the beasts of the field. [45] Then said David to the Philistine, Thou comest to me with a sword, and with a spear, and with a shield: but I come to thee in the name of the LORD of hosts, the God of the armies of Israel, whom thou hast defied. [46] This day will the LORD deliver thee into mine hand; and I will smite thee, and take thine head from thee; and I will give the carcases of the host of the Philistines this day unto the fowls of the air, and to the wild beasts of the earth; that all the earth may know that there is a God in Israel. [47] And all this assembly shall know that the LORD saveth not with sword and spear: for the battle is the LORD's, and he will give you into our hands.

REVELATION 1:6

And hath made us kings and priests unto God and his Father; to him be glory and dominion for ever and ever. Amen.

REVELATION 5:10

And hast made us unto our God kings and priests: and we shall reign on the earth.

1 SAMUEL 17:49-50

And David put his hand in his bag, and took thence a stone, and slang it, and smote the Philistine in his forehead, that the stone sunk into his forehead; and he fell upon his face to the earth. [50] So David prevailed over the Philistine with a sling and with a stone, and smote the Philistine, and slew him; but there was no sword in the hand of David.

The Power of God

I don't always do things perfectly, yet God takes those things and makes them work. I do what I can, and God adds His power and anointing to it.

Little is much when God is in it. The little boy only had five loaves and two fish. It was barely enough for his lunch, let alone the multitude. Yet when he gave it to Jesus, it multiplied, it fed the multitude, and they had more left over after they were all full than when they began (John 6:5-13). That's what you do. You give God the little bit you have, and He takes it and multiplies it to abundantly meet the need.

I believe that's what happened with David. He may have been good, or even average, with his sling, but it wasn't his marksmanship—it was his trust in God. David went out there and slung that stone in faith. The Lord took it and made it hit the mark. Notice that the Word says he…

> …slew him; but there was no sword in the hand of David.
>
> 1 SAMUEL 17:50B

HEAD HELD HIGH

> Therefore David ran, and stood upon the Philistine, and took his sword, and drew it out of the sheath thereof, and slew him, and cut off his head therewith. And when the Philistines saw their champion was dead, they fled.
>
> 1 SAMUEL 17:51

David didn't stop once Goliath was down. He got on top of him, took Goliath's own sword out, cut off his head, and then held it up for all to see. Once the Philistines saw that Goliath was dead, they fled.

The Philistines didn't flee when they saw Goliath fall. They wondered if perhaps he was just wounded and could have gotten back into the fight. He still might have overcome and defeated David. Maybe they thought he just fell. Sometimes big people have trouble lifting their feet and even trip over them. The Philistines who were watching this weren't sure that Goliath was dead. But once David stood on top of him, took his own sword out, cut off his head, and held it up, nobody doubted any more about whether Goliath would get up and fight again. This proved he was dead.

LESSONS FROM DAVID

David didn't just fight his enemy and knock him down. He completely conquered and totally vanquished him! David made sure there was no way Goliath would ever get up and fight again. And once he held that head up, that's when all the Philistines fled. That's when the deliverance came. That's when the Israelites began to chase the Philistines and win this battle!

Many times, we resist the devil and fight just enough to get some relief. We knock him down, but we don't knock him out. So, he rises up and fights us again another day. It's like chasing your enemy over the hill to where they're out of sight. Since you're out of immediate danger, you don't pursue them. You let them go. You allow them to regroup and come back to fight you again.

David didn't do that. He didn't just knock his enemy down. David fought his enemy until they were destroyed. He was taking no prisoners. He was literally out to destroy the enemy.

FINISH THE JOB!

In 1991, the United States, Great Britain, and the coalition forces came against Saddam Hussein's regime in Iraq. They had him on the ropes, but they backed down. Instead of just walking into Baghdad and finishing the job, they pulled out.

There appears to be strong evidence suggesting that Iraq financed terrorists. So, it's possible that if they had finished the job in 1991, there never would have been the terrorist attacks that happened on September 11, 2001. There wouldn't have been airplanes crashing into the World Trade Center and the Pentagon. There wouldn't have been another airplane—one that seemed to be headed for the White House—crashing into a field. There wouldn't have been all this loss of life, or the need for a second war with Iraq in 2003.

But the United States and its allies got an objective accomplished and the immediate pressure relieved. They had humiliated Saddam Hussein and his people and thought that was enough. They didn't pursue their enemy until he was destroyed. Because of that, they had to come back twelve years later and do it again, costing lives, money, resources, world opinion, and a lot of other things that would have been unnecessary if they had just taken care of it the first time.

Don't just resist the devil until you get some relief. Fight him until his work is totally destroyed! If you have arthritis, don't just pray and say, "Well, it's decreased. I can live with it now." No! Fight that thing until there's not a trace of it left. Don't just sit there and say, "Well, I was in absolute poverty. I believed God and now we're okay. We aren't really getting along the way we should, and I certainly can't give the way I'd like to, but we're okay. I think I'll just settle here." No! That's not the right attitude! You need to fight poverty until you destroy it. Keep believing God until you come out on top and truly abound so much that you can give into every good work like it says in 2 Corinthians 9:8. Don't settle with just enough for you. Pursue the manifestation of prosperity to the point that you can become a blessing to other people!

You need to pursue the blessings of God and defeat your Enemy until he cannot rise again! You need to get the attitude that you are taking no prisoners and giving no quarter. You are going to fight the devil and destroy him. You need to get this attitude.

FIGHT NOW OR FIGHT LATER

Once you cut the head off that problem you're fighting and hold it up for all to see, all the other demons will begin to flee. When the Philistines saw David hold up the head of their champion, they fled. But they didn't flee until they were certain he wasn't going to get back up again. Once the Enemy sees that you have this attitude that you are going to totally vanquish him from your life, that's when he and all the other demons will flee.

The only reason the devil fights us so hard is because he's a coward. He knows that if he doesn't fight you now, he'll have to fight you later. So, he'll fight you if he thinks he can get you to back down and cower before him. But once he sees that you're going to take it to him, he just tucks his tail and runs!

David didn't overcome Goliath because of anything natural. It wasn't his talents, skills, looks, or charisma. In the physical realm, he was inadequate in every way. But on the inside, David was a man after God's own heart. He trusted and believed God. He had proven the Lord's promises before and been faithful in the small things. David stood on what had worked for him. He wasn't going to go with someone else's plan. He did what God had shown him to do and pursued the devil until he literally destroyed him.

If you get these attitudes and live them out over a period of time, you'll become a giant killer too!

Outline

V. Little is much when God is in it.
   A. The little boy only had five loaves and two fish, yet when he gave it to Jesus, it multiplied, it fed the multitude, and they had more left over after they were all full than when they began (John 6:5-13).
   B. Give God the little bit you have, and He'll take it and multiply it to abundantly meet the need.
   C. I believe that's what happened with David: He may have been good, or even average, with his sling, but it wasn't his marksmanship—it was his trust in God.
   D. David went out there and slung that stone in faith; the Lord took it and made it hit the mark.

VI. Notice that the Word says David…

   …slew him; but there was no sword in the hand of David.

   1 SAMUEL 17:50B

   A. David didn't stop once Goliath was down.

   Therefore David ran, and stood upon the Philistine, and took his sword, and drew it out of the sheath thereof, and slew him, and cut off his head therewith. And when the Philistines saw their champion was dead, they fled.

   1 SAMUEL 17:51

   B. He got on top of him, took Goliath's own sword out, cut off his head, and then held it up for all to see.
   C. Once the Philistines saw that Goliath was dead, they fled.
   D. David didn't just fight his enemy and knock him down—he completely conquered and totally vanquished him!
   E. David made sure there was no way Goliath would ever get up and fight again.
   F. Many times, we resist the devil and fight just enough to get some relief.
   G. We knock him down, but we don't knock him out.
   H. So, he rises up and fights us again another day.
   I. David fought his enemy until they were destroyed.

VII. Don't just resist the devil until you get some relief.
- A. Fight him until his work is totally destroyed!
- B. You need to pursue the blessings of God and defeat your Enemy until he cannot rise again!
- C. You need to get the attitude that you are taking no prisoners and giving no quarter.
- D. You are going to fight the devil and destroy him.

VIII. Once you cut the head off that problem you're fighting and hold it up for all to see, all the other demons will begin to flee.
- A. When the Philistines saw David hold up the head of their champion, they fled, but they didn't flee until they were certain he wasn't going to get back up again.
- B. Once the Enemy sees that you have this attitude that you are going to totally vanquish him from your life, that's when he and all the other demons will flee.
- C. The only reason the devil fights you so hard is because he's a coward.
- D. He knows that if he doesn't fight you now, he'll have to fight you later.
- E. So, he'll fight you if he thinks he can get you to back down and cower before him.
- F. But once he sees that you're going to take it to him, he just tucks his tail and runs!

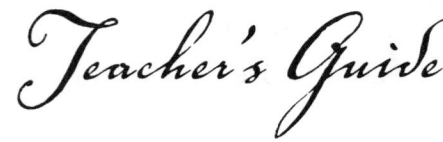

5. Little is much when God is in it. The little boy only had five loaves and two fish, yet when he gave it to Jesus, it multiplied, it fed the multitude, and they had more left over after they were all full than when they began (John 6:5-13). If we give God the little bit we have, He'll take it and multiply it to abundantly meet the need. I believe that's what happened with David: He may have been good, or even average, with his sling, but it wasn't his marksmanship—it was his trust in God. David went out there and slung that stone in faith; the Lord took it and made it hit the mark.

5a. *Discussion question:* Are there any areas of your life where the principles of John 6:5-13 can be applied? In what ways?
   Discussion question

5b. What will happen when you give God the little bit you have?
   He'll take it and multiply it to abundantly meet the need

6. Notice that the Word says David...

   ...slew him; but there was no sword in the hand of David.

   1 SAMUEL 17:50B

David didn't stop once Goliath was down.

Therefore David ran, and stood upon the Philistine, and took his sword, and drew it out of the sheath thereof, and slew him, and cut off his head therewith. And when the Philistines saw their champion was dead, they fled.

1 SAMUEL 17:51

He got on top of him, took Goliath's own sword out, cut off his head, and then held it up for all to see. Once the Philistines saw that Goliath was dead, they fled. David didn't just fight his enemy and knock him down—he completely conquered and totally vanquished him! David made sure there was no way Goliath would ever get up and fight again. Many times, we resist the devil and fight just enough to get some relief. We knock him down, but we don't knock him out. So, he rises up and fights us again another day. David fought his enemy until they were destroyed.

6a. When did the Philistines flee?
   When they saw that Goliath was dead—once David cut off Goliath's head with his own sword and held it up for all to see

6b. *Discussion question:* What enemies in your life have you fought just enough to get some relief? How do you think your battle strategy needs to change so that you can knock those enemies out, not just down?
   Discussion question

6c. David fought his enemy until they were _____.
   Destroyed

7. We can't just resist the devil until we get some relief. Let's fight him until his work is totally destroyed! We need to pursue the blessings of God and defeat our Enemy until he cannot rise again! We need to get the attitude that we are taking no prisoners and giving no quarter. We are going to fight the devil and destroy him.

7a. True or false: You need to pursue the blessings of God and resist the devil until you get some relief.
   False

LESSONS FROM DAVID

8. Once we cut the head off that problem we're fighting and hold it up for all to see, all the other demons will begin to flee. When the Philistines saw David hold up the head of their champion, they fled, but they didn't flee until they were certain he wasn't going to get back up again. Once the Enemy sees that we have this attitude that we are going to totally vanquish him from our lives, that's when he and all the other demons will flee. The only reason the devil fights us so hard is because he's a coward. He knows that if he doesn't fight us now, he'll have to fight us later. So, he'll fight us if he thinks he can get us to back down and cower before him. But once he sees that we're going to take it to him, he just tucks his tail and runs!

8a. What happens once the Enemy sees that you have this attitude that you are going to totally vanquish him from your life?
    A. He will laugh at you and settle in for a long stay
    B. He and all the other demons will flee
    C. His demons will panic but not go anywhere
    D. All of the above
    E. None of the above
    B. He and all the other demons will flee

8b. *Discussion question:* Have you experienced the devil fighting you "now" so he doesn't have to fight you "later"? How have you dealt with that in the past, and how do you plan to deal with it in the future?
Discussion question

Discipleship Questions

13. *Discussion question:* Are there any areas of your life where the principles of John 6:5-13 can be applied? In what ways?

14. What will happen when you give God the little bit you have?

15. When did the Philistines flee?

16. *Discussion question:* What enemies in your life have you fought just enough to get some relief? How do you think your battle strategy needs to change so that you can knock those enemies out, not just down?

17. David fought his enemy until they were _____.

18. True or false: You need to pursue the blessings of God and resist the devil until you get some relief.

19. What happens once the Enemy sees that you have this attitude that you are going to totally vanquish him from your life?
    A. He will laugh at you and settle in for a long stay
    B. He and all the other demons will flee
    C. His demons will panic but not go anywhere
    D. All of the above
    E. None of the above

20. *Discussion question:* Have you experienced the devil fighting you "now" so he doesn't have to fight you "later"? How have you dealt with that in the past, and how do you plan to deal with it in the future?

___
___
___

Answer Key

13. *Discussion question*
14. He'll take it and multiply it to abundantly meet the need
15. When they saw that Goliath was dead—once David cut off Goliath's head with his own sword and held it up for all to see
16. *Discussion question*
17. Destroyed
18. False
19. B. He and all the other demons will flee
20. *Discussion question*

Scriptures

JOHN 6:5-13

When Jesus then lifted up his eyes, and saw a great company come unto him, he saith unto Philip, Whence shall we buy bread, that these may eat? [6] And this he said to prove him: for he himself knew what he would do. [7] Philip answered him, Two hundred pennyworth of bread is not sufficient for them, that every one of them may take a little. [8] One of his disciples, Andrew, Simon Peter's brother, saith unto him, [9] There is a lad here, which hath five barley loaves, and two small fishes: but what are they among so many? [10] And Jesus said, Make the men sit down. Now there was much grass in the place. So the men sat down, in number about five thousand. [11] And Jesus took the loaves; and when he had given thanks, he distributed to the disciples, and the disciples to them that were set down; and likewise of the fishes as much as they would. [12] When they were filled, he said unto his disciples, Gather up the fragments that remain, that nothing be lost. [13] Therefore they gathered them together, and filled twelve baskets with the fragments of the five barley loaves, which remained over and above unto them that had eaten.

1 SAMUEL 17:50-51

So David prevailed over the Philistine with a sling and with a stone, and smote the Philistine, and slew him; but there was no sword in the hand of David. [51] Therefore David ran, and stood upon the Philistine, and took his sword, and drew it out of the sheath thereof, and slew him, and cut off his head therewith. And when the Philistines saw their champion was dead, they fled.

2 CORINTHIANS 9:8

And God is able to make all grace abound toward you; that ye, always having all sufficiency in all things, may abound to every good work.

Encourage Yourself in the Lord

Right before David became king, he was driven from the land of Israel because Saul had been hotly pursuing him. So, he moved into the land of the Philistines and was living among them (1 Sam. 27:1-3). He gained favor with Achish, the Philistine king of Gath, which is the same place Goliath was from. Achish gave David the city of Ziklag to dwell in (1 Sam. 27:5-6). However, when the Philistines were marshaling their forces to go to battle, the princes didn't trust him to go with them, so David and his men were sent home. But as they were returning, they saw that the city had been invaded by the Amalekites, who must've known that the city was unprotected.

> *So David and his men came to the city, and, behold, it was burned with fire; and their wives, and their sons, and their daughters, were taken captives. [4] Then David and the people that were with him lifted up their voice and wept, until they had no more power to weep.*
>
> 1 SAMUEL 30:3-4

This was a terrible situation! Can you imagine experiencing something so tragic that you wept until you couldn't weep anymore? I've done that. And the Scripture also says that the Amalekites had plundered the city and taken spoils (1 Sam. 30:19). David was experiencing a devastating loss. And this was on top of thirteen years of being persecuted, chased, threatened, ridiculed, falsely accused, thought of as crazy—you name it.

Get a picture of this: David was about seventeen years old when Samuel anointed him to be king. This instance in 1 Samuel 30:1-4 is just a day or two shy of when he actually began his reign, at the age of thirty (2 Sam. 5:4). And all the while, he'd operated in integrity and faithfulness. But it was going on thirteen years of him having troubles day in and day out. He'd had problem after problem. Things never got better, only worse. He couldn't even go home to his people in Israel; he had to live among a people that had been his enemy. And on top of all that, all of his wives and children had been taken, and the city had been burned to the ground.

But he wasn't the only one who had been through distress and suffered loss; all of his men had been with him. The Scripture goes on to say:

> *And David was greatly distressed; for the people spake of stoning him, because the soul of all the people was grieved, every man for his sons and for his daughters.*
>
> 1 SAMUEL 30:6A

This just adds insult to injury! The guys who had been with David through all his troubles turned on him, as if it was his fault all of these things had happened! He had provided for them, led them to victory in battle, and how did they repay him? They blamed him for this tragedy! David could have just quit right here. Most people wouldn't have survived this, let alone what he had been through the previous thirteen years. But, you know, this was less than twenty-four or forty-eight hours from him seeing his dreams fulfilled.

DAVID WAS NO FOOL!

If David would have quit and given up, which is what he was tempted to do, he wouldn't have become king. He could have given up and his men would have dispersed, or he could have said "What's the use? What's the point in living now?" and let his men kill him. This is just like what Job's wife told him after they had been through terrible loss:

> *Dost thou still retain thine integrity? curse God, and die.*
>
> JOB 2:9

There's a great lesson in this, and I guarantee you, you will be pushed to a place where it looks like "Why even try anymore? I should just give up." But look at how Job answered:

> *Thou speakest as one of the foolish women speaketh.*
>
> JOB 2:10A

It would have been foolish for David to give up, even in the face of this tragic situation he was in. But David was no fool! He stuck with God no matter what. The Bible tells us how he responded:

> *But David encouraged himself in the L*ORD *his God.*
>
> 1 SAMUEL 30:6B

This is powerful. God has used this to speak to me I couldn't tell you how many times. I've been in situations where in the natural, it looked like I ought to just quit. I have resorted to this passage of Scripture and realized that David was in a worse place than I've ever been in, yet he was able to encourage himself in the Lord. Very few people do this. They're always calling somebody else; they're always depending upon somebody else to encourage them. But you have to get to where you encourage yourself in the Lord. How do you do that? There are a lot of ways. Right here in the very next verse, it says,

> *And David said to Abiathar the priest, Ahimelech's son, I pray thee, bring me hither the ephod. And Abiathar brought thither the ephod to David.*
>
> 1 SAMUEL 30:7

ENCOURAGE YOURSELF IN THE LORD

The ephod was a breastplate that the priests wore, and somehow or another, God could communicate through the stones that were on it. This would be comparable in our day to the Word of God. God speaks to us through the Word. And David encouraged himself by going back to the Word. I've done this exact same thing many times. I just go to the Word, start remembering the promises God gave me, and encourage myself in Him.

SPEAK IN TONGUES

Also, another benefit that I think a lot of Christians do not take advantage of is speaking in tongues. The Scripture says this in 1 Corinthians 14:

He that speaketh in an unknown tongue edifieth himself.

1 CORINTHIANS 14:4A

The word "edify" means to build up. It says something similar in Jude:

But ye, beloved, building up yourselves on your most holy faith, praying in the Holy Ghost.

JUDE 20

That's talking about speaking in tongues too. When you speak in tongues, you are building yourself up on your most holy faith. Now, I know there are a lot of people who don't understand that and think, *Well, what does speaking in tongues have to do with anything? It's total gibberish! I don't see how speaking in tongues would make a difference.* But one of the very reasons that speaking in tongues is so powerful is because it doesn't make sense to the natural mind.

If therefore the whole church be come together into one place, and all speak with tongues, and there come in those that are unlearned, or unbelievers, will they not say that ye are mad?

1 CORINTHIANS 14:23

Your carnal mind will say you're foolish for speaking in tongues. It will try to stop you. But the reason it's so powerful is because if you do it over a prolonged period of time, it forces you to get into your most holy faith. Why? Because you don't know what you're saying.

For he that speaketh in an unknown tongue speaketh not unto men, but unto God: for no man understandeth him; howbeit in the spirit he speaketh mysteries.

1 CORINTHIANS 14:2

When you speak in tongues, there's this tendency not to do it. It takes faith to believe that there's actually a benefit. But as the Scriptures say in 1 Corinthians 14:4, you edify yourself when you speak in tongues—you are building yourself up, and you are promoting spiritual growth. In order to pray in tongues over a prolonged period of time, you have to move into faith because you have to overcome thoughts that it's silly and foolish. But if you persist, you'll move into faith and begin to start edifying yourself.

I say all this to say that for the New Testament believer, when you need encouragement, like David did, you can pray in tongues and build yourself up. If you've been filled with the Spirit, this is a resource you need to use. And it's with you all the time! God has given it to you, and you can speak in tongues anytime you want and receive this benefit. This is tremendous!

There are many Spirit-filled people who will allow themselves to go into depression. They will sit there and feel like, *God, I need something. Would You please send someone my way?* I'm not denying the fact that God can use other people. I believe that God is using me right now to speak to you. If you've been praying "God, what do I do?" here's help coming your way: You need to be like David, to where you can encourage yourself in the Lord. In the New Testament, speaking in tongues is one of the most important things you can possibly do.

HOLD ON!

There's not a single a Christian who is facing something more than they can bear.

> *There hath no temptation taken you but such as is common to man: but God is faithful, who will not suffer you to be tempted above that ye are able; but will with the temptation also make a way to escape, that ye may be able to bear it.*
>
> 1 CORINTHIANS 10:13

Satan doesn't have different things to throw at you. It's the same contents with a different wrapper and a different bow on it. You're not having to endure something you just can't handle. You might be thinking, *That's not true. You don't know my situation.* Well, I know the Word of God, and God promised He would not suffer you to be tempted above what you are able. Everything you're facing is what's common to man. When it seems like you can't stand another minute and you've hit your limits, God is going to make some way of escape so you can survive and come through the thing.

David was in that situation, and if he would have given in to his hurt and pain and just given up hope, he would have done so only hours from what he had been patiently waiting thirteen years for. I'm telling you, if you feel like you should quit, you could be just moments away from seeing the breakthrough you've been looking for.

You've got to encourage yourself in the Lord and stand on the promise that He will not suffer you to be tempted above what you are able. God is telling you to hold on! Don't quit and don't give up! God is going to come through, but you have to encourage yourself in the Lord.

For David, after he encouraged himself, he asked God what he should do about his situation:

And David enquired at the LORD, saying, Shall I pursue after this troop? shall I overtake them? And he answered him, Pursue: for thou shalt surely overtake them, and without fail recover all.

1 SAMUEL 30:8

The rest of this story goes that David took leadership of his men, they submitted unto him, and he pursued the Amalekites, caught them off guard, and completely destroyed them.

This is a great example of what I was talking about in the previous chapter: David pursued his enemies until they couldn't come back! He didn't just fight the Amalekite army until he couldn't see them anymore; he kept going until he utterly destroyed them. We need to learn to do the same.

So, David and his men got back every woman, every child, and all of their livestock—they didn't lose a single life! Plus, they got all the spoil of the Amalekites! God blessed them! Then, in just hours after this, he got news that Saul had been killed in battle, and David was crowned king. So, after thirteen years, and when things were at their worst, David encouraged himself in the Lord, and that's when he saw the breakthrough!

You might be contemplating quitting, but it's like what Peter said:

Lord, to whom shall we go? thou hast the words of eternal life.

JOHN 6:68

Where else can you go? Who else has the words of everlasting life? You don't have anywhere else to go; you just need to stand and believe God. You just need to get to a place where David was. He didn't quit, and because of it, in a relatively short period of time, his dreams began to come to pass. If you will stand your ground and encourage yourself in the Lord, you'll become a victor like David was. You'll outlast what the devil is trying to do in your life. This is one of the great lessons you can learn from the life of David.

LESSONS FROM DAVID

Outline

I. Right before David became king, he was driven from the land of Israel because Saul had been hotly pursuing him.
   A. So, he moved into the land of the Philistines and was living among them (1 Sam. 27:1-3).
   B. He gained favor with Achish, the Philistine king of Gath, and Achish gave David the city of Ziklag to dwell in (1 Sam. 27:5-6).
   C. However, when the Philistines were marshaling their forces to go to battle, the princes didn't trust him to go with them, so David and his men were sent home.
   D. But as they were returning, they saw that the city had been invaded by the Amalekites, who must've known that the city was unprotected.

So David and his men came to the city, and, behold, it was burned with fire; and their wives, and their sons, and their daughters, were taken captives. [4] Then David and the people that were with him lifted up their voice and wept, until they had no more power to weep.
                                                                                                  1 SAMUEL 30:3-4

   E. The Scripture also says that the Amalekites had plundered the city and taken spoils (1 Sam. 30:19).
   F. David was experiencing a devastating loss.
   G. Get a picture of this: David was about seventeen years old when Samuel anointed him to be king, and this instance in 1 Samuel 30:1-4 is just a day or two shy of when he actually began his reign, at the age of thirty (2 Sam. 5:4).
   H. All the while, he'd operated in integrity and faithfulness, but it was going on thirteen years of him having troubles day in and day out.
   I. And on top of all that, all of his wives and children had been taken, and the city had been burned to the ground.
   J. But he wasn't the only one who had been through distress and suffered loss; all of his men had been with him:

And David was greatly distressed; for the people spake of stoning him, because the soul of all the people was grieved, every man for his sons and for his daughters.
                                                                                                  1 SAMUEL 30:6A

   K. David could have just quit right here.
   L. Most people wouldn't have survived this, let alone what he had been through the previous thirteen years.

II. If David would have quit and given up, which is what he was tempted to do, he wouldn't have become king.
    A. He could have given up and his men would have dispersed, or he could have said "What's the use? What's the point in living now?" and let his men kill him.
    B. It would have been foolish for David to give up (see Job 2:9-10), even in the face of this tragic situation he was in.
    C. But David was no fool!
    D. He stuck with God no matter what.

But David encouraged himself in the LORD his God.
1 SAMUEL 30:6B

    E. Very few people encourage themselves in the Lord.
    F. They're always calling somebody else; they're always depending upon somebody else to encourage them.
    G. But we have to get to where we encourage ourselves in the Lord.

And David said to Abiathar the priest, Ahimelech's son, I pray thee, bring me hither the ephod. And Abiathar brought thither the ephod to David.
1 SAMUEL 30:7

    H. The ephod was a breastplate that the priests wore, and somehow or another, God could communicate through the stones that were on it—this would be comparable in our day to the Word of God.
    I. God speaks to us through the Word, and David encouraged himself by going back to the Word.

III. Also, another benefit that I think a lot of Christians do not take advantage of is speaking in tongues.
    A. The Scripture says this in 1 Corinthians 14:

He that speaketh in an unknown tongue edifieth himself.
1 CORINTHIANS 14:4A

    B. The word "edify" means to build up.
    C. It says something similar in Jude about speaking in tongues:

But ye, beloved, building up yourselves on your most holy faith, praying in the Holy Ghost.
JUDE 20

    D. When you speak in tongues, you are building yourself up on your most holy faith.

> *If therefore the whole church be come together into one place, and all speak with tongues, and there come in those that are unlearned, or unbelievers, will they not say that ye are mad?*
>
> 1 CORINTHIANS 14:23

    E. Your carnal mind will say you're foolish for speaking in tongues.

    F. But the reason it's so powerful is because if you do it over a prolonged period of time, it forces you to get into your most holy faith.

> *For he that speaketh in an unknown tongue speaketh not unto men, but unto God: for no man understandeth him; howbeit in the spirit he speaketh mysteries.*
>
> 1 CORINTHIANS 14:2

    G. When you speak in tongues, it takes faith to believe that there's actually a benefit.

    H. I say all this to say that for the New Testament believer, when you need encouragement, like David did, you can pray in tongues and build yourself up.

    I. If you've been filled with the Spirit, this is a resource you need to use.

    J. God has given it to you, and you can speak in tongues anytime you want and receive this benefit.

    K. If you've been praying "God, what do I do?" here's help coming your way: You need to be like David, to where you can encourage yourself in the Lord.

    L. In the New Testament, speaking in tongues is one of the most important things you can possibly do.

IV. There's not a single a Christian who is facing something more than they can bear.

> *There hath no temptation taken you but such as is common to man: but God is faithful, who will not suffer you to be tempted above that ye are able; but will with the temptation also make a way to escape, that ye may be able to bear it.*
>
> 1 CORINTHIANS 10:13

    A. Satan doesn't have different things to throw at you—it's the same contents with a different wrapper and a different bow on it.

    B. You're not having to endure something you just can't handle.

    C. When it seems like you can't stand another minute and you've hit your limits, God is going to make some way of escape so you can survive and come through the thing.

    D. I'm telling you, if you feel like you should quit, you could be just moments away from seeing the breakthrough you've been looking for.

    E. God is going to come through, but you have to encourage yourself in the Lord.

    F. For David, after he encouraged himself, he asked God what he should do about his situation:

And David enquired at the Lord, saying, Shall I pursue after this troop? shall I overtake them? And he answered him, Pursue: for thou shalt surely overtake them, and without fail recover all.

1 SAMUEL 30:8

G. The rest of this story goes that David took leadership of his men, they submitted unto him, and he pursued the Amalekites, caught them off guard, and completely destroyed them.

H. David and his men got back every woman, every child, and all of their livestock; they didn't lose a single life—plus, they got all the spoil of the Amalekites!

I. Then, in just hours after this, he got news that Saul had been killed in battle, and David was crowned king.

J. So, after thirteen years, and when things were at their worst, David encouraged himself in the Lord, and that's when he saw the breakthrough!

K. You might be contemplating quitting, but it's like what Peter said—where else can you go?

Lord, to whom shall we go? thou hast the words of eternal life.

JOHN 6:68

L. You don't have anywhere else to go; you just need to stand and believe God.

M. If you will stand your ground and encourage yourself in the Lord, you'll become a victor like David was—you'll outlast what the devil is trying to do in your life.

N. This is one of the great lessons you can learn from the life of David.

Teacher's Guide

1. Right before David became king, he was driven from the land of Israel because Saul had been hotly pursuing him. So, he moved into the land of the Philistines and was living among them (1 Sam. 27:1-3). He gained favor with Achish, the Philistine king of Gath, and Achish gave David the city of Ziklag to dwell in (1 Sam. 27:5-6). However, when the Philistines were marshaling their forces to go to battle, the princes didn't trust him to go with them, so David and his men were sent home. But as they were returning, they saw that the city had been invaded by the Amalekites, who must've known that the city was unprotected.

> *So David and his men came to the city, and, behold, it was burned with fire; and their wives, and their sons, and their daughters, were taken captives. [4] Then David and the people that were with him lifted up their voice and wept, until they had no more power to weep.*
>
> 1 SAMUEL 30:3-4

The Scripture also says that the Amalekites had plundered the city and taken spoils (1 Sam. 30:19). David was experiencing a devastating loss. Let's get a picture of this: David was about seventeen years old when Samuel anointed him to be king, and this instance in 1 Samuel 30:1-4 is just a day or two shy of when he actually began his reign, at the age of thirty (2 Sam. 5:4). All the while, he'd operated in integrity and faithfulness, but it was going on thirteen years of him having troubles day in and day out. And on top of all that, all of his wives and children had been taken, and the city had been burned to the ground. But he wasn't the only one who had been through distress and suffered loss; all of his men had been with him:

> *And David was greatly distressed; for the people spake of stoning him, because the soul of all the people was grieved, every man for his sons and for his daughters.*
>
> 1 SAMUEL 30:6A

David could have just quit right here. Most people wouldn't have survived this, let alone what he had been through the previous thirteen years.

1a. What was the name of the city Achish gave David?
   A. Gath
   B. Jerusalem
   C. Mizpah
   D. Ziklag
   E. Denver
   D. Ziklag

1b. *Discussion question:* Can you sympathize with David's reaction to the devastating loss he experienced? Why or why not?
   Discussion question

1c. *Discussion question:* What life lessons can you take from this period in David's life—the thirteen years when he operated in integrity and faithfulness yet still faced troubles day in and day out?
   Discussion question

ENCOURAGE YOURSELF IN THE LORD

2. If David would have quit and given up, which is what he was tempted to do, he wouldn't have become king. He could have given up and his men would have dispersed, or he could have said "What's the use? What's the point in living now?" and let his men kill him. It would have been foolish for David to give up (see Job 2:9-10), even in the face of this tragic situation he was in. But David was no fool! He stuck with God no matter what.

> *But David encouraged himself in the LORD his God.*
>
> 1 SAMUEL 30:6B

Very few people encourage themselves in the Lord. They're always calling somebody else; they're always depending upon somebody else to encourage them. But we have to get to where we encourage ourselves in the Lord.

> *And David said to Abiathar the priest, Ahimelech's son, I pray thee, bring me hither the ephod. And Abiathar brought thither the ephod to David.*
>
> 1 SAMUEL 30:7

The ephod was a breastplate that the priests wore, and somehow or another, God could communicate through the stones that were on it—this would be comparable in our day to the Word of God. God speaks to us through the Word, and David encouraged himself by going back to the Word.

2a. True or false: It would have been wise for David to give up, given the tragic situation he was in.
False
2b. True or false: David stuck with God no matter what.
True
2c. *Discussion question:* Why do you think very few people encourage themselves in the Lord?
Discussion question
2d. God speaks to us through the _____, and David _____ himself by going back to the Word.
Word / encouraged

3. Also, another benefit that Andrew thinks a lot of Christians do not take advantage of is speaking in tongues. The Scripture says this in 1 Corinthians 14:

> *He that speaketh in an unknown tongue edifieth himself.*
> 1 CORINTHIANS 14:4A

The word "edify" means to build up. It says something similar in Jude, also talking about speaking in tongues:

> *But ye, beloved, building up yourselves on your most holy faith, praying in the Holy Ghost.*
> JUDE 20

When we speak in tongues, we are building ourselves up on our most holy faith.

> *If therefore the whole church be come together into one place, and all speak with tongues, and there come in those that are unlearned, or unbelievers, will they not say that ye are mad?*
> 1 CORINTHIANS 14:23

Our carnal minds will say we're foolish for speaking in tongues. But the reason it's so powerful is because if we do it over a prolonged period of time, it forces us to get into our most holy faith.

> *For he that speaketh in an unknown tongue speaketh not unto men, but unto God: for no man understandeth him; howbeit in the spirit he speaketh mysteries.*
> 1 CORINTHIANS 14:2

When we speak in tongues, it takes faith to believe that there's actually a benefit. Andrew is saying all this to say that for the New Testament believers, when we need encouragement, like David did, we can pray in tongues and build ourselves up. If we've been filled with the Spirit, this is a resource we need to use. God has given it to us, and we can speak in tongues anytime we want and receive this benefit. If we've been praying "God, what do I do?" here's help coming our way: We need to be like David, to where we can encourage ourselves in the Lord. In the New Testament, speaking in tongues is one of the most important things we can possibly do.

3a. What does 1 Corinthians 14:4a say?
"He that speaketh in an unknown tongue edifieth himself"

3b. What does the word "edify" mean?
   A. To comfort
   B. To build up
   C. To eddy
   D. All of the above
   E. None of the above
B. To build up

3c. *Discussion question:* Meditate on Jude 20 and share your thoughts and revelations.
Discussion question

3d. *Discussion question:* Discuss why speaking in tongues is so important to encouraging yourself in the Lord.
Discussion question

4. There's not a single a Christian who is facing something more than they can bear.

   There hath no temptation taken you but such as is common to man: but God is faithful, who will not suffer you to be tempted above that ye are able; but will with the temptation also make a way to escape, that ye may be able to bear it.

   1 CORINTHIANS 10:13

Satan doesn't have different things to throw at us—it's the same contents with a different wrapper and a different bow on it. We're not having to endure something we just can't handle. When it seems like we can't stand another minute and we've hit our limits, God is going to make some way of escape so we can survive and come through the thing. If we feel like we should quit, we could be just moments away from seeing the breakthrough we've been looking for. God is going to come through, but we have to encourage ourselves in the Lord. For David, after he encouraged himself, he asked God what he should do about his situation:

   And David enquired at the LORD, saying, Shall I pursue after this troop? shall I overtake them? And he answered him, Pursue: for thou shalt surely overtake them, and without fail recover all.

   1 SAMUEL 30:8

The rest of this story goes that David took leadership of his men, they submitted unto him, and he pursued the Amalekites, caught them off guard, and completely destroyed them. David and his men got back every woman, every child, and all of their livestock; they didn't lose a single life—plus, they got all the spoil of the Amalekites! Then, in just hours after this, he got news that Saul had been killed in battle, and David was crowned king. So, after thirteen years, and when things were at their worst, David encouraged himself in the Lord, and that's when he saw the breakthrough! We might be contemplating quitting, but it's like what Peter said—where else can we go?

   Lord, to whom shall we go? thou hast the words of eternal life.

   JOHN 6:68

We don't have anywhere else to go; we just need to stand and believe God. If we will stand our ground and encourage ourselves in the Lord, we'll become victors like David was—we'll outlast what the devil is trying to do in our lives. This is one of the great lessons we can learn from the life of David.

4a. First Corinthians 10:13 says, "There hath no temptation taken you but such as is _____ to man: but God is faithful, who will not suffer you to be tempted above that ye are _____; but will with the temptation also make a way to _____, that ye may be able to bear it."
   "Common" / "able" / "escape"

(continued on next page)

4b. *Discussion question:* Have you ever experienced a situation like David's, where it seemed like you'd hit your limits but God made some way of escape for you? What did you learn from that?
   Discussion question

4c. God is going to come through, but you have to what?
   Encourage yourself in the Lord

4d. If you stand your ground and encourage yourself in the Lord, will you become a victor like David was and outlast what the devil is trying to do in your life?
   Yes

Discipleship Questions

1. What was the name of the city Achish gave David?
   A. Gath
   B. Jerusalem
   C. Mizpah
   D. Ziklag
   E. Denver

2. *Discussion question:* Can you sympathize with David's reaction to the devastating loss he experienced? Why or why not?
   _____
   _____
   _____

3. *Discussion question:* What life lessons can you take from this period in David's life—the thirteen years when he operated in integrity and faithfulness yet still faced troubles day in and day out?
   _____
   _____
   _____

4. True or false: It would have been wise for David to give up, given the tragic situation he was in.

5. True or false: David stuck with God no matter what.

6. *Discussion question:* Why do you think very few people encourage themselves in the Lord?
   _____
   _____
   _____

7. God speaks to us through the _____, and David _____ himself by going back to the Word.

8. What does 1 Corinthians 14:4a say?

9. What does the word "edify" mean?
   A. To comfort
   B. To build up
   C. To eddy
   D. All of the above
   E. None of the above

10. *Discussion question:* Meditate on Jude 20 and share your thoughts and revelations.

11. *Discussion question:* Discuss why speaking in tongues is so important to encouraging yourself in the Lord.

12. First Corinthians 10:13 says, *"There hath no temptation taken you but such as is _____ to man: but God is faithful, who will not suffer you to be tempted above that ye are _____; but will with the temptation also make a way to _____ that ye may be able to bear it."*

13. *Discussion question:* Have you ever experienced a situation like David's, where it seemed like you'd hit your limits but God made some way of escape for you? What did you learn from that?

14. God is going to come through, but you have to what?

15. If you stand your ground and encourage yourself in the Lord, will you become a victor like David was and outlast what the devil is trying to do in your life?

_____
_____
_____

1. D. Ziklag
2. *Discussion question*
3. *Discussion question*
4. False
5. True
6. *Discussion question*
7. Word / encouraged
8. *"He that speaketh in an unknown tongue edifieth himself"*
9. B. To build up
10. *Discussion question*
11. *Discussion question*
12. "Common" / "able" / "escape"
13. *Discussion question*
14. Encourage yourself in the Lord
15. Yes

1 SAMUEL 27:1-3

And David said in his heart, I shall now perish one day by the hand of Saul: there is nothing better for me than that I should speedily escape into the land of the Philistines; and Saul shall despair of me, to seek me any more in any coast of Israel: so shall I escape out of his hand. [2] And David arose, and he passed over with the six hundred men that were with him unto Achish, the son of Maoch, king of Gath. [3] And David dwelt with Achish at Gath, he and his men, every man with his household, even David with his two wives, Ahinoam the Jezreelitess, and Abigail the Carmelitess, Nabal's wife.

1 SAMUEL 27:5-6

And David said unto Achish, If I have now found grace in thine eyes, let them give me a place in some town in the country, that I may dwell there: for why should thy servant dwell in the royal city with thee? [6] Then Achish gave him Ziklag that day: wherefore Ziklag pertaineth unto the kings of Judah unto this day.

1 SAMUEL 30:1-4

And it came to pass, when David and his men were come to Ziklag on the third day, that the Amalekites had invaded the south, and Ziklag, and smitten Ziklag, and burned it with fire; [2] And had taken the women captives, that were therein: they slew not any, either great or small, but carried them away, and went on their way. [3] So David and his men came to the city, and, behold, it was burned with fire; and their wives, and their sons, and their daughters, were taken captives. [4] Then David and the people that were with him lifted up their voice and wept, until they had no more power to weep.

1 SAMUEL 30:19

And there was nothing lacking to them, neither small nor great, neither sons nor daughters, neither spoil, nor any thing that they had taken to them: David recovered all.

1 SAMUEL 30:6-8

And David was greatly distressed; for the people spake of stoning him, because the soul of all the people was grieved, every man for his sons and for his daughters: but David encouraged himself in the LORD his God. [7] And David said to Abiathar the priest, Ahimelech's son, I pray thee, bring me hither the ephod. And Abiathar brought thither the ephod to David. [8] And David enquired at the LORD, saying, Shall I pursue after this troop? shall I overtake them? And he answered him, Pursue: for thou shalt surely overtake them, and without fail recover all.

JOB 2:9-10

Then said his wife unto him, Dost thou still retain thine integrity? curse God, and die. [10] But he said unto her, Thou speakest as one of the foolish women speaketh. What? shall we receive good at the hand of God, and shall we not receive evil? In all this did not Job sin with his lips.

1 CORINTHIANS 14:4

He that speaketh in an unknown tongue edifieth himself; but he that prophesieth edifieth the church.

JUDE 20

But ye, beloved, building up yourselves on your most holy faith, praying in the Holy Ghost.

1 CORINTHIANS 14:23

If therefore the whole church be come together into one place, and all speak with tongues, and there come in those that are unlearned, or unbelievers, will they not say that ye are mad?

1 CORINTHIANS 14:2

For he that speaketh in an unknown tongue speaketh not unto men, but unto God: for no man understandeth him; howbeit in the spirit he speaketh mysteries.

1 CORINTHIANS 10:13

There hath no temptation taken you but such as is common to man: but God is faithful, who will not suffer you to be tempted above that ye are able; but will with the temptation also make a way to escape, that ye may be able to bear it.

JOHN 6:68

Then Simon Peter answered him, Lord, to whom shall we go? thou hast the words of eternal life.

Actions & The Heart

I'd like to contrast Saul, who was the first king of the nation of Israel; David, who has been the focus of our study; and Absalom, David's son who tried to take the kingdom from him by force. These are the three kings we're going to look at.

David is one of the central figures of the Bible. Only Moses had more chapters written by him and about him. This means that by sheer volume, David occupies the attention of a tremendous amount of Scripture. He's the only person the Word calls *"a man after [God's] own heart"* (1 Sam. 13:14, brackets mine).

BORN-AGAIN SPIRIT

As New Testament believers, every one of us who have been born again now have God's heart placed within us. This is a fulfillment of Ezekiel's prophecies:

> *And I will give them one heart, and I will put a new spirit within you; and I will take the stony heart out of their flesh, and will give them an heart of flesh.*
>
> **EZEKIEL 11:19**

> *A new heart also will I give you, and a new spirit will I put within you: and I will take away the stony heart out of your flesh, and I will give you an heart of flesh. [27a] And I will put my spirit within you.*
>
> **EZEKIEL 36:26-27A**

Every born-again Christian has a recreated heart that is superior to what David had. However, not every believer operates in this. Even David himself—the man after God's own heart—didn't always operate in accordance with the Lord. He had flesh flashes that were devastating!

We're going to look at these three kings and give priority to showing that David walked in the superior way. This doesn't mean that everything he did was right. God's Word records his sin too. But we need to look at these three kings in order to see what made David a man after God's own heart.

LESSONS FROM DAVID

AN IMPERFECT RELATIONSHIP

In contrast to both Saul and Absalom, David's *heart* was what made him a man after God's own heart. It wasn't primarily his actions, but his heart.

When talking about what grants us God's favor—things that the Lord looks at and is pleased with—most people today will put the emphasis on actions. Now, the Word does reveal that there is a relationship between our actions and what's in our hearts.

> *But wilt thou know, O vain man, that faith without works is dead?*
> JAMES 2:20

> *For as the body without the spirit is dead, so faith without works is dead also.*
> JAMES 2:26

The Bible calls a person who only says they are something but it never manifests itself in their actions a hypocrite. So, there is a relationship between actions and what is really in someone's heart. However, it isn't necessarily a perfect relationship.

Actions aren't always a 100 percent reflection of what's truly in a person's heart. For instance, David—a man after God's own heart—committed adultery and then murder in order to cover up his adultery. Now certainly, those weren't expressions of God's heart. When David did this, he was unplugged from the Lord. He wasn't walking with Him. Even though he sinned and did these things, David remained a man after God's own heart. You'll see why as we continue our study.

As you and I become people after God's own heart, it'll be reflected in our actions. If someone claims to be something, but there are no actions to back it up, then it's appropriate to call them hypocritical. However, we can have good hearts and still do some stupid things. We can have hearts after God and still have occasional flesh flashes where we do some severely wrong things.

But once David was reproved, the way he responded to his sin—both his attitude and actions in response to his failure—revealed God's heart. In our church world today, I think we're too judgmental of people's actions. We do need to take those actions into account. We can't just separate a person from their actions, because actions are an indication of what's inside. But there's more to it than that. It's a heart issue.

ACTIONS & THE HEART

COMPARATIVE MORALITY

There's no record in Scripture of Saul ever committing adultery. He was never reproved over sexual immorality of any kind. It's possible that there could have been some, but if there was any, it wasn't an issue. And it certainly wasn't a part of why God rejected him.

Before Absalom rebelled against David, there is no record in Scripture of him committing any sexual immorality. As a matter of fact, he was quite offended over his sister Tamar, who was raped by Amnon. Amnon was Absalom and Tamar's half brother. Absalom was so incensed over this that he took Tamar into his own house and cared for her. He even had a daughter that he named Tamar, apparently in honor of his sister. By the way Absalom responded to the sexual abuse of his sister—including his eventual murder of Amnon—we can deduce that he certainly had a high moral standard, at least in respect to his sister.

So, out of these three kings—Saul, David, and Absalom—David is the only one who committed adultery that's recorded in Scripture prior to Absalom's rebellion against David, when he committed adultery with David's wives. And David did it in such a way that he took another man's wife and then had him killed. So, in a sense, Saul and Absalom were more moral in many ways than David was.

Again, that's a relative statement because Saul killed all but one of the sons of a priest—eighty-five men (1 Sam. 22:11-21). That was out-and-out murder! They were ministers. They were unarmed. Even though I disagree with his conclusion, Saul reasoned that they had committed treason. So, this could be looked at as the judicial execution of a group of people who were plotting treason. They weren't, but in his insecurity and deranged frame of mind, I believe Saul could have justified it. What he did wasn't right, but it wasn't any worse than what David did by killing Uriah to try to cover up his sin with Bathsheba.

Absalom murdered his half brother Amnon for raping his sister Tamar. Although this could be viewed as justice or revenge, it doesn't justify what he did.

As far as actions are concerned, David wasn't any better than Saul or Absalom. Therefore, we can conclude that it's not just our actions that reveal whether or not we have a heart after God. It must go deeper than that.

CONSIDER THE HEART

What really set David apart was the attitude of his heart. Integrity begins with an attitude. It doesn't end with it, and that's not all there is to it, but it has to go that deep. David had failures just the same as Saul and Absalom. In some ways, his were worse. But the Word still calls him a man after God's own heart.

LESSONS FROM DAVID

We tend to judge people only by their actions today without looking beyond them to their hearts. Actions are important, but people are more than just physical bodies that act. There are emotional and spiritual parts on the inside of us that drive us to do things. We have to take that into account as well.

I've had certain employees who just had a bad attitude. Their hearts, not just their actions, were wrong. Because of that, they didn't give me a good day's work. They talked about me behind my back, sowed discord among the other employees, etc. When I see that, I'll consider their actions, but I'll also go beyond that and look at their hearts. I'll ask, "Are they vindictive or malicious in doing this? Are they trying to hurt people, or is this just a mistake?" As a leader, I look at and deal with actions because the other employees are watching what's going on. But I try to take into account the person's heart.

I remember one employee in particular who was just as faithful as they could possibly be. Although I paid them for forty hours of work, they'd put in fifty or sixty hours and never charge me overtime. They were just a hard worker with a great attitude, who for years was faithful, faithful, faithful!

Then this person started doing some things that were wrong. At first I wondered, *What's going on?* Then after a while, I had every right to go in and just fire this individual, saying, "That's it! You did this, this, and that, and I've already talked to you about it. You're fired!" But even though I had the right to do that, I knew this person's heart. I knew these actions were inconsistent with their past behavior and what I knew to be their heart.

"THESE ACTIONS ARE INCONSISTENT"

So, instead of blasting them, I went in, sat down, and said, "You've done these things, but I know that's not you. What's going on? Why have you started doing these kinds of things? That's inconsistent with what I know to be your heart." Instead of reproving them, I complimented them and asked, "Is there something I can do to help you work through this? There must be something that's causing you to act this way."

They never did open up and tell me what was wrong, but they humbled themselves and said, "You're absolutely right. I am not treating you right as an employer. You will not have another problem!" Although they didn't choose to open up and tell me what was going on, they repented and promised to straighten it out. They did, and I never had any more problems from that person! Later, I found out this person was having some serious problems at home that caused those actions.

Now, if another person had done the exact same things that this employee did, I might not have handled it the same way. If their heart was wrong and I knew it, then I wouldn't be able to show them as much latitude. If I *made* them submit in these areas, then the problem would just show up again somewhere else because their heart was wrong. The Word says,

For as he thinketh in his heart, so is he.

PROVERBS 23:7A

Therefore, if it's a heart problem, I would just terminate them right then. But for someone with a good heart who is doing things wrong, I deal with them differently.

DEVELOP HIS HEART!

We are human beings—not machines or human doings! We are more than just what we do. We're people who make mistakes. There is more to us than just our actions. So, we're going to focus our attention on David's heart attitudes. If you want to be a person after God's own heart, you're going to have to get beyond just behavior modification and trying to fulfill a set of rules and regulations. You need to get God's heart. You need to develop the characteristics in your heart that are like Him.

This won't guarantee that you'll never do anything wrong. David certainly did some things wrong. However, having this kind of heart will minimize the things you do wrong. And when God reproves you of it, this will cause you to be quick to repent. You'll be able to regain your position and your effectiveness and go on, whereas other people will be destroyed by it.

Outline

I. I'd like to contrast Saul, who was the first king of the nation of Israel; David, who has been the focus of our study; and Absalom, David's son who tried to take the kingdom from him by force.
   A. David is one of the central figures of the Bible.
   B. Only Moses had more chapters written by him and about him.
   C. This means that by sheer volume, David occupies the attention of a tremendous amount of Scripture.
   D. He's the only person the Word calls *"a man after [God's] own heart"* (1 Sam. 13:14, brackets mine).

II. As New Testament believers, every one of us who have been born again now have God's heart placed within us.
   A. This is a fulfillment of Ezekiel's prophecies:

And I will give them one heart, and I will put a new spirit within you; and I will take the stony heart out of their flesh, and will give them an heart of flesh.

EZEKIEL 11:19

A new heart also will I give you, and a new spirit will I put within you: and I will take away the stony heart out of your flesh, and I will give you an heart of flesh. [27a] And I will put my spirit within you.

EZEKIEL 36:26-27A

   B. However, not every believer operates in this.
   C. Even David himself, the man after God's own heart, didn't always operate in accordance with the Lord—he had flesh flashes that were devastating!
   D. We're going to look at these three kings and give priority to showing that David walked in the superior way.
   E. This doesn't mean that everything he did was right; God's Word records his sin too.
   F. But we need to look at these three kings in order to see what made David a man after God's own heart.

III. In contrast to both Saul and Absalom, David's *heart* was what made him a man after God's own heart.
   A. When talking about what grants us God's favor—things that the Lord looks at and is pleased with—most people today will put the emphasis on actions.

ACTIONS & THE HEART

B. Now, the Word does reveal that there is a relationship between our actions and what's in our hearts.

But wilt thou know, O vain man, that faith without works is dead?
JAMES 2:20

For as the body without the spirit is dead, so faith without works is dead also.
JAMES 2:26

C. Actions aren't always a 100 percent reflection of what's truly in a person's heart.
D. For instance, David—a man after God's own heart—committed adultery and then murder in order to cover up his adultery.
  i. Now certainly, those weren't expressions of God's heart.
  ii. When David did this, he was unplugged from the Lord; he wasn't walking with Him.
  iii. Even though he sinned and did these things, David remained a man after God's own heart—we'll see why as we continue our study.
E. As you and I become people after God's own heart, it'll be reflected in our actions.
F. If someone claims to be something, but there are no actions to back it up, then it's appropriate to call them hypocritical.
G. However, we can have good hearts and still do some stupid things.
H. In our church world today, I think we're too judgmental based on people's actions.
I. We do need to take those actions into account; we can't just separate a person from their actions, because actions are an indication of what's inside.
J. But there's more to it than that—it's a heart issue.

IV. There's no record in Scripture of Saul ever being reproved over sexual immorality of any kind.
  A. It's possible that there could have been some, but if there was any, it wasn't an issue.
  B. Before Absalom rebelled against David, there is no record in Scripture of him committing any sexual immorality.
  C. As a matter of fact, by the way Absalom responded to the sexual abuse of his sister Tamar—including his eventual murder of their half brother Amnon—we can deduce that he certainly had a high moral standard, at least in respect to his sister.
  D. So, out of these three kings—Saul, David, and Absalom—David is the only one who committed adultery that's recorded in Scripture prior to Absalom's rebellion against David, when he committed adultery with David's wives.
  E. And David did it in such a way that he took another man's wife and then had him killed.
  F. So, in a sense, Saul and Absalom were more moral in many ways than David was.
  G. Again, that's a relative statement because Saul killed all but one of the sons of a priest—eighty-five men (1 Sam. 22:11-21).

     H. Absalom murdered his half brother Amnon for raping his sister Tamar.
     I. As far as actions are concerned, David wasn't any better than Saul or Absalom.
     J. Therefore, we can conclude that it's not just our actions that reveal whether or not we have a heart after God—it must go deeper than that.

V. Integrity begins with an attitude.
     A. It doesn't end with it, and that's not all there is to it, but it has to go that deep.
     B. We tend to judge people only by their actions today without looking beyond them to their hearts.
     C. Actions are important, but people are more than just physical bodies that act.
     D. There are emotional and spiritual parts on the inside of us that drive us to do things.
     E. We have to take that into account as well.

VI. As a leader, I look at and deal with actions because the other employees are watching what's going on, but I try to take into account the person's heart.
     A. If their heart was wrong and I knew it, then I wouldn't be able to show them as much latitude.
     B. If I *made* them submit in these areas, then the problem would just show up again somewhere else because their heart was wrong.

For as he thinketh in his heart, so is he.
PROVERBS 23:7A

     C. Therefore, if it's a heart problem, I would just terminate them right then.
     D. But for someone with a good heart who is doing things wrong, I deal with them differently.

VII. You are more than just what you do.
     A. If you want to be a person after God's own heart, you're going to have to get beyond just behavior modification and trying to fulfill a set of rules and regulations.
     B. You need to develop the characteristics in your heart that are like Him.
     C. This won't guarantee that you'll never do anything wrong.
     D. However, having this kind of heart will minimize the things you do wrong.
     E. And when God reproves you of it, this will cause you to be quick to repent.
     F. You'll be able to regain your position and your effectiveness and go on, whereas other people will be destroyed by it.

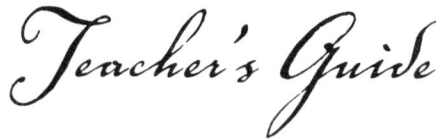

Teacher's Guide

1. Andrew would like to contrast Saul, who was the first king of the nation of Israel; David, who has been the focus of our study; and Absalom, David's son who tried to take the kingdom from him by force. David is one of the central figures of the Bible. Only Moses had more chapters written by him and about him. This means that by sheer volume, David occupies the attention of a tremendous amount of Scripture. He's the only person the Word calls *"a man after [God's] own heart"* (1 Sam. 13:14, brackets mine).

1a. _____ is one of the central figures of the Bible—only _____ had more chapters written by him and about him.
   David / Moses

ACTIONS & THE HEART

2. As New Testament believers, every one of us who have been born again now have God's heart placed within us. This is a fulfillment of Ezekiel's prophecies:

And I will give them one heart, and I will put a new spirit within you; and I will take the stony heart out of their flesh, and will give them an heart of flesh.

EZEKIEL 11:19

A new heart also will I give you, and a new spirit will I put within you: and I will take away the stony heart out of your flesh, and I will give you an heart of flesh. [27a] And I will put my spirit within you.

EZEKIEL 36:26-27A

However, not every believer operates in this. Even David himself, the man after God's own heart, didn't always operate in accordance with the Lord—he had flesh flashes that were devastating! We're going to look at these three kings and give priority to showing that David walked in the superior way. This doesn't mean that everything he did was right; God's Word records his sin too. But we need to look at these three kings in order to see what made David a man after God's own heart.

2a. As a born-again, New Testament believer, what do you have?
God's heart placed within you
2b. This is a fulfillment of whose prophecies?
- A. Ezekiel's
- B. Isaiah's
- C. Jeremiah's
- D. Jesus'
- E. Nostradamus'

A. Ezekiel's
2c. *Discussion question:* Give some reasons that not every believer operates in what God has given them.
Discussion question

3. In contrast to both Saul and Absalom, David's *heart* was what made him a man after God's own heart. When talking about what grants us God's favor—things that the Lord looks at and is pleased with—most people today will put the emphasis on actions. Now, the Word does reveal that there is a relationship between our actions and what's in our hearts.

> *But wilt thou know, O vain man, that faith without works is dead?*
>
> **JAMES 2:20**

> *For as the body without the spirit is dead, so faith without works is dead also.*
>
> **JAMES 2:26**

Actions aren't always a 100 percent reflection of what's truly in a person's heart. For instance, David—a man after God's own heart—committed adultery and then murder in order to cover up his adultery. Now certainly, those weren't expressions of God's heart. When David did this, he was unplugged from the Lord; he wasn't walking with Him. Even though he sinned and did these things, David remained a man after God's own heart—we'll see why as we continue our study. As we become people after God's own heart, it'll be reflected in our actions. If someone claims to be something, but there are no actions to back it up, then it's appropriate to call them hypocritical. However, we can have good hearts and still do some stupid things. In our church world today, we're too judgmental based on people's actions. We do need to take those actions into account; we can't just separate a person from their actions, because actions are an indication of what's inside. But there's more to it than that—it's a heart issue.

3a. *Discussion question:* Why do you think most people today put the emphasis on actions?
   Discussion question
3b. What are two scriptures that reveal there is a relationship between your actions and what is in your heart?
   James 2:20 and 26
3c. _____ aren't always a 100 percent reflection of what's _____ in a person's _____.
   Actions / truly / heart
3d. *Discussion question:* Explain why it's possible to have a good heart but still do some stupid things.
   Discussion question

ACTIONS & THE HEART

4. There's no record in Scripture of Saul ever being reproved over sexual immorality of any kind. It's possible that there could have been some, but if there was any, it wasn't an issue. Before Absalom rebelled against David, there is no record in Scripture of him committing any sexual immorality. As a matter of fact, by the way Absalom responded to the sexual abuse of his sister Tamar—including his eventual murder of their half brother Amnon—we can deduce that he certainly had a high moral standard, at least in respect to his sister. So, out of these three kings—Saul, David, and Absalom—David is the only one who committed adultery that's recorded in Scripture prior to Absalom's rebellion against David, when he committed adultery with David's wives. And David did it in such a way that he took another man's wife and then had him killed. So, in a sense, Saul and Absalom were more moral in many ways than David was. Again, that's a relative statement because Saul killed all but one of the sons of a priest—eighty-five men (1 Sam. 22:11-21). Absalom murdered his half brother Amnon for raping his sister Tamar. As far as actions are concerned, David wasn't any better than Saul or Absalom. Therefore, we can conclude that it's not just our actions that reveal whether or not we have a heart after God—it must go deeper than that.

4a. Why can it be concluded that it's not just your actions that reveal whether or not you have a heart after God?
Because as far as actions are concerned, David wasn't any better than Saul or Absalom—David committed adultery and murder, Saul had eighty-five men killed, and Absalom murdered his half brother

5. Integrity begins with an attitude. It doesn't end with it, and that's not all there is to it, but it has to go that deep. We tend to judge people only by their actions today without looking beyond them to their hearts. Actions are important, but people are more than just physical bodies that act. There are emotional and spiritual parts on the inside of us that drive us to do things. We have to take that into account as well.

5a. Integrity begins with what?
Attitude

5b. *Discussion question:* Why is it so important to remember that people are more than just physical bodies that act?
Discussion question

6. As a leader, Andrew looks at and deals with actions because the other employees are watching what's going on, but he tries to take into account the person's heart. If their heart was wrong and Andrew knew it, then he wouldn't be able to show them as much latitude. If he *made* them submit in these areas, then the problem would just show up again somewhere else because their heart was wrong.

> *For as he thinketh in his heart, so is he.*
> PROVERBS 23:7A

Therefore, if it's a heart problem, he would just terminate them right then. But for someone with a good heart who is doing things wrong, he deals with them differently.

6a. Read Proverbs 23:7. "For as he _____ in his heart, so is he."
   "Thinketh"
6b. *Discussion question:* What difference does it make if a person has a good heart or a wrong heart?
   Discussion question

7. We are more than just what we do. If we want to be people after God's own heart, we're going to have to get beyond just behavior modification and trying to fulfill a set of rules and regulations. We need to develop the characteristics in our hearts that are like Him. This won't guarantee that we'll never do anything wrong. However, having this kind of heart will minimize the things we do wrong. And when God reproves us of it, this will cause us to be quick to repent. We'll be able to regain our position and your effectiveness and go on, whereas other people will be destroyed by it.

7a. If you want to be a person after God's own heart, you're going to have to do what?
   A. Get all the self-help books you can and attend every seminar and conference you can find
   B. Get beyond just behavior modification and trying to fulfill a set of rules and regulations
   C. Go to church every time the doors are open and volunteer in every area you can
   D. All of the above
   E. None of the above
   B. Get beyond just behavior modification and trying to fulfill a set of rules and regulations
7b. Will having characteristics in your heart that are like Him guarantee that you'll never do anything wrong?
   No
7c. *Discussion question:* What sort of impact do you think having God's own heart will make on your life?
   Discussion question

ACTIONS & THE HEART

Discipleship Questions

1. _____ is one of the central figures of the Bible—only _____ had more chapters written by him and about him.

2. As a born-again, New Testament believer, what do you have?
   _____
   _____
   _____

3. This is a fulfillment of whose prophecies?
   A. Ezekiel's
   B. Isaiah's
   C. Jeremiah's
   D. Jesus'
   E. Nostradamus'

4. *Discussion question:* Give some reasons that not every believer operates in what God has given them.
   _____
   _____
   _____

5. *Discussion question:* Why do you think most people today put the emphasis on actions?
   _____
   _____
   _____

6. What are two scriptures that reveal there is a relationship between your actions and what is in your heart?
   _____
   _____
   _____

7. _____ aren't always a 100 percent reflection of what's _____ in a person's _____.

ACTIONS & THE HEART

8. *Discussion question:* Explain why it's possible to have a good heart but still do some stupid things.

9. Why can it be concluded that it's not just your actions that reveal whether or not you have a heart after God?

10. Integrity begins with what?

11. *Discussion question:* Why is it so important to remember that people are more than just physical bodies that act?

12. Read Proverbs 23:7. "For as he _____ in his heart, so is he."

13. *Discussion question:* What difference does it make if a person has a good heart or a wrong heart?

14. If you want to be a person after God's own heart, you're going to have to do what?
    A. Get all the self-help books you can and attend every seminar and conference you can find
    B. Get beyond just behavior modification and trying to fulfill a set of rules and regulations
    C. Go to church every time the doors are open and volunteer in every area you can
    D. All of the above
    E. None of the above

15. Will having characteristics in your heart that are like Him guarantee that you'll never do anything wrong?

16. *Discussion question:* What sort of impact do you think having God's own heart will make on your life?

Answer Key

1. David / Moses
2. God's heart placed within you
3. A. Ezekiel's
4. *Discussion question*
5. *Discussion question*
6. James 2:20 and 26
7. Actions / truly / heart
8. *Discussion question*
9. Because as far as actions are concerned, David wasn't any better than Saul or Absalom—David committed adultery and murder, Saul had eighty-five men killed, and Absalom murdered his half brother
10. Attitude
11. *Discussion question*
12. "Thinketh"
13. *Discussion question*
14. B. Get beyond just behavior modification and trying to fulfill a set of rules and regulations
15. No
16. *Discussion question*

1 SAMUEL 13:14
But now thy kingdom shall not continue: the Lord hath sought him a man after his own heart, and the Lord hath commanded him to be captain over his people, because thou hast not kept that which the Lord commanded thee.

EZEKIEL 11:19
And I will give them one heart, and I will put a new spirit within you; and I will take the stony heart out of their flesh, and will give them an heart of flesh.

EZEKIEL 36:26-27
A new heart also will I give you, and a new spirit will I put within you: and I will take away the stony heart out of your flesh, and I will give you an heart of flesh. [27] And I will put my spirit within you, and cause you to walk in my statutes, and ye shall keep my judgments, and do them.

JAMES 2:20
But wilt thou know, O vain man, that faith without works is dead?

JAMES 2:26
For as the body without the spirit is dead, so faith without works is dead also.

1 SAMUEL 22:11-21
Then the king sent to call Ahimelech the priest, the son of Ahitub, and all his father's house, the priests that were in Nob: and they came all of them to the king. [12] And Saul said, Hear now, thou son of Ahitub. And he answered, Here I am, my lord. [13] And Saul said unto him, Why have ye conspired against me, thou and the son of Jesse, in that thou hast given him bread, and a sword, and hast enquired of God for him, that he should rise against me, to lie in wait, as at this day? [14] Then Ahimelech answered the king, and said, And who is so faithful among all thy servants as David, which is the king's son in law, and goeth at thy bidding, and is honourable in thine house? [15] Did I then begin to enquire of God for him? be it far from me: let not the king impute any thing unto his servant, nor to all the house of my father: for thy servant knew nothing of all this, less or more. [16] And the king said, Thou shalt surely die, Ahimelech, thou, and all thy father's house. [17] And the king said unto the footmen that stood about him, Turn, and slay the priests of the Lord; because their hand also is with David, and because they knew when he fled, and did not shew it to me. But the servants of the king would not put forth their hand to fall upon the priests of the Lord. [18] And the king said to Doeg, Turn thou, and fall upon the priests. And Doeg the Edomite turned, and he fell upon the priests, and slew on

---

ACTIONS & THE HEART

that day fourscore and five persons that did wear a linen ephod. [19] And Nob, the city of the priests, smote he with the edge of the sword, both men and women, children and sucklings, and oxen, and asses, and sheep, with the edge of the sword. [20] And one of the sons of Ahimelech the son of Ahitub, named Abiathar, escaped, and fled after David. [21] And Abiathar shewed David that Saul had slain the Lord's priests.

PROVERBS 23:7
For as he thinketh in his heart, so is he: Eat and drink, saith he to thee; but his heart is not with thee.

"It's My Fault!"

David had a relationship with God on a heart level. There were qualities, characteristics, and attitudes in his heart that set him apart from Saul and Absalom.

In 1 Samuel 15, God told Saul—through Samuel—to execute judgment upon the Amalekites. These people had attacked and shown no mercy to the Israelites while they were wandering in the wilderness. Due to this, the Lord had determined their absolute destruction. Many years after this transgression, God—through Samuel—sent Saul on a mission to utterly destroy everything of the Amalekites—their men, women, children, cattle, sheep, oxen, etc. This wasn't a battle to get spoils or a conquest where they could acquire property; this was for vengeance and punishment. Therefore, God commanded, "Wipe out everything that breathes!"

However, Saul didn't do it. He claimed to have obeyed God, but he didn't. He saved Agag, king of the Amalekites, and brought all of the best sheep, oxen, and cattle back with him. Samuel went to see Saul after this mission.

> *And Samuel came to Saul: and Saul said unto him, Blessed be thou of the LORD: I have performed the commandment of the LORD. [14] And Samuel said, What meaneth then this bleating of the sheep in mine ears, and the lowing of the oxen which I hear?*
>
> 1 SAMUEL 15:13-14

In other words, the command included killing *all* of the animals. Yet Samuel could hear both sheep and oxen.

SACRIFICE?

> *And Saul said, They have brought them from the Amalekites: for the people spared the best of the sheep and of the oxen, to sacrifice unto the LORD thy God; and the rest we have utterly destroyed.*
>
> 1 SAMUEL 15:15

Saul claimed that he had performed everything the Lord had told him to do, but Samuel reproved him by saying, "No, you didn't. These animals are still alive." Then Saul answered, "The people spared the best."

Picture this! Saul was the king. He had been given a command to kill everything that breathed. Yet here he was, saying, "The people spared" these. Who was the king? Who was in the position of authority? Saul was. So, the people couldn't have done this if Saul had not tolerated it. At the very least, Saul had to give his approval. More likely, he was the instigator of it. However, Saul wasn't accepting responsibility for what he had done. Instead, he pushed this off onto the people.

Saul placed the blame on somebody else and then tried to whitewash it by saying, "Well, we might not have killed the animals the way you told us to, but we brought them back here so we could slaughter them as sacrifices. Instead of just killing them and letting their deaths be in vain, we wanted to bring them back and offer them to the Lord."

If—and that's a big "if"—what Saul was saying was truly what they meant to do, then they were planning to offer a sacrifice to the Lord that cost them nothing. Maybe they said, "Let's bring back some of the enemy's herds and offer them to God. Then we won't suffer a depletion of our own herds when we celebrate this victory. Besides, we're just going to kill them anyway." This is totally an ungodly way of doing things. David shows us why.

NO POSITIVE SPIN

Later in life, David came to Araunah's threshing floor to offer a sacrifice to the Lord (2 Sam. 24:18-25). However, Araunah basically said, "Here, take my oxen. Take my yokes and use them for fire. Take all of these things—I give them to you!"

But David answered, "No, I'm going to pay you for it."

Araunah continued, "No, I want to give them to you!"

> *And the king* [David] *said unto Araunah, Nay; but I will surely buy it of thee at a price: neither will I offer burnt offerings unto the* LORD *my God of that which doth cost me nothing.*
> 2 SAMUEL 24:24, BRACKETS MINE

What a great attitude! You can't take your neighbor's sheep and offer it as a sacrifice to God. If you aren't giving of yourself, of your own substance—it's not costing you anything and it really isn't a "sacrifice."

So, if this was truly what motivated them to bring back the Amalekites' oxen and sheep, then they were trying to find a cheap way of fulfilling their duty to offer sacrifices to the Lord for His protection in this battle: "Let's not offer our animals but theirs for the sacrifice!" Even if this was what they truly intended to do, there was no way to whitewash their disobedience and put a positive spin on it.

"IT'S MY FAULT!"

THE FIRST CAREER POLITICIAN

Then Samuel said unto Saul, Stay, and I will tell thee what the LORD hath said to me this night. And he said unto him, Say on. [17] And Samuel said, When thou wast little in thine own sight, wast thou not made the head of the tribes of Israel, and the LORD anointed thee king over Israel? [18] And the LORD sent thee on a journey, and said, Go and utterly destroy the sinners the Amalekites, and fight against them until they be consumed. [19] Wherefore then didst thou not obey the voice of the LORD, but didst fly upon the spoil, and didst evil in the sight of the LORD? [20] And Saul said unto Samuel, Yea, I have obeyed the voice of the LORD, and have gone the way which the LORD sent me, and have brought Agag the king of Amalek, and have utterly destroyed the Amalekites. [21a] But the people took of the spoil, sheep and oxen, the chief of the things which should have been utterly destroyed.

1 SAMUEL 15:16-21A

Saul was acknowledging that he understood the command was to utterly destroy them, and yet he didn't do it. So, this wasn't a deception; it was a lie. He was putting his spin on things. Saul was the first real career politician. You could ask him a question, but the answer he would give you would depend on which side of his mouth he used. (Now, that's not true of every politician but certainly a large number of them.)

But the people took of the spoil, sheep and oxen, the chief of the things which should have been utterly destroyed, to sacrifice unto the LORD thy God in Gilgal. [22] And Samuel said, Hath the LORD as great delight in burnt offerings and sacrifices, as in obeying the voice of the LORD? Behold, to obey is better than sacrifice, and to hearken than the fat of rams. [23] For rebellion is as the sin of witchcraft, and stubbornness is as iniquity and idolatry. Because thou hast rejected the word of the LORD, he hath also rejected thee from being kin.

1 SAMUEL 15:21-23

The prophet reproved Saul for his disobedience.

"I'M RESPONSIBLE!"

David also disobeyed the Lord: He committed adultery, murdered the woman's husband, and then took her as his wife in an attempt to cover up the adultery and make it look like the child was actually legally the husband's. What he did was terribly wrong! But once he was reproved, he repented in sackcloth and ashes. He didn't point the finger at anyone else. David accepted the blame and took responsibility for his actions.

LESSONS FROM DAVID

It takes two to commit adultery. Although Bathsheba was involved in this too, David never said anything like, "She enticed me. It's her fault. Bathsheba shouldn't have been washing herself on the roof without her clothes on. She's the one who exposed herself to me!" Neither did he say, "Joab helped me kill her husband." You don't find any of that in the Bible.

David wrote Psalm 51, when he repented of this sin. The subscript reveals it:

> *To the chief Musician, A Psalm of David, when Nathan the prophet came unto him, after he had gone in to Bathsheba.*

Verse 4 really shows David's heart during this time:

> *Against thee, thee only, have I sinned, and done this evil in thy sight: that thou mightest be justified when thou speakest, and be clear when thou judgest.*

All through Psalm 51, David was saying, "God, it's my fault! I did this. I'm responsible." Whenever David sinned, he took responsibility for his actions by saying, "Lord, I'm the one who numbered the people. I'm the one who transgressed against You. But these sheep, what have they done?" (2 Sam. 24:17) Again, he was accepting responsibility.

FEELING JUSTIFIED

Contrast this with Saul in 1 Samuel 15. Twice he said, "It's the people who did this. They made me do it!" He just wouldn't admit he was wrong. He refused to accept responsibility and kept pointing the finger at someone else.

Absalom also refused to own up to his sin. He simply would not acknowledge that his problems and his estrangement from his father, David, happened because he murdered his brother Amnon (2 Sam. 13:20-29). Instead, Absalom contended that it was David's fault: "Why didn't my father punish Amnon? If he would have done what he was supposed to do, I wouldn't have had to bring vengeance upon Amnon for what he did to my sister!" Once Amnon was dead, Absalom went into a self-imposed exile for three years because he was afraid of what would happen to him for the murder of his brother (2 Sam. 13:37-38).

David allowed Absalom to come back to the nation of Israel, but for two whole years, David didn't see him (2 Sam. 14:21-24 and 28). Finally, Absalom imposed upon Joab to get him an audience with the king. Although David came in, hugged him, and kissed him, it isn't mentioned that they reconciled. David didn't say, "Well, everything's okay now."

After David refused to whitewash what had happened, Absalom began his treason and eventually caused a civil war. He tried to kill his own father and then committed adultery with his father's concubines, in broad daylight (2 Sam. 15-18).

Absalom was full of hatred, and he blamed his father for all of his woes: "It's because he didn't punish Amnon. It's because he didn't accept me back. It's because he allowed this thing to go on." Absalom felt justified in doing what he was doing. He felt like he was getting vengeance on his father for ruining his life.

DEFYING LOGIC

This is an important difference between David, Saul, and Absalom. David never did transpose his problems onto other people; he accepted responsibility for his actions. Saul and Absalom didn't.

One of the most important issues facing our society today is the fact that people will not accept responsibility for their actions. It has just become standard fare that nobody will say, "It's my fault." Somebody takes the lid off of their boiling hot coffee from McDonald's, puts it between their legs, and drives off. Then, when it splashes out, instead of saying "That was stupid. I burned myself. How could I have done this?"—they go and sue McDonald's. That's crazy enough, but then the jury blamed McDonald's and made them responsible for this person's stupid actions. If someone shoots someone, people say it's not the fault of the person who pulled the trigger; it's now the responsibility of the company that manufactured the gun. Guns don't kill people any more than forks make people fat. People are making cigarette companies responsible for those who smoke cigarettes. People are making fast food chains responsible for obesity, saying, "They should have put a warning label on there and told me I shouldn't eat here every single day, three meals a day." That's just stupid. It defies logic.

You can't blame somebody else for the stupid things you do. You have a responsibility over your own life.

No longer is a person made responsible for being an alcoholic or a drug addict; people say, "It's because I have a genetic disposition." People contend that genes control whether someone will become an addicted gambler or not. They say, "Gambling is an addiction. I can't control it. I just happen to be inferior to other people." They're saying the same thing about emotional issues, like depression: "It's not me. It's not my choices. It's just a chemical imbalance. Give me a pill and put me into a stupor to control my emotions."

I know there are people who take exception to this and get very upset with me because I say that it's not genetics or chemical imbalances that cause depression, alcoholism, gambling, or drug addiction.

They say, "Who are you? All of these educated experts have done all of these studies." I don't care how many degrees someone has after their name, or how they became deified in the secular world. If what they say goes contrary to the Word, they're wrong!

Let God be true, but every man a liar.

ROMANS 3:4

ALWAYS REJOICE!

Because thou servedst not the Lord thy God with joyfulness, and with gladness of heart, for the abundance of all things; [48] Therefore shalt thou serve thine enemies which the Lord shall send against thee.

DEUTERONOMY 28:47-48

As born-again believers, the Lord doesn't send "enemies" against us. However, we—ourselves—can open up a door to the devil by grumbling and complaining. That's why we're commanded to…

Rejoice in the Lord alway: and again I say, Rejoice.

PHILIPPIANS 4:4

Emphasizing this word *"alway,"* Psalm 34:1 says…

I will bless the Lord at all times: *his praise shall* continually *be in my mouth.*

EMPHASIS MINE

NOT TROUBLED BY TROUBLE

On the night before His crucifixion, Jesus told His disciples they would have trouble but not to be troubled by it:

In the world ye shall have tribulation: but be of good cheer; *I have overcome the world.*

JOHN 16:33B, EMPHASIS MINE

The Lord acknowledged tribulation. He didn't just say, "Be of good cheer when everything goes good. I'm going to remove all problems so you'll never have a reason to be discouraged ever again." No, He was saying, "There will be tribulation. But in the midst of that negative circumstance, be of good cheer!"

"IT'S MY FAULT!"

God would be unjust to command us to do something that we are genetically incapable of doing. However, this mindset of not accepting responsibility has spread like a cancer throughout our society. It has even infected Christians! We say, "It's because they said this about me, I was born into an underprivileged home, it's because of the color of my skin, I don't have an education, or the devil made me do it." And if we can't find something else to blame it on, we just blame it on our dysfunctional families. It's totally subjective. We can justify murder, rape, adultery—anything—because of the way we were potty trained, because we didn't get a birthday cake when we were three, etc. That's absurd! It's unbelievable that people fall for that. Yet it's being said so often in our society that even Christians are being influenced by it. That's absolutely wrong!

If you want to be a person after God's own heart, you're going to have to unplug from the way this world thinks, quit excusing your actions, and accept responsibility. David humbled himself and said, "God, it's me! I'm the one who sinned." This is one of the heart attitudes that stand out in stark contrast to both Saul and Absalom. David accepted responsibility for his own actions.

ANDREW'S RECOMMENDATIONS FOR FURTHER STUDY

God's Word is a greater authority in my life than what anybody else has to say. In fact, the Word teaches us that the Lord will hold us accountable for our emotions. My book entitled *Harnessing Your Emotions* goes into much more detail on this topic. God made us accountable for our emotions and actually punished people for not rejoicing.

If you or someone you know is facing a crisis situation, I recommend my teaching entitled the *Christian Survival Kit*. This is an indepth study of John 14, 15, and 16—Jesus' last words to His disciples before His arrest and crucifixion. These messages have helped many people overcome.

Outline

I. David had qualities that set him apart from Saul and Absalom.
  A. God sent Saul on a mission to destroy all the Amalekites, but he didn't do it.
  B. He claimed he had performed everything the Lord had told him to do, and he blamed the people.
  C. The people couldn't have done this if Saul had not tolerated it; Saul had to give his approval.
  D. Saul whitewashed it, calling it a sacrifice: "Instead of letting the deaths of these animals be in vain, we wanted to offer them to the Lord."
  E. When David offered a sacrifice to the Lord (2 Sam. 24:18-25), Araunah basically said, "Take my oxen. Take my yokes and use them for the fire."
    i. David answered,

Nay; but I will surely buy it of a price: neither will I offer burnt offerings unto the LORD my God of that which doth cost me nothing.
2 SAMUEL 24:24

    ii. What a great attitude!
  F. If you aren't giving of yourself—of your own substance—if it's not costing you anything, then it really isn't a sacrifice.

II. David also disobeyed the Lord.
  A. He committed adultery, murdered, and then tried to cover up his sins.
  B. What he did was terribly wrong, but once he was reproved, he repented in sackcloth and ashes.
  C. He didn't point the finger at Bathsheba and say, "She enticed me; she shouldn't have been washing herself on the roof!"
  D. Neither did he say, "Joab helped me kill her husband."
  E. David wrote in Psalm 51:4,

Against thee, thee only, have I sinned, and done this evil in thy sight.

III. Absalom also refused to own up to his sin.
  A. He would not acknowledge that his problems happened because he murdered his brother Amnon.
  B. Absalom contended that it was his father David's fault, saying, "Why didn't my father punish Amnon? Then I wouldn't have had to bring vengeance for what he did to my sister."

"IT'S MY FAULT!"

C. David refused to whitewash what had happened, so Absalon committed treason by trying to kill him and committing adultery with his concubines.
D. Yet he blamed his father for it because David didn't accept him back.

IV. One of the most important issues facing our society is the fact that people will not accept responsibility for their actions.
   A. It has become standard fare that nobody will say, "It's my fault":
      i. Somebody takes the lid off their boiling hot coffee, and when it splashes out, they sue McDonald's.
      ii. If someone shoots someone, people say it's not the fault of the person who pulled the trigger; it's now the responsibility of the company that manufactured the gun.
      iii. People are making cigarette companies responsible for those who smoke cigarettes and fast food chains responsible for obesity.
   B. I know there are people who take exception to this and get very upset with me because I say that it's not genetics or chemical imbalances that cause depression, alcoholism, gambling, or drug addiction.
   C. I don't care how many degrees someone has after their name; if what they say goes contrary to the Word, they're wrong!

Let God be true and every man a liar.

ROMANS 3:4

V. The Word teaches that the Lord will hold us accountable for our emotions and that He actually punished people for not rejoicing.

Because thou servedst not the LORD thy God with joyfulness, and with gladness of heart, for the abundance of all things; [48] Therefore shalt thou serve thine enemies which the LORD shall send against thee.

DEUTERONOMY 28:47-48

   A. As born-again believers, the Lord doesn't send "enemies" against us; however, we can open up a door to the devil by complaining.
   B. We are commanded to...

Rejoice in the Lord alway: and again I say, rejoice.

PHILIPPIANS 4:4

   C. Psalm 34:1 emphasizes this word *"alway"*:

LESSONS FROM DAVID

*I will bless the L*ORD *at all times: his praise shall continually be in my mouth.*
PSALM 34:1, EMPHASIS MINE

VI. On the night before His crucifixion, Jesus told His disciples that they would have trouble but not to be troubled by it.

In the world ye shall have tribulation: but be of good cheer; I have overcome the world.
JOHN 16:33, EMPHASIS MINE

    A. God would not command you to do something that you are genetically incapable of doing.
    B. The mindset of not accepting responsibility has even infected Christians.
    C. People can justify anything, and that's absolutely wrong!
    D. If you want to be a person after God's own heart, you're going to have to unplug from the way the world thinks.
    E. David's humility is one of the heart attitudes that stands out in stark contrast to Saul's and Absalom's heart attitudes.

ANDREW'S RECOMMENDATIONS FOR FURTHER STUDY

God's Word is a greater authority in my life than what anybody else has to say. In fact, the Word teaches us that the Lord will hold us accountable for our emotions. My book entitled *Harnessing Your Emotions* goes into much more detail on this topic. God made us accountable for our emotions and actually punished people for not rejoicing.

If you or someone you know is facing a crisis situation, I recommend my teaching entitled the *Christian Survival Kit*. This is an indepth study of John 14, 15, and 16—Jesus' last words to His disciples before His arrest and crucifixion. These messages have helped many people overcome.

"IT'S MY FAULT!"

Teacher's Guide

1. David had qualities that set him apart from Saul and Absalom. God sent Saul on a mission to destroy all the Amalekites, but he didn't do it. He claimed he had performed everything the Lord had told him to do, and he blamed the people. The people couldn't have done this if Saul had not tolerated it; Saul had to give his approval. Saul whitewashed it, calling it a sacrifice: "Instead of letting the deaths of these animals be in vain, we wanted to offer them to the Lord." When David offered a sacrifice to the Lord (2 Sam. 24:18-25), Araunah basically said, "Take my oxen. Take my yokes and use them for the fire." David answered,

> *Nay; but I will surely buy it of a price: neither will I offer burnt offerings unto the* LORD *my God of that which doth cost me nothing.*
>
> 2 SAMUEL 24:24

What a great attitude! If we aren't giving of ourselves—of our own substance—if it's not costing us anything, then it really isn't a sacrifice.

1a. *Discussion question:* What was it about Saul that made it possible for him to rationalize disobedience?
   Discussion question
1b. What did God send Saul to do?
   A. Talk to the Amalekites about their merciless behavior
   B. Kill the Amalekite men
   C. Deliver a pizza
   D. Get spoils
   E. Obey His command exactly by wiping out every trace of the Amalekites
   E. Obey His commands exactly by wiping out every trace of the Amalekites
1c. Read 2 Samuel 24:18-25. What was David's attitude about sacrificing to the Lord?
   A. He bartered to get the best deal on the best animal
   B. He thought, *Well, my heart's right, so God will understand if I don't pay for this sacrifice*
   C. He would not offer the Lord something that cost him nothing
   D. He looked to the people to help him obey God and supply the offering
   E. He didn't want to put forth the effort
   C. He would not offer the Lord something that cost him nothing

---

LESSONS FROM DAVID

2. David also disobeyed the Lord. He committed adultery, murdered, and then tried to cover up his sins. What he did was terribly wrong, but once he was reproved, he repented in sackcloth and ashes. He didn't point the finger at Bathsheba and say, "She enticed me; she shouldn't have been washing herself on the roof!" Neither did he say, "Joab helped me kill her husband." David wrote in Psalm 51:4, *"Against thee, thee only, have I sinned, and done this evil in thy sight."*

2a. *Discussion question:* When you stumble and sin, do you immediately think, *Against you, you only, have I sinned*? Why or why not?
   Discussion question

2b. David knew _____.
   A. He was too busy to be watching Bathsheba take a bath
   B. He could wiggle his way out of any trouble that might come from his adultery
   C. Bathsheba should have been bathing inside of a tent
   D. He was terribly wrong
   E. It didn't matter what he'd done
   D. He was terribly wrong

2c. Read Psalm 51:4. David sinned against whom?
   A. God
   B. Bathsheba
   C. Bathsheba's husband
   D. All of the above
   E. None of the above
   A. God

"IT'S MY FAULT!"

3. Absalom also refused to own up to his sin. He would not acknowledge that his problems happened because he murdered his brother Amnon. Absalom contended that it was his father David's fault, saying, "Why didn't my father punish Amnon? Then I wouldn't have had to bring vengeance for what he did to my sister." David refused to whitewash what had happened, so Absalom committed treason by trying to kill him and committing adultery with his concubines. Yet he blamed his father for it because David didn't accept him back.

3a. *Discussion question:* Consider the ways you may have blamed others for your transgressions. How did you realize the truth?
Discussion question

3b. Why did Absalom refuse to own up to his sin?
   A. It was easier that way
   B. It was his responsibility to take care of Amnon's wrong
   C. He had an undeniable passion for justice
   D. He blamed his father
   E. He had been spoiled as a child
   D. He blamed his father

3c. David refused to _____ what had happened with Absalom.
   Whitewash

4. One of the most important issues facing our society is the fact that people will not accept responsibility for their actions. It has just become standard fare that nobody will say, "It's my fault": Somebody takes the lid off their boiling coffee, and when it splashes out, they sue McDonald's. If someone shoots someone, people say it's not the fault of the person who pulled the trigger—it's now the responsibility of the company that manufactured the gun. People are making cigarette companies responsible for those who smoke cigarettes and fast food chains responsible for obesity. There are people who take exception to this and get very upset with Andrew because he says that it's not genetics or chemical imbalances that cause depression, alcoholism, gambling, or drug addiction. It doesn't matter how many degrees someone has after their name; if what they say goes contrary to the Word, they're wrong!

> *Let God be true and every man a liar.*
>
> ROMANS 3:4

4a. *Discussion question:* Why is it important to take responsibility for your actions?
Discussion question

4b. It has become standard fare that nobody will say _____.
"It's my fault"

4c. If what someone says is contrary to the Word of God, they are _____!
Wrong

5. The Word teaches that the Lord will hold us accountable for our emotions and that He actually punished people for not rejoicing:

> *Because thou servedst not the* Lord *thy God with joyfulness, and with gladness of heart, for the abundance of all things; [48] therefore shalt thou serve thine enemies which the* Lord *shall send against thee.*
>
> DEUTERONOMY 28:47-48

As born-again believers, the Lord doesn't send "enemies" against us; however, we can open up a door to the devil by complaining. We are commanded to *"rejoice in the Lord alway: and again I say, Rejoice"* (Phil. 4:4). Psalm 34:1 emphasizes this word *"alway"*:

> *I will bless the* Lord *at* all *times: his praise shall* continually *be in my mouth.*
>
> EMPHASIS MINE

5a. *Discussion question:* Why do you think it is right for the Lord to hold you accountable for your emotions?
   Discussion question
5b. Does the Lord send enemies against you?
   No
5c. You are _____ to rejoice.
   Commanded

"IT'S MY FAULT!"

6. On the night before His crucifixion, Jesus told His disciples that they would have trouble, but not to be troubled by it.

In the world ye shall have tribulation: but be of good cheer; *I have overcome the world.*
JOHN 16:33, EMPHASIS MINE

God would not command us to do something that we are genetically incapable of doing, and yet the mindset of not accepting responsibility has even infected Christians. People can justify anything, and that's absolutely wrong! If we want to be people after God's own heart, we're going to have to unplug from the way the world thinks. David's humility is one of the heart attitudes that stands out in stark contrast to Saul's and Absalom's heart attitudes.

6a. *Discussion question:* Do you believe that God would not command you to do anything that you were genetically incapable of doing? Why or why not?
<u>Discussion question</u>

6b. If you want to be a person after God's own heart, you are going to have to _____ from the way this world thinks.
<u>Unplug</u>

6c. David's humility is one of the heart attitudes that stands out in stark contrast to what?
  A. The Hollywood elite and most of society
  B. Presbyterians and Baptists
  C. The president
  D. Saul's and Absalom's heart attitudes
  E. Everyone else's
D. Saul's and Absalom's heart attitudes

Discipleship Questions

1. *Discussion question:* What was it about Saul that made it possible for him to rationalize disobedience?
   _____
   _____
   _____

2. What did God send Saul to do?
   A. Talk to the Amalekites about their merciless behavior
   B. Kill the Amalekite men
   C. Deliver a pizza
   D. Get spoils
   E. Obey His command exactly by wiping out every trace of the Amalekites

3. Read 2 Samuel 24:18-25. What was David's attitude about sacrificing to the Lord?
   A. He bartered to get the best deal on the best animal
   B. He thought, *Well, my heart's right, so God will understand if I don't pay for this sacrifice*
   C. He would not offer the Lord something that cost him nothing
   D. He looked to the people to help him obey God and supply the offering
   E. He didn't want to put forth the effort

4. When you stumble and sin, do you immediately think, *Against you, and you only have I sinned*? Why or Why not?
   _____
   _____
   _____

5. David knew _____.
   A. He was too busy to be watching Bathsheba take a bath
   B. He could wiggle his way out of any trouble that might come from his adultery
   C. Bathsheba should have been bathing inside of a tent
   D. He was terribly wrong
   E. It didn't matter what he'd done

6. Read Psalm 51:4. David sinned against whom?
   A. God
   B. Bathsheba
   C. Bathsheba's husband
   D. All of the above
   E. None of the above

7. *Discussion question:* Consider the ways you may have blamed others for your transgressions. How do you realize the truth?
   _____
   _____
   _____

8. Why did Absalom refuse to own up to his sin?
   A. It was easier that way
   B. It was his responsibility to take care of Amnon's wrong
   C. He had an undeniable passion for justice
   D. He blamed his father
   E. He had been spoiled as a child

9. David refused to _____ what happened with Absalom.

10. *Discussion question:* Why is it important to take responsibility for your actions?
    _____
    _____
    _____

11. It has become standard fare that nobody will say _____.

12. If what someone says is contrary to the Word of God, they are _____!

13. *Discussion question:* Why do you think it is right for the Lord to hold you accountable for your emotions?
    _____
    _____
    _____

"IT'S MY FAULT!"

14. Does the Lord send enemies against you?
_____
_____
_____

15. You are _____ to rejoice.

16. *Discussion question:* Do you believe that God would not command you to do anything that you were genetically incapable of doing? Why or why not?
_____
_____
_____

17. If you want to be a person after God's own heart, you are going to have to _____ from the way the world thinks.

18. David's humility is one of the heart attitudes that stands out in stark contrast to what?
   A. The Hollywood Elite and most of society
   B. Presbyterians and Baptists
   C. The president
   D. Saul's and Absalom's heart attitudes
   E. Everyone else's

Answer Key

1. *Discussion question*
2. E. Obey His commands exactly by wiping out every trace of the Amalekites
3. C. He would not offer the Lord something that cost him nothing
4. *Discussion question*
5. D. He was terribly wrong
6. A. God
7. *Discussion question*
8. D. He blamed his father
9. Whitewash
10. *Discussion question*
11. "It's my fault"
12. Wrong
13. *Discussion question*
14. No
15. Commanded
16. *Discussion question*
17. Unplug
18. Saul's and Absalom's heart attitudes

"IT'S MY FAULT!"

Scriptures

1 SAMUEL 15:13-23

And Samuel came to Saul: and Saul said unto him, Blessed be thou of the Lord: I have performed the commandment of the Lord. [14] And Samuel said, What meaneth then this bleating of the sheep in mine ears, and the lowing of the oxen which I hear? [15] And Saul said, They have brought them from the Amalekites: for the people spared the best of the sheep and of the oxen, to sacrifice unto the Lord thy God; and the rest we have utterly destroyed. [16] Then Samuel said unto Saul, Stay, and I will tell thee what the Lord hath said to me this night. And he said unto him, Say on. [17] And Samuel said, When thou wast little in thine own sight, wast thou not made the head of the tribes of Israel, and the Lord anointed thee king over Israel? [18] And the Lord sent thee on a journey, and said, Go and utterly destroy the sinners the Amalekites, and fight against them until they be consumed. [19] Wherefore then didst thou not obey the voice of the Lord, but didst fly upon the spoil, and didst evil in the sight of the Lord? [20] And Saul said unto Samuel, Yea, I have obeyed the voice of the Lord, and have gone the way which the Lord sent me, and have brought Agag the king of Amalek, and have utterly destroyed the Amalekites. [21] But the people took of the spoil, sheep and oxen, the chief of the things which should have been utterly destroyed. [22] And Samuel said, Hath the Lord as great delight in burnt offerings and sacrifices, as in obeying the voice of the Lord? Behold, to obey is better than sacrifice, and to hearken than the fat of rams. [23] For rebellion is as the sin of witchcraft, and stubbornness is as iniquity and idolatry. Because thou hast rejected the word of the Lord, he hath also rejected thee from being king.

2 SAMUEL 24:17-25

And David spake unto the Lord when he saw the angel that smote the people, and said, Lo, I have sinned, and I have done wickedly: but these sheep, what have they done? let thine hand, I pray thee, be against me, and against my father's house. [18] And Gad came that day to David, and said unto him, Go up, rear an altar unto the Lord in the threshingfloor of Araunah the Jebusite. [19] And David, according to the saying of Gad, went up as the Lord commanded. [20] And Araunah looked, and saw the king and his servants coming on toward him: and Araunah went out, and bowed himself before the king on his face upon the ground. [21] And Araunah said, Wherefore is my lord the king come to his servant? And David said, To buy the threshingfloor of thee, to build an altar unto the Lord, that the plague may be stayed from the people. [22] And Araunah said unto David, Let my lord the king take and offer up what seemeth good unto him: behold, here be oxen for burnt sacrifice, and threshing instruments and other instruments of the oxen for wood. [23] All these things did Araunah, as a king, give unto the king. And Araunah said unto the king, The Lord thy God accept thee. [24] And the king said unto Araunah, Nay; but I will surely buy it of thee at a price: neither will I offer burnt offerings unto the Lord my God of that which doth cost me nothing. So David bought the threshingfloor and the oxen for fifty shekels of silver. [25] And David built there an altar unto the Lord, and offered burnt offerings and peace offerings. So the Lord was intreated for the land, and the plague was stayed from Israel.

PSALM 51:4

Against thee, thee only, have I sinned, and done this evil in thy sight: that thou mightest be justified when thou speakest, and be clear when thou judgest.

2 SAMUEL 13:20-29

And Absalom her brother said unto her, Hath Amnon thy brother been with thee? but hold now thy peace, my sister: he is thy brother; regard not this thing. So Tamar remained desolate in her brother Absalom's house. [21] But when king David heard of all these things, he was very wroth. [22] And Absalom spake unto his brother Amnon neither good nor bad: for Absalom hated Amnon, because he had forced his sister Tamar. [23] And it came to pass after two full years, that Absalom had sheepshearers in Baalhazor, which is beside Ephraim: and Absalom invited all the king's sons. [24] And Absalom came to the king, and said, Behold now, thy servant hath sheepshearers; let the king, I beseech thee, and his servants go with thy servant. [25] And the king said to Absalom, Nay, my son, let us not all now go, lest we be chargeable unto thee. And he pressed him: howbeit he would not go, but blessed him. [26] Then said Absalom, If not, I pray thee, let my brother Amnon go with us. And the king said unto him, Why should he go with thee? [27] But Absalom pressed him, that he let Amnon and all the king's sons go with him. [28] Now Absalom had commanded his servants, saying, Mark ye now when Amnon's heart is merry with wine, and when I say unto you, Smite Amnon; then kill him, fear not: have not I commanded you? be courageous, and be valiant. [29] And the servants of Absalom did unto Amnon as Absalom had commanded. Then all the king's sons arose, and every man gat him up upon his mule, and fled.

2 SAMUEL 13:37-38

But Absalom fled, and went to Talmai, the son of Ammihud, king of Geshur. And David mourned for his son every day. [38] So Absalom fled, and went to Geshur, and was there three years.

2 SAMUEL 14:21-24

And the king said unto Joab, Behold now, I have done this thing: go therefore, bring the young man Absalom again. [22] And Joab fell to the ground on his face, and bowed himself, and thanked the king: and Joab said, To day thy servant knoweth that I have found grace in thy sight, my lord, O king, in that the king hath fulfilled the request of his servant. [23] So Joab arose and went to Geshur, and brought Absalom to Jerusalem. [24] And the king said, Let him turn to his own house, and let him not see my face. So Absalom returned to his own house, and saw not the king's face.

"IT'S MY FAULT!"

2 SAMUEL 14:28

So Absalom dwelt two full years in Jerusalem, and saw not the king's face.

ROMANS 3:4

Let God be true, but every man a liar.

DEUTERONOMY 28:47-48

Because thou servedst not the Lord thy God with joyfulness, and with gladness of heart, for the abundance of all things; [48] therefore shalt thou serve thine enemies which the Lord shall send against thee.

PHILIPPIANS 4:4

Rejoice in the Lord alway: and again I say, Rejoice.

PSALM 34:1

I will bless the Lord at all times: his praise shall continually be in my mouth.

JOHN 16:33

In the world ye shall have tribulation: but be of good cheer; I have overcome the world.

A Snare

Accepting responsibility is one of the greatest signs of whether someone has truly repented or not. David humbled himself, accepted responsibility, and refused to blame anybody else. Saul eventually admitted "I've sinned" because he was argued and forced into it (1 Sam. 15:24). However, he was still placing blame and pointing the finger, saying, "But you don't understand. The people did this. It's their fault!" Saul hadn't truly repented.

The prodigal son truly repented. Notice what he purposed in his heart to tell his father:

> *I will arise and go to my father, and will say unto him, Father, I have sinned against heaven, and before thee, [19] And am no more worthy to be called thy son: make me as one of thy hired servants.*
>
> LUKE 15:18-19

He was saying, "Father, I was wrong, and I don't have any justification. I don't have any claim on your goodness. I have voided everything, but I'm asking for mercy." He didn't come to his father and say, "I think I've made a mistake, but it's your fault too. You shouldn't have given me all this money. You shouldn't have allowed this to happen. You're the one who drove me away. You're the one who gave me my inheritance early!" He didn't point the finger at his father and say, "You don't understand what happened when I was in this foreign land. People took advantage of me. I had to eat pig's food just to survive!" No, the prodigal son had truly repented. He didn't try to blame things on anyone else; he took responsibility for his own actions.

Failure to accept responsibility and pointing the finger while saying "It's someone else's fault!" is a sure sign that their heart hasn't changed and there isn't genuine repentance. I've seen many people in the Christian community who got in trouble and had their sins exposed, whether moral, ethical, or civil. Perhaps they were going to lose something—like their spouse or family—or they had to go to court or jail. I've seen people who were humiliated, who cried, who were sorry and said they repented, but there was this thread running through everything they said. "Yes, I'm wrong. I can't believe I did this. But you just don't understand. I was raised to be this way. My family was always like this. This person drove me to do this. With the way my spouse treated me, I just couldn't help it." As long as there are these little threads of blaming someone else, then true, genuine, heartfelt repentance hasn't occurred yet. They are only sorry they got caught. In order to be a person after God's own heart, you're going to have to move beyond that.

WHAT DAVID WANTED

Unlike Saul and Absalom, David didn't care about anyone else's opinion. He was a God pleaser, not a man pleaser. The Lord was foremost in his life. Let that sink in for a moment. God can't be seen. As far as the physical realm is concerned, He's intangible. But when David humbled himself before God and repented of his sin with Bathsheba, he said *"I have sinned against the LORD"* (2 Sam. 12:13) and *"Against thee, thee only, have I sinned, and done this evil in thy sight"* (Ps. 51:4).

David confessed, "Against You, and You only, Lord, have I sinned!" God's opinion of him was the only thing he was concerned about. There is no indication in the Scripture that David ever publicly told everybody everything that had happened, but there is also zero indication that he hid it. He exposed himself and brought it out in the open. David didn't do this in an imprudent way. He didn't just go around every day asking everyone, "Have you heard yet what I've done?" But he didn't try to conceal it or cover it up anymore either. David wanted relationship with God more than man's approval.

"IT'S OVER!"

Contrast this with Saul. In the second half of 1 Samuel 15:23, Samuel continued his reproof of Saul, saying,

> *Because thou hast rejected the word of the LORD, he hath also rejected thee from being king.*

Then Saul responded,

> *I have sinned: for I have transgressed the commandment of the LORD, and thy words: because I feared the people, and obeyed their voice.*
>
> 1 SAMUEL 15:24

Saul was forced to admit, "All right, I'm wrong. But it was the people who made me do it!" He was still pointing the finger. There wasn't genuine repentance. He still refused to take responsibility for his own actions.

> *Now therefore, I pray thee, pardon my sin, and turn again with me, that I may worship the LORD. [26] And Samuel said unto Saul, I will not return with thee: for thou hast rejected the word of the LORD, and the LORD hath rejected thee from being king over Israel*
>
> 1 SAMUEL 15:25-26

A SNARE

In our day and age, people are elected president. And as long as they have their popularity—or force—they can maintain it. But, in Saul's day, it was a theocracy. Saul had been chosen by God to rule, but he only had this power as long as the Lord gave it to him. Here was the messenger of God, saying, "It's over! You've lost everything. Not only are you going to cease being king, but your children will never inherit the kingdom. Your dynasty is over. God is going to raise up another king!" Now, that's a severe judgment.

MAN PLEASER

And as Samuel turned about to go away, he [Saul] laid hold upon the skirt of his [Samuel's] mantle, and it rent. [28] And Samuel said unto him, The LORD hath rent the kingdom of Israel from thee this day, and hath given it to a neighbour of thine, that is better than thou.

1 SAMUEL 15:27-28, BRACKETS MINE

As the kingdom has just been taken away from him, Saul grabbed Samuel's robe and it tore. Samuel used that as a word picture to illustrate what God had just done in the spirit: "He just tore the kingdom right out of your hand!" Look how Saul reacted with this terrible judgment pronounced upon him:

I have sinned: yet honour me now, I pray thee, before the elders of my people, and before Israel, and turn again with me, that I may worship the LORD thy God.

1 SAMUEL 15:30

Do you see what Saul was doing? He said, "All right, I've lost the kingdom. God has rejected me. He's punishing me, but that's not really what's important in my life. Please honor me so I'll still look good in the sight of the people!"

Saul's problem was that he was a man pleaser. The evidence is right here. He had lost everything, but instead of repenting and saying "Lord, forgive me! How could I do this? I love You more than anything else. I must have Your acceptance," he was willing to let all that go. The main issue for Saul wasn't the Lord's favor but rather honor in the sight of the people.

ARE YOU A GOD PLEASER?

God's Word is very clear about the fear of man:

The fear of man bringeth a snare: but whoso putteth his trust in the LORD shall be safe.

PROVERBS 29:25

LESSONS FROM DAVID

Being a man pleaser brings a snare. This is talking about a trap that was used to catch animals and birds. Satan goes about *"seeking whom he may devour"* (1 Pet. 5:8). When we become a man pleaser, we open the door for the enemy to come in and devour us. This happens when we seek to receive our approval and validation from people more than God. We need to seek first His kingdom and His righteousness (Matt. 6:33). We need to seek the Lord's acceptance and approval more than man's acceptance and approval. We need to make God first place in our lives and be more concerned about pleasing Him than our own reputations. That's how we can avoid this trap of the devil.

In a sense, we've all become the politicians that we abhor. Many politicians—not all, but many—constantly keep their finger in the air to check which way the public opinion polls are blowing. And whatever it is that the people want to hear, that's what they have to say. They're like chameleons—void of any convictions of their own. They change and do whatever will buy them enough votes to get them re-elected. They're out to please people 100 percent of the time! They have no integrity. You can't tell what they're going to do in a particular situation because it just depends on how the polls are. That's terrible!

You're probably thinking, *Yes, Andrew, that's wrong. You ought to be a person of conviction, etc.* But may I ask you a personal question? Is that the way you are? It's easy to judge politicians, but what about you? If you were applying for a job or a promotion at work and you had to be really candid about something in your background that might affect whether you receive the job or promotion, would you be honest and open about it? If you were applying for a loan, would you tell them the things they want to know, even if they could be used against you? Are you a God pleaser or a man pleaser?

If I was being considered for a job and had something in my past like a police record, I wouldn't conceal it. I would be open and honest and tell people up front. I am not a man pleaser. My security is in God. Because of this, I'm secure. I'm safe. The Lord is my Provider, and He will provide me with a job (Ps. 90:16-17).

COMPLETELY TRANSPARENT

This is a major difference between David and many Christians today. David humbled himself and accepted responsibility for what he did. He didn't try to cover it up or blame someone else. David was so God conscious that it didn't matter to him if the entire nation knew what had happened. What mattered to him was getting his relationship with God back to where it should be.

To be a person after God's own heart, you need to quit covering up, hiding, and concealing sin and failure in your life. Of course, you need to use wisdom. Don't just go out there and announce it like it's something you're proud of. But if you're applying for something and they expect you to put down any past problems you've had—be honest. Trust God and tell the people.

The Bible doesn't say, "Thou shalt not lie"; it says, *"Thou shalt not bear false witness"* (Ex. 20:16). Therefore, if you're filling out an application and you fail to put something there that should be, you bore false witness. You may say, "But I didn't lie!" Well, yes, you did. You gave a false representation of yourself. You need to be candid. Don't just carry a sign down the street that says "I've committed adultery" or "I went to prison," but if something needs to be said, be honest and courageous enough to expose it to the light.

Sometimes you need to tell someone else in order to help them. Perhaps somebody you are dealing with has a similar problem to what you've had. You desire to keep these dark things concealed in your life and don't want them to be known. But if you shared them, you could minister hope and encouragement to this other person. You could testify of how the Lord forgave you and your life went on, how He healed your heart, how He restored your marriage, etc. If you won't share something just because you don't want anyone else to know about it, then you're still a man pleaser. You're still ensnared by the fear of man.

Jesus spoke the truth. He didn't enjoy upsetting people. He didn't rebuke them because He loved controversy, strife, and criticism. Some of today's talk shows just love controversy because it sells, it draws people in, and it improves their ratings. The Lord wasn't like that. Jesus was absolutely free to tell the truth to people who had the authority to hurt him (Luke 22:66-23:3). He was fearless. There was zero snare in His life, because He didn't care about man's opinion. Jesus was out to only please His Father.

That's how we need to be too. We need to be completely transparent.

BE WHO GOD WANTS YOU TO BE!

Are you willing to do anything the Lord wants you to do? Will you maintain your integrity in the face of negative peer pressure from your fellow employees, or if it means possibly being passed over for a promotion at work? Do you have that kind of attitude?

I remember hearing a fifteen-year-old girl give a testimony at the local church I attend. For the past two years of her Christian life, she had been living a life of compromise. She hated who she had become and what she was doing. However, she wanted to be accepted by certain peers. She went on a missions trip to Costa Rica, and while there, they visited a girls' home. They met young ladies who had been beaten, raped, were impoverished, and had all kinds of disadvantages. This caused her to see how blessed she really was. The Lord had given her a good home, loving parents, a church, and all these things. So, she became ashamed of the fact that she wanted the approval of these other teenagers more than God. All of a sudden, it just clicked inside of her, and she declared, "I'm going to start being true to myself. I'm going to be who I want to be—who God wants me to be!" In a sense, she was saying, "I'm going to start pleasing God more than people." This girl arrived at a conclusion that most adult believers never have—choosing to be a God pleaser instead of a man pleaser.

David lived to please God, but Saul and Absalom lived to please man. If you want to be a person after God's own heart, then you're going to have to get to the place where you love God and value His acceptance and approval more than man's. When David was reproved for his sin, what broke his heart was how he had broken his relationship with God. He didn't care what anyone thought. He wanted that relationship back more than anything. It didn't matter about his kingdom. *Let somebody else take it,* he figured. David just wanted God.

Saul didn't value his relationship with God that way. When the Lord forsook him, quit responding to him, and wouldn't answer him, Saul just went and consulted a witch (1 Sam. 28:3-19). He didn't care how he got his answer. His relationship with God just wasn't that important. Saul wanted results. This is exactly the reason many people aren't a man or woman after God's own heart today.

Outline

I. Accepting responsibility is one of the greatest signs of whether someone has truly repented or not.
   A. Saul eventually admitted "I have sinned," but he was still saying, "It's their fault!"
   B. The prodigal son truly repented:

   I will arise and go to my father, and will say unto him, Father, I have sinned against heaven, and before thee, [19] And am no more worthy to be called thy son: make me as one of thy hired servants.

   LUKE 15:18-19

   i. The prodigal son didn't tell his father, "You shouldn't have given me all this money; it's your fault too."

II. I've seen people who were humiliated, who cried, who were sorry and said they repented, but there was a thread running through everything they said.
   A. They'd say "Yes, I'm wrong, but you just don't understand; I was raised to be this way" or "With the way my spouse treated me, I just couldn't help it."
   B. As long as there are threads of blaming someone else, then true, genuine, heartfelt repentance hasn't occurred.
   C. In order to be a person after God's own heart, you're going to have to move beyond that mindset.

III. When David humbled himself before God and repented of his sin with Bathsheba, he said *"I have sinned against the LORD"* (2 Sam. 12:13) and *"Against thee, thee only, have I sinned, and done this evil in thy sight"* (Ps. 51:4).
   A. God's opinion of him was the only thing he cared about.
   B. Contrast this with Saul, who feared the people:

   I have sinned: for I have transgressed the commandment of the LORD, and thy words: because I feared the people, and obeyed their voice.

   1 SAMUEL 15:24

   C. Saul's problem was that he was a man pleaser.

IV. God's Word is very clear about the fear of man:

   The fear of man bringeth a snare: but whoso putteth his trust in the LORD shall be safe.

   PROVERBS 29:25

      A. Being a man pleaser brings a snare—like a trap that is used to catch animals—and it opens the door for the enemy to come destroy you.
      B. Seek the Lord's approval more than man's; that's how you can avoid this trap of the devil.
      C. Are you a God pleaser or a man pleaser?

V.   To be a person after God's own heart, you need to quit covering up, hiding, and concealing sin and failure in your life.
      A. The Bible doesn't say, "Thou shalt not lie"; it says, *"Thou shalt not bear false witness"* (Ex. 20:16).
         i. If you're filling out an application and you fail to put something there that should be, you bore false witness.
         ii. If something needs to be said, be honest and courageous enough to expose it to the light.
      B. Sometimes you need to tell someone else about your sin in order to help them.
         i. You could testify of how the Lord forgave you and your life went on, how He healed your heart, how He restored your marriage, etc.
         ii. If you won't share something just because you don't want anyone else to know about it, then you're still a man pleaser; you're still ensnared by the fear of man.

Teacher's Guide

1. Accepting responsibility is one of the greatest signs of whether someone has truly repented or not. Saul eventually admitted "I have sinned," but he was still saying, "It's their fault." The prodigal son truly repented:

> *I will arise and go to my father, and will say unto him, Father, I have sinned against heaven, and before thee, [19] And am no more worthy to be called thy son: make me as one of thy hired servants.*
>
> LUKE 15:18-19

The prodigal didn't tell his father, "You shouldn't have given me all this money; it's your fault too."

1a. *Discussion question:* What is the benefit of accepting responsibility for your transgressions? What is the cost of not accepting responsibility?
   Discussion question
1b. Saul finally admitted he was wrong, but he didn't let go of saying, "_____."
   "It's their fault"
1c. The prodigal son recognized that he had sinned against _____ and before his _____.
   Heaven / father

2. Andrew has seen people who were humiliated, who cried, who were sorry and said they repented, but there was a thread running through everything they said. They'd say "Yes, I'm wrong, but you just don't understand; I was raised to be this way" or "With the way my spouse treated me, I just couldn't help it." As long as there are threads of blaming someone else, then true, genuine, heartfelt repentance hasn't occurred. In order to be people after God's own heart, we're going to have to move beyond that mindset.

2a. *Discussion question:* Why shouldn't you try to justify yourself when you've sinned?
   Discussion question
2b. To be a person after God's own heart, you are going to have to move beyond the _____ of blaming someone else.
   Mindset

LESSONS FROM DAVID

3. When David humbled himself before God and repented of his sin with Bathsheba, he said *"I have sinned against the LORD"* (2 Sam. 12:13) and *"Against thee, thee only, have I sinned, and done this evil in thy sight"* (Ps. 51:4). God's opinion of him was the only thing he cared about. Let's contrast this with Saul, who feared the people:

> *I have sinned: for I have transgressed the commandment of the LORD, and thy words: because I feared the people, and obeyed their voice.*
>
> 1 SAMUEL 15:24

Saul's problem was that he was a man pleaser.

3a. David _____ himself before God.
Humbled

3b. Saul was a man pleaser, meaning he _____ the people.
   A. Feared
   B. Loathed
   C. Pleased
   D. Tolerated
   E. Loved
   A. Feared

4. God's Word is very clear about the fear of man:

> *The fear of man bringeth a snare: but whoso putteth his trust in the LORD shall be safe.*
>
> PROVERBS 29:25

Being a man pleaser brings a snare—like a trap that is used to catch animals—and it opens the door for the Enemy to come destroy us. We need to seek the Lord's approval more than man's; that's how we can avoid this trap of the devil. Are we God pleasers or man pleasers?

4a. Read Proverbs 29:25. What does being a man pleaser do?
   It brings a snare and it opens the door for the Enemy to come destroy you
4b. How can you avoid this trap of the devil?
   Seek the Lord's approval more than man's

A SNARE

5. To be people after God's own heart, we need to quit covering up, hiding, and concealing sin and failure in our lives. The Bible doesn't say, "Thou shalt not lie"; it says, *"Thou shalt not bear false witness"* (Ex. 20:16). If we're filling out an application and we fail to put something there that should be, we bore false witness. If something needs to be said, we need to be honest and courageous enough to expose it to the light. Sometimes we need to tell someone about our sin in order to help them. We could testify of how the Lord forgave us and our lives went on, how He healed our hearts, how He restored our marriages, etc. If we won't share something just because we don't want anyone else to know about it, then we're still man pleasers; we're still ensared by the fear of man.

5a. If something needs to be said, you should be _____ and _____ enough to expose it to the light.
   Honest / courageous

5b. If you won't share something just because you don't want anyone else to know about it, then you are what?
   A. Timid
   B. Needing psychiatric help
   C. Confused about what is right and wrong
   D. A man pleaser
   E. A very private person who doesn't need others to affirm you
   D. A man pleaser

Discipleship Questions

1. What is the benefit of accepting responsibility for our transgressions? What is the cost of not accepting responsibility?
   _____
   _____
   _____

2. Saul finally admitted he was wrong, but he didn't let go of saying, "_____"

3. The prodigal son recognized that he had sinned against _____, and before his _____.

4. *Discussion question:* Why shouldn't you try to justify yourself when you've sinned?
   _____
   _____
   _____

5. To be a person after God's own heart, you are going to have to move beyond the _____ of blaming someone else.

6. David _____ himself before God.

7. Saul was a man pleaser, meaning he _____ the people.
   A. Feared
   B. Loathed
   C. Pleased
   D. Tolerated
   E. Loved

8. What does being a man pleaser do?
   _____
   _____
   _____

   _____

A SNARE

9. How can you avoid this trap of the devil?
_____
_____
_____

10. If something needs to be said, you should be _____ and _____ enough to expose it to the light.

11. If you won't share something just because you don't want anyone else to know about it, then you are what?
    A. Timid
    B. Needing psychiatric help
    C. Confused about what is right and wrong
    D. A man pleaser
    E. A very private person who doesn't need others to affirm you

Answer Key

1. *Discussion question*
2. "It's their fault"
3. Heaven / father
4. *Discussion question*
5. Mindset
6. Humbled
7. A. Feared
8. It brings a snare and it opens the door for the Enemy to come destroy you
9. Seek the Lord's approval more than man's
10. Honest / courageous
11. D. A man pleaser

Scriptures

LUKE 15:18-19
I will arise and go to my father, and will say unto him, Father, I have sinned against heaven, and before thee, [19] And am no more worthy to be called thy son: make me as one of thy hired servants.

2 SAMUEL 12:13
I have sinned against the Lord.

PSALMS 51:4
Against thee, thee only, have I sinned, and done this evil in thy sight

1 SAMUEL 15:24-28
I have sinned: for I have transgressed the commandment of the Lord, and thy words: because I feared the people, and obeyed their voice. [25] Now therefore, I pray thee, pardon my sin, and turn again with me, that I may worship the Lord. [26] And Samuel said unto Saul, I will not return with thee: for thou hast rejected the word of the Lord, and the Lord hath rejected thee from being king over Israel. [27] And as Samuel turned about to go away, he laid hold upon the skirt of his mantle, and it rent. [28] And Samuel said unto him, The Lord hath rent the kingdom of Israel from thee this day, and hath given it to a neighbour of thine, that is better than thou.

1 SAMUEL 15:30
Then he said, I have sinned: yet honour me now, I pray thee, before the elders of my people, and before Israel, and turn again with me, that I may worship the Lord thy God.

PROVERBS 29:25
The fear of man bringeth a snare: but whoso putteth his trust in the Lord shall be safe.

1 PETER 5:8
Be sober, be vigilant; because your adversary the devil, as a roaring lion, walketh about, seeking whom he may devour:

MATTHEW 6:33
But seek ye first the kingdom of God, and his righteousness; and all these things shall be added unto you.

PSALM 90:16-17

Let thy work appear unto thy servants, and thy glory unto their children. [17] And let the beauty of the LORD our God be upon us: and establish thou the work of our hands upon us; yea, the work of our hands establish thou it.

EXODUS 20:16

Thou shalt not bear false witness against thy neighbour.

LUKE 22:66-71

And as soon as it was day, the elders of the people and the chief priests and the scribes came together, and led him into their council, saying, [67] Art thou the Christ? tell us. And he said unto them, If I tell you, ye will not believe: [68] And if I also ask you, ye will not answer me, nor let me go. [69] Hereafter shall the Son of man sit on the right hand of the power of God. [70] Then said they all, Art thou then the Son of God? And he said unto them, Ye say that I am. [71] And they said, What need we any further witness? for we ourselves have heard of his own mouth.

LUKE 23:1-3

And the whole multitude of them arose, and led him unto Pilate. [2] And they began to accuse him, saying, We found this fellow perverting the nation, and forbidding to give tribute to Caesar, saying that he himself is Christ a King. [3] And Pilate asked him, saying, Art thou the King of the Jews? And he answered him and said, Thou sayest it.

1 SAMUEL 28:3-19

Now Samuel was dead, and all Israel had lamented him, and buried him in Ramah, even in his own city. And Saul had put away those that had familiar spirits, and the wizards, out of the land. [4] And the Philistines gathered themselves together, and came and pitched in Shunem: and Saul gathered all Israel together, and they pitched in Gilboa. [5] And when Saul saw the host of the Philistines, he was afraid, and his heart greatly trembled. [6] And when Saul enquired of the LORD, the LORD answered him not, neither by dreams, nor by Urim, nor by prophets. [7] Then said Saul unto his servants, Seek me a woman that hath a familiar spirit, that I may go to her, and enquire of her. And his servants said to him, Behold, there is a woman that hath a familiar spirit at Endor. [8] And Saul disguised himself, and put on other raiment, and he went, and two men with him, and they came to the woman by night: and he said, I pray thee, divine unto me by the familiar spirit, and bring me him up, whom I shall name unto thee. [9] And the woman said unto him, Behold, thou knowest what Saul hath done, how he hath cut off those that have familiar spirits, and the wizards, out of the land: wherefore then layest thou a snare for my life, to cause me to die? [10] And Saul sware to her by the LORD, saying, As the LORD liveth, there shall no punishment happen to thee for this thing. [11] Then said the woman, Whom shall I bring up unto thee? And he said, Bring me up Samuel. [12] And when the woman saw Samuel, she cried with a loud voice: and the woman spake to Saul, saying, Why hast thou deceived me? for thou art Saul. [13] And the king said unto her, Be not afraid: for what sawest thou? And the woman said unto Saul, I saw gods ascending out of the earth. [14] And he said unto her, What form is he of? And she said, An old man cometh up; and he is covered with a mantle. And Saul perceived that it was Samuel, and he stooped with his face to the ground, and bowed himself. [15] And Samuel said to Saul, Why hast thou disquieted me, to bring me up? And Saul answered, I am sore distressed; for the Philistines make war against me, and God is departed from me, and answereth me no more, neither by prophets, nor by dreams: therefore I have called thee, that thou mayest make known unto me what I shall do. [16] Then said Samuel, Wherefore then dost thou ask of me, seeing the Lord is departed from thee, and is become thine enemy? [17] And the Lord hath done to him, as he spake by me: for the Lord hath rent the kingdom out of thine hand, and given it to thy neighbour, even to David: [18] Because thou obeyedst not the voice of the Lord, nor executedst his fierce wrath upon Amalek, therefore hath the Lord done this thing unto thee this day. [19] Moreover the Lord will also deliver Israel with thee into the hand of the Philistines: and to morrow shalt thou and thy sons be with me: the Lord also shall deliver the host of Israel into the hand of the Philistines.

A Purpose Bigger than Yourself

David was a man after God's own heart. This wasn't always obvious from his actions, but it was definitely evidenced by the attitude of his heart. David accepted responsibility and was accountable for his actions. He always sought God's acceptance and approval, not man's. Also, David had a cause that was bigger than himself.

In other words, David wasn't the center of his universe. He wasn't the focus of his life. David knew he was where he was to serve God's purposes, not his own. He didn't just use God to get his way but longed for the Lord to use him to accomplish His purposes. This important trait helped make David a man after God's own heart.

If you live a self-centered life, you will never be a person after God's own heart. Take, for instance, the business realm. If you're running neck and neck with someone for a promotion at work, are you thinking, *What's best for this company?* or *Who cares about the company—what's best for me? I need this promotion. I need this money. What about me? What about my ego?* This self-serving, self-centered kind of attitude is completely inconsistent with God's heart. If you are all wrapped up in yourself, you make a very small package! And I'm afraid that's where most people are today.

THE ARK STAYS

David didn't have a selfish attitude. Serving God benefited and promoted him in life. It brought him from being a shepherd boy to being king. But this was just a fringe benefit. These things came as byproducts of his relationship with God. David's heart was to serve the Lord.

Even when Absalom revolted against him, David's heart was to serve the Lord. Absalom invested years into winning the hearts of the people. He was a handsome, gifted individual, and the people loved him. He literally stole their hearts away from his father, David (2 Sam. 15:6). Absalom invited certain nobles to join with him and proclaimed himself as king. When David got wind of this, he had to flee for his life from Jerusalem, or he would have been trapped there and killed by Absalom (2 Sam. 15:13-14). While leaving with those still loyal to him…

> …*the king said unto Zadok* [the priest], *Carry back the ark of God into the city: if I shall find favour in the eyes of the* LORD, *he will bring me again, and show me both it, and his*

habitation: [26] But if he thus say, I have no delight in thee; behold, here am I, let him do to me as seemeth good unto him.

2 SAMUEL 15:25-26, BRACKETS MINE

What a tremendous passage of Scripture! What a revelation into David's heart. Here David was, fleeing for his life, fleeing from the shame of his own son who was rebelling against him, fleeing for the sake of the kingdom. Yet when the Ark—which would have given him a great advantage—was offered to go with him, David said, "No. Take the Ark back to its place in the tabernacle. If God is pleased to return me as king over Israel, then I'll come back to it. But if the Lord is through with me, then let Him do what He wants." In other words, David was saying, "If God wants me to be king, I'll come back to Jerusalem and the Ark. But if not, then let the Ark stay here and serve God's people."

David had a purpose that was bigger than himself. Although he was king, it wasn't for his ego or how it would benefit him. He was king to serve the Lord and the nation of Israel. This was God's call on his life. So, David stepped up to the plate when his nation was impoverished and oppressed by the Philistines. He didn't fight Goliath for himself, but to serve God by overcoming the armies of the Philistines and by bringing deliverance to the Israelites. David was king for the same reason—to serve God and His people. This was his purpose. David wasn't just consumed with self. Self was not the god of his life!

In order to truly understand this, the Holy Spirit must reveal it to you. This trait would make you a person after God's own heart. You must die to yourself and come alive to something that's bigger than you.

FOCUS ON THE MESSAGE!

There are so many ways you are tempted to exalt yourself in everyday situations. If you can overcome in the small things, then you'll be able to handle the big temptations when they come. However, we just miss it in so many ways.

The year 2003 marked our twenty-fifth anniversary of the incorporation of Andrew Wommack Ministries. It was also the thirty-fifth anniversary of God supernaturally touching my life. We produced an anniversary magazine detailing some of the things the Lord had done. We also stated our vision for the future in this magazine.

As we were preparing this magazine, members of our Production Department came to me with a list of questions they wanted Jamie and me to answer. Some of them were things like, "What is your favorite

---

A PURPOSE BIGGER THAN YOURSELF

color? What are your hobbies? What do you like to do on your days off?" etc. Now, I understand that these are questions that people would want to ask a leader in a newspaper type of article, but I had to tell them, "Look, I understand what you're doing, but you're missing something here. This ministry isn't about me. It's not about what my favorite color is or what I like to do in my free time. This is about the message God has given me to share with the entire world!"

All of our ministry expansion, including this new building and the multiplying of Bible colleges all around the world, isn't about me. It's not about me looking at something and saying, "Look what I've built!" No! All these things are just tools to get the job done. What's important is getting the Word out about God's unconditional love, and the balance of grace and faith. The reason I get excited when I see that building, when the schools multiply and grow, and when new radio and television stations are added is because the message the Lord has put in my heart to share is changing people's lives. It excites me to know we're accomplishing what God has called us to do!

I have a purpose that's bigger than me. It's not about having a large facility, being recognized by millions of people, or anything like that. It's about the message! That's why I redirected my staff and said, "Ask me questions about the ministry, how it started, some of the hardships we've been through, and lessons we've learned that could help someone else overcome their hardships. But keep it focused on the message!" We must always stay focused on the message—not the messenger!

A MAN OF PURPOSE

I use a lot of personal examples when I minister. In fact, I just used one in the last few paragraphs. But my purpose in doing so isn't to bring attention to myself; it's to illustrate my points. I've found that personal examples are one of the best ways people can relate to, understand, and apply the message I'm trying to communicate.

Ronald Reagan was one of the best presidents we've ever had. He's credited with ending the Cold War, among many other things. Although I don't necessarily agree with everything he did, he was a great president. As he was leaving public office, there was a tremendous amount of recognition. As people started thinking about his legacy, one of the questions often directed toward him was, "What made you such a great man?" Almost every time, without fail, he responded by saying, "There's nothing great about me. I'm an ordinary person—but I had an extraordinary message! I'm not a great man. I'm a man who had great ideas and great purpose!"

Ronald Reagan wasn't out to build his legacy. He had a philosophy and a goal of less government and more personal responsibility. He had a vision of overcoming the Soviet Union and the Cold War problems through strength and refusing to back down. It wasn't just détente or business as usual. Reagan's purpose—which was bigger than himself—drove him and caused him to succeed.

In the same way, my God-given purpose motivates and spurs me on. The Lord touched me and changed my life. He burned a revelation in my heart, and I'm doing everything I can to get this message out. These truths I'm sharing about David have become real to me and have transformed my life. I believe that the Lord wants them to become real to you and impact your life—and the lives of millions of others—too. That's what drives me!

If I were in ministry just for my own personal benefit, I would have quit a long time ago. It's true—we are prospering and enjoying a certain measure of success right now. However, I've been in ministry for over forty-five years. We've lived through decades of hardships and trials. If this was about me, I would have given up and changed careers decades ago. There are other ways I could have taken care of myself and my family. I could have done something else and made a mark. But this isn't about me; it's about serving the Lord and accomplishing His goals. I have a God-given purpose that is bigger than myself!

"I CHOOSE TO SERVE GOD"

This is one of the reasons David was a man after God's own heart: When it was literally his life on the line, his kingdom on the line, or his legacy on the line, what mattered to David was serving God. He didn't care about all those other things. He basically said, "If it pleases God and that's what's best for the nation, then I'll come back. But if the Lord is through with me and it's better for the nation that I be gone and Absalom rule, then that's fine with me!"

I can truthfully testify to you today that if God were to tell me that I was doing more damage than good and it were better for the body of Christ that I do something else besides minister, I would. I'm not saying I would completely like it. I wouldn't necessarily enjoy it, any more than David enjoyed facing death and having his own son try to kill him. I'm not saying it would be pleasant. But I can honestly say that if I felt that it was to the kingdom of God's advantage that I no longer minister, then I wouldn't. If it would please God and glorify Him to use someone else, and to have me promote them and help them succeed ahead of me, I would do it with all my heart. Not many people can say that!

What about you? Have you been accepting responsibility for your actions, or do you still shift the blame? Are you claiming that it's your dysfunctional family, hormones, genetics, chemical imbalance, etc. that makes you that way? Examine your heart.

If you've been guilty of these things I've been talking about, you can repent and start changing your heart. The place where you begin is dying to yourself and saying, "Lord, please help me get to the place where serving, exalting, and pleasing You is more important to me than doing my own thing." If you honestly did that, this process of change will begin.

You can change your heart—you really can—but you can't do it by yourself. It has to be God who changes your heart. It requires His power, but it's your choice whether that power functions or not.

You must stop exalting yourself and living by your own self-will. Quit acting like Saul and saying, "It's their fault. They made me do it!" and "I don't care if I lose everything from God, but just make me look good in the eyes of people." Stop acting like Absalom and saying, "It's all my father's, mother's, sister's, brother's—somebody else's fault. It's not mine!" You aren't accepting the fact that you are the one who started this whole process. Therefore, you feel justified, and it's vengeance on your part. That's not a person after God's own heart. You need to change that!

The good news is you can change. It starts with a decision, but it doesn't end there. You have to walk it out.

CULTIVATE A SENSITIVE HEART

The contrasts between these three kings really brings out and magnifies what made David a man after God's own heart and how you and I can become people after God's own heart today. But it's up to you. You choose what your heart is going to be like. Whatever your heart is like right now is the result of the choices you have made in the past. You might not have intentionally and with understanding said "I want to be a hard-hearted person," but you have made choices that have hardened your heart toward Him. You can start making choices today that will soften and sensitize your heart toward God.

ANDREW'S RECOMMENDATIONS FOR FURTHER STUDY

Again, I refer you to my booklet entitled *Self-Centeredness: The Source of All Grief*. This book goes into much more detail about this. I encourage you to get it!

Also, my book entitled *Hardness of Heart* would go right along with this. It will instruct you on how to cultivate and keep a sensitive heart toward the Lord.

Outline

I. David was a man after God's own heart because of the attitude of his heart.
   A. He had a cause that was bigger than himself.
   B. David knew he was where he was to serve God's purposes, not his own.
      i. This important trait helped make David a man after God's own heart.
   C. If you live a self-centered life, you will never be a person after God's own heart.
   D. If you are all wrapped up in yourself, you make a very small package!

II. Even when Absalom revolted against him, David's heart was to serve the Lord.
   A. David had to flee for his life from Jerusalem, or he would have been trapped there and killed by Absalom (2 Sam. 15:13-14).
   B. While leaving with those still loyal to him…

…the king said unto Zadok [the priest], Carry back the ark of God into the city: if I shall find favour in the eyes of the Lord, he will bring me again, and show me both it, and his habitation: [26] But if he thus say, I have no delight in thee; behold, here am I, let him do to me as seemeth good unto him.

2 SAMUEL 15:25-26, BRACKETS MINE

   C. What a revelation into David's heart.
      i. When the Ark—which would have given him a great advantage—was offered to go with him, David said, "No. Take the Ark back to its place in the tabernacle. If God is pleased to return me as king over Israel, then I'll come back to it. But if the Lord is through with me, then let Him do what He wants."
   D. Although he was king, it wasn't for his ego or how it would benefit him; it was to serve the Lord and the nation of Israel.

III. There are so many ways you are all tempted to exalt yourself in everyday situations.
   A. If you can overcome in the small things, then you'll be able to handle the big temptations when they come.
   B. All of our ministry expansion, including this new building and the multiplying of Bible colleges all around the world, isn't about me.
   C. What's important is getting the Word out about God's unconditional love, and the balance of grace and faith.

A PURPOSE BIGGER THAN YOURSELF

- D. These truths I'm sharing about David have become real to me and have transformed my life, and I believe that the Lord wants them to become real to you and impact your life—that's what drives me!
- E. If I were in ministry just for my own personal benefit, I would have quit a long time ago.
    - i. We've lived through decades of hardships and trials.
- F. But it's about serving the Lord and accomplishing His goals.

IV. When it was literally his life on the line, his kingdom on the line, or his legacy on the line, what mattered to David was serving God.
- A. Have you been accepting responsibility for your actions, or do you still shift the blame?
- B. If you've been guilty of these things I've been talking about, you can repent.
- C. It's God's power that changes your heart, but it's your choice whether that power functions or not.
- D. You must stop exalting yourself and living by your own self-will.
- E. It starts with a decision, but you have to walk it out.

V. The contrasts between these three kings really brings out and magnifies what made David a man after God's own heart and how you and I can become people after God's own heart today.
- A. You choose what your heart is going to be like.
- B. Whatever your heart is like right now is the result of the choices you have made in the past.
- C. You can start making choices today that will soften and sensitize your heart toward God.

ANDREW'S RECOMMENDATIONS FOR FURTHER STUDY

Again, I refer you to my booklet entitled *Self-Centeredness: The Source of All Grief*. This book goes into much more detail about this. I encourage you to get it!

Also, my book entitled *Hardness of Heart* would go right along with this. It will instruct you on how to cultivate and keep a sensitive heart toward the Lord.

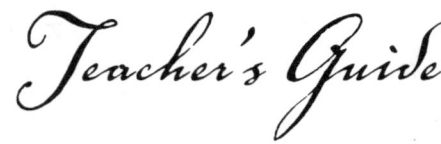

1. David was a man after God's own heart because of the attitude of his heart. He had a cause that was bigger than himself. David knew he was where he was to serve God's purposes, not his own. This important trait helped make David a man after God's own heart. If we live self-centered lives, we will never be people after God's own heart. If we are all wrapped up in ourselves, we make very small packages!

1a. *Discussion question:* Identify a cause in your life that is bigger than yourself. How did this become your cause?
   <u>Discussion question</u>

1b. True or false: If you live a self-centered life, you're still a person after God's own heart.
   <u>False</u>

A PURPOSE BIGGER THAN YOURSELF

2. Even when Absalom revolted against him, David's heart was to serve the Lord. David had to flee for his life from Jerusalem, or he would have been trapped there and killed by Absalom (2 Sam. 15:13-14). While leaving with those still loyal to him…

> …*the king said unto Zadok* [the priest], *Carry back the ark of God into the city: if I shall find favour in the eyes of the LORD, he will bring me again, and show me both it, and his habitation: [26] But if he thus say, I have no delight in thee; behold, here am I, let him do to me as seemeth good unto him.*
>
> 2 SAMUEL 15:25-26, BRACKETS MINE

What a revelation into David's heart. When the Ark—which would have given him a great advantage—was offered to go with him, David said, "No. Take the Ark back to its place in the tabernacle. If God is pleased to return me as king over Israel, then I'll come back to it. But if the Lord is through with me, then let Him do what He wants." Although he was king, it wasn't for his ego or how it would benefit him; it was to serve the Lord and the nation of Israel.

2a. When Absalom revolted, David had to _____.
    A. Flee for his life
    B. Stay trapped in Jerusalem
    C. Hide in a barrel
    D. Act like he was crazy
    E. Plot a counterattack
    A. Flee for his life

2b. Why didn't David want to take the Ark with him?
    A. He wasn't serving as king in order to feed his ego
    B. He did not want to use it for his own advantage
    C. He believed the Ark should stay in the tabernacle
    D. All of the above
    E. None of the above
    D. All of the above

2c. If God wasn't pleased with David, what did he want Him to do?
    A. Kill him
    B. Whatever seemed good to Him
    C. Nothing
    D. Replace him
    E. Give him something better to do
    B. Whatever seemed good to Him

3. There are so many ways we are tempted to exalt ourselves in everyday situations. If we can overcome in the small things, then we'll be able to handle the big temptations when they come. All of Andrew Wommack Ministries' expansion, including this new building and the multiplying of Bible colleges all around the world, isn't about Andrew. What's important is getting the Word out about God's unconditional love, and the balance of grace and faith. These truths Andrew is sharing about David have become real to him and have transformed his life, and he believes that the Lord wants them to become real to us and impact our lives—that's what drives him! If he were in ministry just for his own personal benefit, he would have quit a long time ago. He has lived through decades of hardships and trials. But it's about serving the Lord and accomplishing His goals.

3a. True or false: Only people who are wildly successful are tempted to exalt themselves.
   False
3b. Why does Andrew want the truths about David to become real to others?
   A. Because they transformed his life
   B. Because he believes the Lord wants them to impact your life
   C. Because he is driven by personal benefit
   D. A and B
   E. A and C
   D. A and B

4. When it was literally his life on the line, his kingdom on the line, or his legacy on the line, what mattered to David was serving God. Have we been accepting responsibility for our actions, or do we still shift the blame? If we've been guilty of these things Andrew has been talking about, we can repent. It's God's power that changes our hearts, but it's our choice whether that power functions or not. We must stop exalting ourselves and living by our own self-will. It starts with a decision, but we have to walk it out.

4a. What mattered to David?
   A. Serving dinner to others out of his great riches
   B. Staying alive and keeping his kingdom
   C. Having a spotless legacy
   D. Serving God
   E. Being appreciated
   D. Serving God

4b. In order to accept responsibility for your actions, you must do what?
   A. Assess where all the blame lies with all the people involved
   B. Feel guilty
   C. Shift the blame around to protect your reputation
   D. All of the above
   E. None of the above
   E. None of the above

4c. It's God's power that changes your heart, but _____.
   A. He doesn't mind you living in your own self-will
   B. It's your choice whether that power functions or not
   C. It's okay for you to keep exalting yourself a little
   D. As long as you confess your sin in public, you don't need to change
   E. You have to use it sparingly
   B. It's your choice whether that power functions or not

5. The contrasts between these three kings really brings out and magnifies what made David a man after God's own heart and how we can become people after God's own heart today. We choose what our hearts are going to be like. Whatever our hearts are like right now are the result of the choices we have made in the past. We can start making choices today that will soften and sensitize our hearts toward God.

5a. The contrast between these three kings magnifies how you can become _____.
   A. Cynical
   B. A king as well
   C. A person everyone likes
   D. A person after God's own heart
   E. Rich and famous
   D. A person after God's own heart

5b. You can start making choices today that will do what?
   Soften and sensitize your heart toward God

Discipleship Questions

1. *Discussion question:* Identify a cause in your life that is bigger than yourself. How did this become your cause?
   _____
   _____
   _____

2. True or false: If you live a self-centered life, you're still a person after God's own heart.

3. When Absalom revolted, David had to _____.
   A. Flee for his life
   B. Stay trapped in Jerusalem
   C. Hide in a barrel
   D. Act like he was crazy
   E. Plot a counterattack

4. Why didn't David want to take the Ark with him?
   A. He wasn't serving as king in order to feed his ego
   B. He did not want to use it for his own advantage
   C. He believed the Ark should stay in the tabernacle
   D. All of the above
   E. None of the above

5. If God wasn't pleased with David, what did he want Him to do?
   A. Kill him
   B. Whatever seemed good to Him
   C. Nothing
   D. Replace him
   E. Give him something better to do

6. True or false: Only people who are wildly successful are tempted to exalt themselves.

LESSONS FROM DAVID

7. Why does Andrew want the truths about David to become real to others?
   A. Because they transformed his life
   B. Because he believes the Lord wants them to impact your life
   C. Because he is driven by personal benefit
   D. A and B
   E. A and C

8. What mattered to David?
   A. Serving dinner to others out of his great riches
   B. Staying alive and keeping his kingdom
   C. Having a spotless legacy
   D. Serving God
   E. Being appreciated

9. In order to accept responsibility for your actions, you must do what?
   A. Assess where all the blame lies with all the people involved
   B. Feel guilty
   C. Shift the blame around to protect your reputation
   D. All of the above
   E. None of the above

10. It's God's power that changes your heart, but _____.
    A. He doesn't mind you living in your own self-will
    B. It's your choice whether that power functions or not
    C. It's okay for you to keep exalting yourself a little
    D. As long as you confess your sin in public, you don't need to change
    E. You have to use it sparingly

11. The contrast between these three kings magnifies how you can become _____.
    A. Cynical
    B. A king as well
    C. A person everyone likes
    D. A person after God's own heart
    E. Rich and famous

12. You can start making choices today that will do what?
    _____
    _____
    _____
    _____

A PURPOSE BIGGER THAN YOURSELF

Answer Key

1. *Discussion question*
2. False
3. A. Flee for his life
4. D. All of the above
5. B. Whatever seemed good to Him
6. False
7. D. A and B
8. D. Serving God
9. E. None of the above
10. B. It's your choice whether that power functions or not
11. D. A person after God's own heart
12. Soften and sensitize your heart toward God

LESSONS FROM DAVID

Scriptures

2 SAMUEL 15:6

And on this manner did Absalom to all Israel that came to the king for judgment: so Absalom stole the hearts of the men of Israel.

2 SAMUEL 15:13-14

And there came a messenger to David, saying, The hearts of the men of Israel are after Absalom. [14] And David said unto all his servants that were with him at Jerusalem, Arise, and let us flee; for we shall not else escape from Absalom: make speed to depart, lest he overtake us suddenly, and bring evil upon us, and smite the city with the edge of the sword.

2 SAMUEL 15:25-26

The king said unto Zadok, Carry back the ark of God into the city: if I shall find favour in the eyes of the Lord, he will bring me again, and show me both it, and his habitation: [26] But if he thus say, I have no delight in thee; behold, here am I, let him do to me as seemeth good unto him.

Follow God's Order

The Ark of the Covenant was made in Moses' day, approximately 400 years before David's story. By the time David was king, it had been sitting for years in Abinadab's house, in Kirjathjearim (1 Sam. 7:1), or what is called Gibeah (2 Sam. 6:3).

After David was king, he intended to bring the Ark of the Covenant to Jerusalem, the city he had chosen as his royal city and residence. The Ark symbolized God's presence, and it didn't seem good to him not to have it in Jerusalem (1 Chr. 13:2-3). So, he had the Ark placed on a cart that was pulled by oxen, and they started for Jerusalem. It was a great company of people, and they were rejoicing and praising God with instruments. But while they were on the way, something terrible happened—

> *And when they came to Nachon's threshingfloor, Uzzah put forth his hand to the ark of God, and took hold of it; for the oxen shook it. [7] And the anger of the LORD was kindled against Uzzah; and God smote him there for his error; and there he died by the ark of God.*
>
> 2 SAMUEL 6:6-7

This judgment upon Uzzah looks harsh, and the Scripture says, *"David was displeased, because the LORD had made a breach upon Uzzah"* (2 Sam. 6:8a). You might be able to identify with David here. I know many people who feel like God failed them, and they are mad at Him or, at the least, "displeased" as David was.

But God is never wrong. There was a reason for what happened. David didn't know what it was at the time, but he later came to realize he, not God, had missed it. We should learn a lesson from David here. From our point of view, it sometimes looks like God's promises aren't true, but that's never the case. Whether we know the reason or not, there was something the Lord told us to do that we failed to do if some of His promises didn't come to pass. Never forget that.

David didn't realize it, but there was a prescribed order as to how the Ark was supposed to be approached and handled (Num. 4:15). It had to be kept behind a veil in a place called the holy of holies, which was in the tabernacle. And on either side of the mercy seat of the Ark were two gold cherubims—warrior angels. They were there as a symbol to let people know that angels kept people from the presence of God. The meaning was that there was a separation between a holy God and unholy man.

Only the high priest could go in to where the Ark was, and he could only do that once a year to make atonement for the people's sins and for his own (Lev. 16:34). And if he didn't do everything just right in

---

LESSONS FROM DAVID

there, God would smite him. A first-century historian named Josephus recorded that they actually had a rope tied around the high priest's ankle, with the end of it trailing out beyond the veil, so that if he was struck dead, they could drag him out. They certainly couldn't go in after him to get him—they'd be struck dead too!

Now, later, when Jesus made atonement for our sins, this veil separating man from the Ark was rent in two (Matt. 27:51). We now have direct access to God! But in the Old Testament, this separation between a holy God and unholy man had to be enforced. People couldn't just approach God. None of us are worthy, as the Scripture says, *"All have sinned, and come short of the glory of God"* (Rom. 3:23).

I tell you, there are a lot of people today who don't understand and appreciate these things, and they talk about God in a way that doesn't reverence Him. They think God is love (1 John 4:8) and therefore God's just going to accept them. But God is a holy God, too, and the reason you have access to God today is because a price was paid. The Scripture says that *"the wages of sin is death"* (Rom. 6:23a). A price had to be paid, and before that price was paid, man could not just come into the presence of God.

THERE IS A PRESCRIBED ORDER

God had specific instructions about how to handle the Ark of the Covenant. It was to be carried between two poles by the Levites so that it would be supported properly and couldn't fall (Ex. 25:12-15 and Num. 4). This also kept it out of reach so no one could bump into it and bring judgment on themselves. But David was bringing it to Jerusalem on a cart that could easily bounce and tip over. And, sure enough, that's exactly what happened: The oxen stumbled, and the Ark was about to fall over. Then Uzzah, trying to brace it, reached out and touched it, totally violating God's prescribed order. So, God struck him dead.

See, sin's price had not yet been paid. No one could touch the presence of God and get away with it. However, David got very upset at this. His intentions were good. The Lord could have adjusted to what he wanted. But that's not how it works. We have to conform our actions to God and not the other way around.

Likewise, we sometimes think the Lord is too bound to His word. Our intentions are good, so we think the Lord should just go ahead and perform our every wish even though we are full of doubt or fear or bitterness or whatever. The temptation is to blame God. But the next verse says,

> *And David was afraid of the Lord that day, and said, How shall the ark of the Lord come to me?*
>
> 2 SAMUEL 6:9

FOLLOW GOD'S ORDER

David humbled himself before the Lord. That's one of the qualities that made him a man after God's own heart (1 Sam. 13:14). Instead of being mad, David feared the Lord. David quickly realized there's only one God and he wasn't Him. That's a very wise thing to do when it looks like God's not coming through for us. We should humble ourselves and proclaim God's faithfulness, even when it doesn't look like that to us.

David then had the Ark moved to Obededom's house. After three months, he was told that Obededom was being blessed because of the Ark, and David once again wanted to bring it to Jerusalem. He said,

> *None ought to carry the ark of God but the Levites: for them hath the LORD chosen to carry the ark of God, and to minister unto him for ever.*
>
> 1 CHRONICLES 15:2

This indicates that David had finally gone back and asked God, "What happened with Uzzah? Why didn't this work?" He went back to God's Word and found the proper way to carry the Ark. David revealed to the Levites what God told him:

> *Ye are the chief of the fathers of the Levites: sanctify yourselves, both ye and your brethren, that ye may bring up the ark of the LORD God of Israel unto the place that I have prepared for it. [13] For because ye did it not at the first, the LORD our God made a breach upon us, for that we sought him not after the due order.*
>
> 1 CHRONICLES 15:12-13

Uzzah died because David didn't follow the prescribed order. He hadn't sought the Lord the first time about how to handle the Ark. There are a lot of applications I can make from this, but one of them is that many people, even so-called Christians, say, "It doesn't matter how you seek the Lord. You can be a Buddhist, a Hindu, a Muslim, or whatever. There's only one God, but there are many paths that lead to Him. Just as long as you believe in some divine being and as long as you do your best, that's good enough." Boy, if you are paying attention to this example from David's life, you can see that there *is* a proper order to seeking the Lord. David desired a good end, but because he didn't do it the proper way, a man died needlessly.

I have talked to many people who have had this attitude that *It doesn't matter the way you get there, just as long as you believe there's a God. I believe that God is a good God, so He's going to accept you regardless of which way you choose.* But that's not right. There *is* a right way and a wrong way to relate to God.

Acts 4:12 says,

Neither is there salvation in any other: for there is no other name under heaven given among men, whereby we must be saved.

In John 14:6, Jesus said,

I am the way, the truth, and the life: no man cometh unto the Father, but by me.

JUST ASK UZZAH!

However, most people do not let the Bible get in the way of what they believe. But I'm telling you, if you're going to really connect with the Lord, the Bible is the instruction manual. It is God telling you how you are to relate to Him, and you have to do it according to the pattern He gives. That's really simple, but I guarantee you, there are a lot of people today who have accepted the mindset that they can relate to God any way they want.

That's what David started off thinking. He wanted to do something good, but he thought, *It doesn't really matter whether we follow the instructions of the Word of God. A cart can travel faster than a man. It's going to be a long trip, and it'd be much easier for the oxen to carry the Ark than for people to carry it.* But quick and easy isn't always the best way. The Bible prescribes the way to do things. Just ask Uzzah! I'm telling you, you need to accept the Word of God and recognize that there's a reason He gives the instructions He gives.

David finally saw that and did it the way God told him, so the Scripture goes on to say,

So David went and brought up the ark of God from the house of Obededom into the city of David with gladness. [13] And it was so, that when they that bare the ark of the LORD had gone six paces, he sacrificed oxen and fatlings. [14] And David danced before the LORD with all his might; and David was girded with a linen ephod. [15] So David and all the house of Israel brought up the ark of the LORD with shouting, and with the sound of the trumpet.
2 SAMUEL 6:12B-15

David went back to praising God! He didn't stop worshiping because of this incident with Uzzah. Things just work out when you do it God's way. This is a major lesson to learn from the life of David. Do it God's way—the first time—and you'll avoid unnecessary problems.

Outline

I. After David was king, he intended to bring the Ark of the Covenant to Jerusalem (1 Sam. 7:1 and 2 Sam. 6:3), the city he had chosen as his royal city and residence.
   A. The Ark symbolized God's presence, and it didn't seem good to him not to have it in Jerusalem (1 Chr. 13:2-3).
   B. So, he had the Ark placed on a cart that was pulled by oxen, and they started for Jerusalem.
   C. But while they were on the way, something terrible happened—

And when they came to Nachon's threshingfloor, Uzzah put forth his hand to the ark of God, and took hold of it; for the oxen shook it. [7] And the anger of the LORD was kindled against Uzzah; and God smote him there for his error; and there he died by the ark of God.

2 SAMUEL 6:6-7

   D. This judgment upon Uzzah looks harsh, and the Scripture says, *"David was displeased, because the LORD had made a breach upon Uzzah"* (2 Sam. 6:8a).
   E. We might be able to identify with David here, but God is never wrong—there was a reason for what happened.
   F. From our point of view, it sometimes looks like God's promises aren't true, but that's never the case.
   G. Whether we know the reason or not, there was something the Lord told us to do that we failed to do if some of His promises didn't come to pass.
   H. David didn't realize it, but there was a prescribed order as to how the Ark was supposed to be approached and handled (Num. 4:15).
   I. In the Old Testament, this separation between a holy God and unholy man had to be enforced—people couldn't just approach God.

All have sinned, and come short of the glory of God.

ROMANS 3:23

   J. There are a lot of people today who don't understand and appreciate these things, and they think God is love (1 John 4:8) and therefore God's just going to accept them.
   K. But God is a holy God, too, and the reason you have access to God today is because a price was paid.
   L. A price had to be paid (Rom. 6:23a), and before that price was paid, man could not just come into the presence of God.

LESSONS FROM DAVID

II. God had specific instructions about how to handle the Ark of the Covenant.
   A. It was to be carried between two poles by the Levites so that it would be supported properly and couldn't fall (Ex. 25:12-15 and Num. 4); this also kept it out of reach so no one could bump into it and bring judgment on themselves.
   B. But David was bringing it to Jerusalem on a cart that could easily bounce and tip over, and sure enough, that's exactly what happened: The oxen stumbled, and the Ark was about to fall over.
   C. Then Uzzah, trying to brace it, reached out and touched it, totally violating God's prescribed order, so God struck him dead.
   D. Sin's price had not yet been paid—no one could touch the presence of God and get away with it.
   E. However, David got very upset at this.
   F. His intentions were good; the Lord could have adjusted to what he wanted.
   G. But that's not how it works.
   H. We have to conform our actions to God and not the other way around.

III. Likewise, we sometimes think the Lord is too bound to His word.
   A. Our intentions are good, so we think the Lord should just go ahead and perform our every wish even though we are full of doubt or fear or bitterness or whatever.
   B. The temptation is to blame God, but the Word says,

And David was afraid of the LORD that day, and said, How shall the ark of the LORD come to me?

2 SAMUEL 6:9

   C. Instead of being mad, David feared the Lord.
   D. That's a very wise thing to do when it looks like God's not coming through for us—we should humble ourselves and proclaim God's faithfulness, even when it doesn't look like that to us.
   E. After three months, David once again wanted to bring it to Jerusalem.

Then David said, None ought to carry the ark of God but the Levites: for them hath the LORD chosen to carry the ark of God, and to minister unto him for ever.

1 CHRONICLES 15:2

   F. This indicates that David had finally gone back to God's Word and found the proper way to carry the Ark.

And [David] said unto them, Ye are the chief of the fathers of the Levites: sanctify yourselves, both ye and your brethren, that ye may bring up the ark of the LORD God of Israel unto the place that I have prepared for it. [13] For because ye did it not at the first, the LORD our God made a breach upon us, for that we sought him not after the due order.

1 CHRONICLES 15:12-13, BRACKETS MINE

    G. Uzzah died because David didn't follow the prescribed order—he hadn't sought the Lord the first time about how to handle the Ark.

    H. If we are paying attention to this example from David's life, we can see that there *is* a proper order to seeking the Lord.

    I. There *is* a right way and a wrong way to relate to God.

    J. Acts 4:12 says,

Neither is there salvation in any other: for there is no other name under heaven given among men, whereby we must be saved.

    K. In John 14:6, Jesus said,

I am the way, the truth, and the life: no man cometh unto the Father, but by me.

IV. If you're going to really connect with the Lord, the Bible is the instruction manual.
    A. It is God telling you how you are to relate to Him, and you have to do it according to the pattern He gives.
    B. That's really simple, but there are a lot of people today who have accepted the mindset that they can relate to God any way they want.
    C. That's what David started off thinking.
    D. But what's quick and easy isn't always the best way.
    E. You need to accept the Word of God and recognize that there's a reason He gives the instructions He gives.
    F. David finally saw that and did it the way God told him, so the Scripture goes on to say,

So David went and brought up the ark of God from the house of Obededom into the city of David with gladness. [13] And it was so, that when they that bare the ark of the LORD had gone six paces, he sacrificed oxen and fatlings. [14] And David danced before the LORD with all his might; and David was girded with a linen ephod. [15] So David and all the house of Israel brought up the ark of the LORD with shouting, and with the sound of the trumpet.

2 SAMUEL 6:12B-15

    G. Things just work out when you do it God's way.

    H. This is a major lesson to learn from the life of David: Do it God's way—the first time—and you'll avoid unnecessary problems.

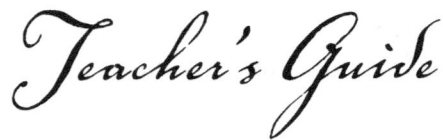

1. After David was king, he intended to bring the Ark of the Covenant to Jerusalem (1 Sam. 7:1 and 2 Sam. 6:3), the city he had chosen as his royal city and residence. The Ark symbolized God's presence, and it didn't seem good to him not to have it in Jerusalem (1 Chr. 13:2-3). So, he had the Ark placed on a cart that was pulled by oxen, and they started for Jerusalem. But while they were on the way, something terrible happened—

> *And when they came to Nachon's threshingfloor, Uzzah put forth his hand to the ark of God, and took hold of it; for the oxen shook it. [7] And the anger of the LORD was kindled against Uzzah; and God smote him there for his error; and there he died by the ark of God.*
>
> 2 SAMUEL 6:6-7

This judgment upon Uzzah looks harsh, and the Scripture says, *"David was displeased, because the LORD had made a breach upon Uzzah"* (2 Sam. 6:8a). We might be able to identify with David here, but God is never wrong—there was a reason for what happened. From our point of view, it sometimes looks like God's promises aren't true, but that's never the case. Whether we know the reason or not, there was something the Lord told us to do that we failed to do if some of His promises didn't come to pass. David didn't realize it, but there was a prescribed order as to how the Ark was supposed to be approached and handled (Num. 4:15). In the Old Testament, this separation between a holy God and unholy man had to be enforced—people couldn't just approach God.

> *All have sinned, and come short of the glory of God.*
>
> ROMANS 3:23

There are a lot of people today who don't understand and appreciate these things, and they think God is love (1 John 4:8) and therefore God's just going to accept them. But God is a holy God, too, and the reason we have access to God today is because a price was paid. A price had to be paid (Rom. 6:23a), and before that price was paid, man could not just come into the presence of God.

1a. How did David first try to bring the Ark to Jerusalem?
   On a cart pulled by oxen
1b. According to 2 Samuel 6:6-7, what happened to Uzzah?
   Uzzah touched the Ark, to steady it as it was shaken by the oxen, and God killed him for his error
1c. *Discussion question:* What are your thoughts regarding this judgment on Uzzah?
   Discussion question
1d. *Discussion question:* Discuss the difference between how people approached God in the Old Testament and how they can approach him now that the price has been paid.
   Discussion question

FOLLOW GOD'S ORDER

2. God had specific instructions about how to handle the Ark of the Covenant. It was to be carried between two poles by the Levites so that it would be supported properly and couldn't fall (Ex. 25:12-15 and Num. 4); this also kept it out of reach so no one could bump into it and bring judgment on themselves. But David was bringing it to Jerusalem on a cart that could easily bounce and tip over, and sure enough, that's exactly what happened: The oxen stumbled, and the Ark was about to fall over. Then Uzzah, trying to brace it, reached out and touched it, totally violating God's prescribed order, so God struck him dead. Sin's price had not yet been paid—no one could touch the presence of God and get away with it. However, David got very upset at this. His intentions were good; the Lord could have adjusted to what he wanted. But that's not how it works. We have to conform our actions to God and not the other way around.

2a. *Discussion question:* How would things have been different if they had followed God's specific instructions for carrying the Ark?
Discussion question
2b. Why did David get upset at Uzzah's death?
His intentions were good; the Lord could have adjusted to what he wanted
2c. You have to conform your _____ to God and _____ the other way around.
Actions / not

3. Likewise, we sometimes think the Lord is too bound to His word. Our intentions are good, so we think the Lord should just go ahead and perform our every wish even though we are full of doubt or fear or bitterness or whatever. The temptation is to blame God, but the Word says,

> *And David was afraid of the L*ORD *that day, and said, How shall the ark of the L*ORD *come to me?*
> 2 SAMUEL 6:9

Instead of being mad, David feared the Lord. That's a very wise thing to do when it looks like God's not coming through for us—we should humble ourselves and proclaim God's faithfulness, even when it doesn't look like that to us. After three months, David once again wanted to bring it to Jerusalem.

> *Then David said, None ought to carry the ark of God but the Levites: for them hath the L*ORD *chosen to carry the ark of God, and to minister unto him for ever.*
> 1 CHRONICLES 15:2

This indicates that David had finally gone back to God's Word and found the proper way to carry the Ark.

> *And* [David] *said unto them, Ye are the chief of the fathers of the Levites: sanctify yourselves, both ye and your brethren, that ye may bring up the ark of the L*ORD *God of Israel unto the place that I have prepared for it.* [13] *For because ye did it not at the first, the L*ORD *our God made a breach upon us, for that we sought him not after the due order.*
> 1 CHRONICLES 15:12-13, BRACKETS MINE

Uzzah died because David didn't follow the prescribed order—he hadn't sought the Lord the first time about how to handle the Ark. If we are paying attention to this example from David's life, we can see that there *is* a proper order to seeking the Lord. There *is* a right way and a wrong way to relate to God. Acts 4:12 says,

> *Neither is there salvation in any other: for there is no other name under heaven given among men, whereby we must be saved.*

In John 14:6, Jesus said,

> *I am the way, the truth, and the life: no man cometh unto the Father, but by me.*

3a. *Discussion question:* Why do people sometimes think that since their intentions are good, the Lord should just go ahead and perform their every wish?
   Discussion question

(continued on next page)

3b. Instead of being mad, what was David's reaction?
   A. He broke down crying
   B. He carried on as though nothing had happened
   C. He feared the Lord
   D. All of the above
   E. None of the above
   C. He feared the Lord
3c. What did David do when he again wanted to bring the Ark to Jerusalem?
   He went back to God's Word, found the proper way to carry the Ark, and followed the prescribed order
3d. True or false: There really is no proper order to seeking the Lord.
   False

4. If we're going to really connect with the Lord, the Bible is the instruction manual. It is God telling us how we are to relate to Him, and we have to do it according to the pattern He gives. That's really simple, but there are a lot of people today who have accepted the mindset that they can relate to God any way they want. That's what David started off thinking. But quick and easy isn't always the best way. We need to accept the Word of God and recognize that there's a reason He gives the instructions He gives. David finally saw that and did it the way God told him, so the Scripture goes on to say,

> So David went and brought up the ark of God from the house of Obededom into the city of David with gladness. [13] And it was so, that when they that bare the ark of the LORD had gone six paces, he sacrificed oxen and fatlings. [14] And David danced before the LORD with all his might; and David was girded with a linen ephod. [15] So David and all the house of Israel brought up the ark of the LORD with shouting, and with the sound of the trumpet.
> 2 SAMUEL 6:12B-15

Things just work out when you do it God's way. This is a major lesson to learn from the life of David: If we do it God's way—the first time—we'll avoid unnecessary problems.

4a. *Discussion question:* If you're going to really connect with the Lord, why is the Bible so important?
   Discussion question
4b. Do things just work out when you do it God's way?
   Yes
4c. Do it God's way—the _____ time—and you'll avoid _____ _____.
   First / unnecessary problems

LESSONS FROM DAVID

Discipleship Questions

1. How did David first try to bring the Ark to Jerusalem?

2. According to 2 Samuel 6:6-7, what happened to Uzzah?

3. *Discussion question*: What are your thoughts regarding this judgment on Uzzah?

4. *Discussion question*: Discuss the difference between how people approached God in the Old Testament and how they can approach Him now that the price has been paid.

5. *Discussion question*: How would things have been different if they had followed God's specific instructions for carrying the Ark?

6. Why did David get upset at Uzzah's death?

7. You have to conform your _____ to God and _____ the other way around.

FOLLOW GOD'S ORDER

8. *Discussion question*: Why do people sometimes think that since their intentions are good, the Lord should just go ahead and perform their every wish?
___
___
___

9. Instead of being mad, what was David's reaction?
   A. He broke down crying
   B. He carried on as though nothing had happened
   C. He feared the Lord
   D. All of the above
   E. None of the above

10. What did David do when he again wanted to bring the Ark to Jerusalem?
___
___
___

11. True or false: There really is no proper order to seeking the Lord.

12. *Discussion question*: If you're going to really connect with the Lord, why is the Bible so important?
___
___
___

13. Do things just work out when you do it God's way?
___
___
___

14. Do it God's way—the _____ time—and you'll avoid _____ _____.

LESSONS FROM DAVID

#

1. On a cart pulled by oxen
2. Uzzah touched the Ark, to steady it as it was shaken by the oxen, and God killed him for his error
3. *Discussion question*
4. *Discussion question*
5. *Discussion question*
6. His intentions were good; the Lord could have adjusted to what he wanted
7. Actions / not
8. *Discussion question*
9. C. He feared the Lord
10. He went back to God's Word, found the proper way to carry the Ark, and followed the prescribed order
11. False
12. *Discussion question*
13. Yes
14. First / unnecessary problems

FOLLOW GOD'S ORDER

Scriptures

1 SAMUEL 7:1
And the men of Kirjathjearim came, and fetched up the ark of the Lord, and brought it into the house of Abinadab in the hill, and sanctified Eleazar his son to keep the ark of the Lord.

2 SAMUEL 6:3
And they set the ark of God upon a new cart, and brought it out of the house of Abinadab that was in Gibeah: and Uzzah and Ahio, the sons of Abinadab, drave the new cart.

1 CHRONICLES 13:2-3
And David said unto all the congregation of Israel, If it seem good unto you, and that it be of the Lord our God, let us send abroad unto our brethren every where, that are left in all the land of Israel, and with them also to the priests and Levites which are in their cities and suburbs, that they may gather themselves unto us: [3] And let us bring again the ark of our God to us: for we enquired not at it in the days of Saul.

2 SAMUEL 6:6-9
And when they came to Nachon's threshingfloor, Uzzah put forth his hand to the ark of God, and took hold of it; for the oxen shook it. [7] And the anger of the Lord was kindled against Uzzah; and God smote him there for his error; and there he died by the ark of God. [8] And David was displeased, because the Lord had made a breach upon Uzzah: and he called the name of the place Perezuzzah to this day. [9] And David was afraid of the Lord that day, and said, How shall the ark of the Lord come to me?

LEVITICUS 16:34
And this shall be an everlasting statute unto you, to make an atonement for the children of Israel for all their sins once a year. And he did as the Lord commanded Moses.

ROMANS 3:23
For all have sinned, and come short of the glory of God.

ROMANS 6:23
For the wages of sin is death; but the gift of God is eternal life through Jesus Christ our Lord.

EXODUS 25:12-15

And thou shalt cast four rings of gold for it, and put them in the four corners thereof; and two rings shall be in the one side of it, and two rings in the other side of it. [13] And thou shalt make staves of shittim wood, and overlay them with gold. [14] And thou shalt put the staves into the rings by the sides of the ark, that the ark may be borne with them. [15] The staves shall be in the rings of the ark: they shall not be taken from it.

1 CHRONICLES 15:2

Then David said, None ought to carry the ark of God but the Levites: for them hath the Lord chosen to carry the ark of God, and to minister unto him for ever.

1 CHRONICLES 15:12-13

And said unto them, Ye are the chief of the fathers of the Levites: sanctify yourselves, both ye and your brethren, that ye may bring up the ark of the Lord God of Israel unto the place that I have prepared for it. [13] For because ye did it not at the first, the Lord our God made a breach upon us, for that we sought him not after the due order.

2 SAMUEL 6:12-15

And it was told king David, saying, The Lord hath blessed the house of Obededom, and all that pertaineth unto him, because of the ark of God. So David went and brought up the ark of God from the house of Obededom into the city of David with gladness. [13] And it was so, that when they that bare the ark of the Lord had gone six paces, he sacrificed oxen and fatlings. [14] And David danced before the Lord with all his might; and David was girded with a linen ephod. [15] So David and all the house of Israel brought up the ark of the Lord with shouting, and with the sound of the trumpet.

FOLLOW GOD'S ORDER

Follow God's Order

And as the ark of the LORD came into the city of David, Michal Saul's daughter looked through a window, and saw king David leaping and dancing before the LORD; and she despised him in her heart.

2 SAMUEL 6:16

Michal was David's wife. She had been given to him by Saul, the previous king who was her father. Saul had given Michal to David to be a snare to him (1 Sam. 18:21), implying that this woman probably had some really bad attitudes. Saul saw giving her to him as a punishment. But the Scripture says Michal loved David (1 Sam. 18:20), and she saved his life from her father (1 Sam. 19:11-18). Then Saul took her and gave her to be the wife of Phalti (1 Sam. 25:44). Women during those days were treated as property and had no choice in matters like this.

When David became king, probably thirteen or fourteen years later, he took Michal from her husband (2 Sam. 3:14-15). The Scriptures don't give us all the details, but it's obvious she was hurt by this. Here was a king's daughter—a princess—who had been married to a man she loved and then ripped from him and given to another man. By the time David took her back, she had probably adjusted and even learned to love Phalti. In other words, she was over David. She probably wondered, *Why did you take me from my husband after it's been so long? Where were you when I was given to Phalti? Where have you been?* She might have even been jealous that David had since married and she had to share him with his other wives. She was used to having a husband only to herself.

This instance in 2 Samuel 6 makes it obvious that Michal was bitter over the abuse that had happened in her life. And when she saw David dancing and twirling around, she directed this bitterness at him, and the Scripture says *"she despised him in her heart."* She didn't wait for David to come to her. She was hot. She went out to meet him and began criticizing him, saying,

> *How glorious was the king of Israel to day, who uncovered himself to day in the eyes of the handmaids of his servants, as one of the vain fellows shamelessly uncovereth himself!*
>
> 2 SAMUEL 6:20B

This was totally sarcastic of her. She thought David was ruining the kingship. Her father had certainly never acted like David was acting. But the truth is, Saul would never have danced before the Lord like this because he was a man pleaser, not a God pleaser. David was a completely different king from Saul. What he was doing was for the Lord! Michal didn't recognize that.

When she said David shamelessly uncovered himself, she meant he uncovered himself in an improper way. It's possible that he took off an outer garment, but was totally clothed, while he was dancing. In his exuberance, he might have exposed something he wasn't supposed to reveal, but she was unjustly criticizing him. And here is his response:

> It was before the LORD, which chose me before thy father, and before all his house, to appoint me ruler over the people of the LORD, over Israel: therefore will I play before the LORD. [22] And I will yet be more vile than thus, and will be base in mine own sight: and of the maidservants which thou hast spoken of, of them shall I be had in honour.
> 2 SAMUEL 6:21-22

Regardless of the injustices done to her, she didn't get a pass for criticizing David. He was the one who was worshiping God! She totally missed praising God and was blinded by her bitterness.

This is one of the things that made David a man after God's own heart: He loved God and wasn't ashamed to show his commitment and affection to Him publicly. He basically said, "I was worshiping God, and frankly, I don't give a rip what people think. I was doing this for the Lord, and I'll become even more undignified than this!" Contrary to what Michal thought, he *had* learned to do things the prescribed way. He wasn't going to stop worshiping God for anything! He referred to how God had blessed him, and he was not ashamed to show his love, his commitment, and his worship to God in front of people. This has direct applications to our lives.

If you want to be a man or a woman after God's own heart, then you need to learn that your love and commitment to God ought to trump any other relationship. You shouldn't be a man pleaser, no matter what. David was thankful that God had allowed him to take the Ark—literally, His presence—into Jerusalem. Everybody should have been shouting about this!

STAND UP FOR THE LORD

In John 5:44, Jesus said,

> How can ye believe, which receive honour one of another, and seek not the honour that cometh from God only?

People act like they have never read this. Most don't realize that being a man pleaser stops them from believing God. They are intimidated by what other people think. They are afraid to stand up for what His Word says. And you know what? They are exactly opposite of how David was here. I'm not saying you

---

FOLLOW GOD'S ORDER

should attack people who are ungodly. You should love them. But you should not be ashamed to stand up for the Lord and His standards.

David didn't care that he was thought of as a fool for showing that kind of affection and commitment to God. But he turned the tables on this criticism. This is one of the lessons you can learn from him: Instead of you being intimidated by the people who don't love God, whose standards are totally wrong, instead of you feeling strange, they ought to feel strange. You're not the weird one, amen? They are. You're the one who loves God and believes that He's alive and that miracles happen. That's normal. You shouldn't be the one who feels awkward and out of place!

Look at what happened to David and Michal after this:

> *Therefore Michal the daughter of Saul had no child unto the day of her death.*
> 2 SAMUEL 6:23

In other words, that was the end of her relationship with David. She let this bitterness ruin her relationship with the man after God's own heart. She'd had some bad things happen to her, but she vented this bitterness, and it cost her dearly for the rest of her life.

Here's another lesson that you can learn from this situation: You may have had bad things happen to you, but you have a choice as to whether you'll become bitter or better. If you allow this bitterness to fester, the Scripture says that a root of bitterness will spring up and defile the whole body and many people will be defiled because of it (Heb. 12:15). You need to run to the Lord and let Him take care of this bitterness you might have. You don't need to spew it out, because it'll keep you from being fruitful the rest of your life. There are a lot of things to learn here, but you don't have to learn them from your own hard knocks—the Bible is full of examples like this one, to show you how to do things and be who He's called you to be.

Outline

V. Michal was David's wife.

*And as the ark of the L*ORD *came into the city of David, Michal Saul's daughter looked through a window, and saw king David leaping and dancing before the L*ORD*; and she despised him in her heart.*

2 SAMUEL 6:16

A. This instance in 2 Samuel 6 makes it obvious that Michal was bitter over the abuse that had happened in her life (see 1 Sam. 18:20-21, 19:11-18, 25:44; and 2 Sam. 3:14-15).
B. And when she saw David dancing and twirling around, she directed this bitterness at him, and the Scripture says *"she despised him in her heart."*
C. She went out to meet him and began criticizing him, saying,

How glorious was the king of Israel to day, who uncovered himself to day in the eyes of the handmaids of his servants, as one of the vain fellows shamelessly uncovereth himself!

2 SAMUEL 6:20B

D. She thought David was ruining the kingship—her father had certainly never acted like David was acting.
E. But the truth is, Saul would never have danced before the Lord like this because he was a man pleaser, not a God pleaser.
F. David was a completely different king from Saul.
G. Michal didn't recognize that what David was doing was for the Lord.
H. When she said David shamelessly uncovered himself, she meant he uncovered himself in an improper way.
I. Here is his response to her unjust criticism:

*It was before the L*ORD*, which chose me before thy father, and before all his house, to appoint me ruler over the people of the L*ORD*, over Israel: therefore will I play before the L*ORD*. [22] And I will yet be more vile than thus, and will be base in mine own sight: and of the maidservants which thou hast spoken of, of them shall I be had in honour.*

2 SAMUEL 6:21-22

J. In his exuberance, he might have exposed something he wasn't supposed to reveal, but she was unjustly criticizing him.

FOLLOW GOD'S ORDER

VI. This is one of the things that made David a man after God's own heart: He loved God and wasn't ashamed to show his commitment and affection to Him publicly.
- A. Contrary to what Michal thought, he *had* learned to do things the prescribed way.
- B. He wasn't going to stop worshiping God for anything!
- C. He referred to how God had blessed him, and he was not ashamed to show his love, his commitment, and his worship to God in front of people.
- D. If you want to be a man or a woman after God's own heart, then you need to learn that your love and commitment to God ought to trump any other relationship.
- E. You shouldn't be a man pleaser, no matter what.

VII. In John 5:44, Jesus said,

How can ye believe, which receive honour one of another, and seek not the honour that cometh from God only?

- A. Most don't realize that being a man pleaser stops them from believing God.
- B. They are intimidated by what other people think; they are afraid to stand up for what His Word says.
- C. They are exactly opposite of how David was here.
- D. You should not be ashamed to stand up for the Lord and His standards.
- E. Instead of you being intimidated by the people who don't love God, whose standards are totally wrong, instead of you feeling strange, they ought to feel strange.
- F. Look at what happened to David and Michal after this:

Therefore Michal the daughter of Saul had no child unto the day of her death.
2 SAMUEL 6:23

- G. In other words, that was the end of her relationship with David; she let this bitterness ruin her relationship with the man after God's own heart.
- H. You may have had bad things happen to you, but you have a choice as to whether you'll become bitter or better.
- I. If you allow this bitterness to fester, the Scripture says that a root of bitterness will spring up and defile the whole body and many people will be defiled because of it (Heb. 12:15).
- J. You need to run to the Lord and let Him take care of this bitterness you might have.
- K. You don't have to learn things from your own hard knocks—the Bible is full of examples like this one, to show you how to do things and be who He's called you to be.

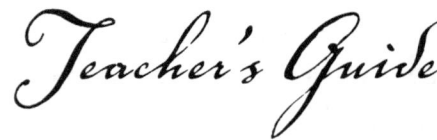

5. Michal was David's wife.

> *And as the ark of the L*ORD *came into the city of David, Michal Saul's daughter looked through a window, and saw king David leaping and dancing before the L*ORD*; and she despised him in her heart.*
>
> 2 SAMUEL 6:16

This instance in 2 Samuel 6 makes it obvious that Michal was bitter over the abuse that had happened in her life (see 1 Sam. 18:20-21, 19:11-18, 25:44; and 2 Sam. 3:14-15). And when she saw David dancing and twirling around, she directed this bitterness at him, and the Scripture says *"she despised him in her heart."* She went out to meet him and began criticizing him, saying,

> *How glorious was the king of Israel to day, who uncovered himself to day in the eyes of the handmaids of his servants, as one of the vain fellows shamelessly uncovereth himself!*
>
> 2 SAMUEL 6:20B

She thought David was ruining the kingship—her father had certainly never acted like David was acting. But the truth is, Saul would never have danced before the Lord like this because he was a man pleaser, not a God pleaser. David was a completely different king from Saul. Michal didn't recognize that what David was doing was for the Lord. When she said David shamelessly uncovered himself, she meant he uncovered himself in an improper way. Here is his response to her unjust criticism:

> *It was before the L*ORD*, which chose me before thy father, and before all his house, to appoint me ruler over the people of the L*ORD*, over Israel: therefore will I play before the L*ORD*. [22] And I will yet be more vile than thus, and will be base in mine own sight: and of the maidservants which thou hast spoken of, of them shall I be had in honour.*
>
> 2 SAMUEL 6:21-22

In his exuberance, he might have exposed something he wasn't supposed to reveal, but she was unjustly criticizing him.

5a. What was Michal bitter about?
 The abuse that had happened in her life
5b. What did she do with that bitterness?
 She directed it at David
5c. *Discussion question:* What difference can being a man pleaser make, especially in worshiping the Lord?
 Discussion question
5d. *Discussion question:* Read David's response to Michal in 2 Samuel 6:21-22. What would your response be to criticism like Michal's? Would you respond as David did? Why or why not?
 Discussion question

FOLLOW GOD'S ORDER

6. This is one of the things that made David a man after God's own heart: He loved God and wasn't ashamed to show his commitment and affection to Him publicly. Contrary to what Michal thought, he *had* learned to do things the prescribed way. He wasn't going to stop worshiping God for anything! He referred to how God had blessed him, and he was not ashamed to show his love, his commitment, and his worship to God in front of people. If we want to be men or a women after God's own heart, then we need to learn that our love and commitment to God ought to trump any other relationship. We shouldn't be man pleasers, no matter what.

6a. What was one of the things that made David a man after God's own heart?
He loved God and wasn't ashamed to show his commitment and affection to Him publicly

6b. You shouldn't be a _____ _____, no matter what.
Man pleaser

7. In John 5:44, Jesus said,

    How can ye believe, which receive honour one of another, and seek not the honour that cometh from God only?

Most don't realize that being a man pleaser stops them from believing God. They are intimidated by what other people think; they are afraid to stand up for what His Word says. They are exactly opposite of how David was here. We should not be ashamed to stand up for the Lord and His standards. Instead of us being intimidated by the people who don't love God, whose standards are totally wrong, instead of us feeling strange, they ought to feel strange. Let's look at what happened to David and Michal after this:

Therefore Michal the daughter of Saul had no child unto the day of her death.
2 SAMUEL 6:23

In other words, that was the end of her relationship with David; she let this bitterness ruin her relationship with the man after God's own heart. We may have had bad things happen to us, but we have a choice as to whether we'll become bitter or better. If we allow this bitterness to fester, the Scripture says that a root of bitterness will spring up and defile the whole body and many people will be defiled because of it (Heb. 12:15). We need to run to the Lord and let Him take care of this bitterness we might have. We don't have to learn things from our own hard knocks—the Bible is full of examples like this one, to show us how to do things and be who He's called us to be.

7a. *Discussion question*: Why does being a man pleaser stop you from believing God?
    Discussion question
7b. What did Michal's bitterness bring about in her life (2 Sam. 6:23)?
    The end of her relationship with David, the man after God's own heart, and for the rest of her life, she had no children
7c. Do you have a choice as to whether you become bitter or better?
    Yes
7d. *Discussion question*: Discuss why bitterness can be so destructive.
    Discussion question
7e. What is the solution for bitterness?
    You need to run to the Lord and let Him take care of it

Discipleship Questions

15. What was Michal bitter about?

16. What did she do with that bitterness?

17. *Discussion question:* What difference can being a man pleaser make, especially in worshiping the Lord?

18. *Discussion question:* Read David's response to Michal in 2 Samuel 6:21-22. What would your response be to criticism like Michal's? Would you respond as David did? Why or why not?

19. What was one of the things that made David a man after God's own heart?

20. You shouldn't be a _____ _____, no matter what.

21. *Discussion question:* Why does being a man pleaser stop you from believing God?

22. What did Michal's bitterness bring about in her life (2 Sam. 6:23)?

23. Do you have a choice as to whether you become bitter or better?

24. *Discussion question:* Discuss why bitterness can be so destructive.

25. What is the solution for bitterness?

Answer Key

15. The abuse that had happened in her life
16. She directed it at David
17. *Discussion question*
18. *Discussion question*
19. He loved God and wasn't ashamed to show his commitment and affection to Him publicly
20. Man pleaser
21. *Discussion question*
22. The end of her relationship with David, the man after God's own heart, and for the rest of her life, she had no children
23. Yes
24. *Discussion question*
25. You need to run to the Lord and let Him take care of it

Scriptures

2 SAMUEL 6:16

And as the ark of the LORD came into the city of David, Michal Saul's daughter looked through a window, and saw king David leaping and dancing before the LORD; and she despised him in her heart.

1 SAMUEL 18:20-21

And Michal Saul's daughter loved David: and they told Saul, and the thing pleased him. [21] And Saul said, I will give him her, that she may be a snare to him, and that the hand of the Philistines may be against him. Wherefore Saul said to David, Thou shalt this day be my son in law in the one of the twain.

1 SAMUEL 19:11-18

Saul also sent messengers unto David's house, to watch him, and to slay him in the morning: and Michal David's wife told him, saying, If thou save not thy life to night, to morrow thou shalt be slain. [12] So Michal let David down through a window: and he went, and fled, and escaped. [13] And Michal took an image, and laid it in the bed, and put a pillow of goats' hair for his bolster, and covered it with a cloth. [14] And when Saul sent messengers to take David, she said, He is sick. [15] And Saul sent the messengers again to see David, saying, Bring him up to me in the bed, that I may slay him. [16] And when the messengers were come in, behold, there was an image in the bed, with a pillow of goats' hair for his bolster. [17] And Saul said unto Michal, Why hast thou deceived me so, and sent away mine enemy, that he is escaped? And Michal answered Saul, He said unto me, Let me go; why should I kill thee? [18] So David fled, and escaped, and came to Samuel to Ramah, and told him all that Saul had done to him. And he and Samuel went and dwelt in Naioth.

1 SAMUEL 25:44

But Saul had given Michal his daughter, David's wife, to Phalti the son of Laish, which was of Gallim.

2 SAMUEL 3:14-15

And David sent messengers to Ishbosheth Saul's son, saying, Deliver me my wife Michal, which I espoused to me for an hundred foreskins of the Philistines. [15] And Ishbosheth sent, and took her from her husband, even from Phaltiel the son of Laish.

2 SAMUEL 6:20-23

Then David returned to bless his household. And Michal the daughter of Saul came out to meet David, and said, How glorious was the king of Israel to day, who uncovered himself to day in the eyes of the handmaids of his servants, as one of the vain fellows shamelessly uncovereth himself! [21] And David said unto Michal, It was before the Lord, which chose me before thy father, and before all his house, to appoint me ruler over the people of the Lord, over Israel: therefore will I play before the Lord. [22] And I will yet be more vile than thus, and will be base in mine own sight: and of the maidservants which thou hast spoken of, of them shall I be had in honour. [23] Therefore Michal the daughter of Saul had no child unto the day of her death.

JOHN 5:44

How can ye believe, which receive honour one of another, and seek not the honour that cometh from God only?

HEBREWS 12:15

Looking diligently lest any man fail of the grace of God; lest any root of bitterness springing up trouble you, and thereby many be defiled.

The Danger of Prosperity

Although David achieved many great and godly accomplishments, he also experienced a great downfall. The man after God's own heart sinned and transgressed against the Lord.

The Bible is very candid, even with major characters like David. Instead of glossing over his failures, the Scriptures are very plain. The Lord's purpose for this is to benefit you and me today. We can learn many lessons, even from the negative aspects of David's life.

Have you ever been through a major moral failure? If so, there are some things in David's life that will help you recover, especially as you see how God dealt with him and was able to continue using him. If not, then you can receive instruction through David's life regarding how much his sin cost him and damaged those around him. It will definitely inspire you not to go that route. So, whether you've been through a major moral failure in your life or not, there are lessons God wants you to learn from David.

When David sinned with Bathsheba, he didn't just make a mistake. It wasn't that he was only human and failed to do one little thing that he should have done. David literally turned from God and went the other way. He rebelled.

SIN MUST BE CONCEIVED

David didn't have a major departure from God "accidentally." There were reasons why this happened.

> *But every man is tempted, when he is drawn away of his own lust, and enticed. [15] Then when lust hath conceived, it bringeth forth sin: and sin, when it is finished, bringeth forth death.*
>
> JAMES 1:14-15

Sin must be conceived, just a like a baby is conceived. A stork doesn't bring a baby, and you can't get pregnant by drinking water after someone else. Conception isn't something you catch from another person, like a cold. A seed must be planted.

David began with a pure heart, a heart after God Himself. Despite all of the hardships and challenging circumstances, he remained faithful. While being pursued by his father-in-law, King Saul, David refused to be influenced by the ungodly counsel around him and stayed sensitive to the Lord. Throughout all

---

LESSONS FROM DAVID

of the battles and overwhelming circumstances, David kept his faith steadfastly in God. However, this episode with Bathsheba was an anomaly—totally contrary to how his heart was most of his life.

DAVID LOST HIS VISION

And it came to pass, after the year was expired, at the time when kings go forth to battle, that David sent Joab, and his servants with him, and all Israel; and they destroyed the children of Ammon, and besieged Rabbah. But David tarried still at Jerusalem.

2 SAMUEL 11:1

David was anointed by God to be king. Part of the king's job was to serve as commander-in-chief and supreme general over all the troops. As king, he should have been out there with his armies running the battles. However, David delegated this role to Joab, his highest-ranking general, and chose to stay home instead.

This is our first clue as to why David had this major moral failure. He wasn't doing what the Lord had called him to do. David had lost his vision.

When you're under pressure and it looks like your goal is nearly unobtainable, it creates a hunger on the inside of you to achieve it. When what you're pursuing seems so far-fetched and far away from where you are, it keeps you intent and focused on the things of God. When you have a goal out in front of you, it keeps an energy and an enthusiasm alive on the inside of you. But once you begin to obtain your goal, it is a dangerous time because you no longer have purpose.

One of the things that had made David such a great man was that he had a purpose that was bigger than himself. He served a higher purpose. He wasn't in it for himself. David's goal was to liberate God's people and bring the nation of Israel to the place of prominence and power that the Lord intended. He occupied himself with this as long as he saw himself as God's appointed minister, and he kept that goal out in front of him.

BORED

One of the best defenses against temptation is just being focused on what God has called you to do. Be occupied with your heavenly Father's business. It's very beneficial to have a purpose and a goal that consumes your time, energy, and attention. When you get bored, you open yourself up to many things from the devil.

THE DANGER OF PROSPERITY

As the popular saying goes, "Idleness is the devil's workshop." Although it's not in the Bible, I believe it's still a godly principle. You need to be doing something. You need to have a purpose, a goal, and an aim for your life.

David had quit doing what God had called him to do. He had won many victories, and the kingdom was now established. He prospered and wanted to build God a temple. The prophet had told him that one of his sons was going to do it. The Lord had given him tremendous prophecies about how his kingdom would endure and that he would always have a son sitting on the throne. All of this brought David to an apex—he was at the top of his game. Everything he had wanted for the nation, for himself, and for his heirs was all being done. David had reached his goal and fulfilled what he set out to do.

Now he was so prosperous that he could send his armies into battle and stay home. Besides, this battle with Ammon was just a minor skirmish. It wasn't a major thing. There really wasn't any chance of Israel losing in this battle, because they had superior power. Since victory was certain, David didn't have to go. He didn't think he had to do what God had told him to do.

Now that the pressure was off, David let up. He quit seeking the Lord with the same intensity. Since he wasn't doing what God had told him to do, David basically became bored.

HARDSHIP VS. PROSPERITY

And it came to pass in an eveningtide, that David arose from off his bed, and walked upon the roof of the king's house: and from the roof he saw a woman washing herself; and the woman was very beautiful to look upon.

2 SAMUEL 11:2

David was getting up out of bed when most people who have a job—a purpose—and have worked all day—are getting off, going home, and going to bed! In other words, David wasn't doing anything. He wasn't overwhelmed with the affairs of the state. He was sleeping, napping during the day. David didn't have much to do, because he had already reached his goal. That's dangerous!

Seasons of prosperity are more dangerous than seasons of pressure. When all pressure is removed and things are going well, you're the most vulnerable to the devil. Conventional wisdom says, "You'll find out what's in someone when they're in difficult circumstances and under tremendous pressure." I disagree. Of course, it takes faith and character to be able to persevere through hard times, but temptation is worse in times of prosperity.

In hardship, you know you need the Lord. When you're facing something overwhelming, it amplifies the reality of your need for God. You know you're incapable and can't deal with this—it's bigger than you. Even someone with a low commitment to God will run to Him in hardship and ask Him for help. It's easy to seek the Lord and be God dependent in a time of need.

Think about it! When do you pray the most? If you're typical, you pray the most when you're under pressure. Trouble drives people to God! Anybody who knows He exists and He wants to help them will turn to Him when the chips are down. But what happens when the pressure is removed?

What happened when everything was going so good that David could just send in his generals to fight the battle without him? He was so blessed and prosperous that he didn't have to do it anymore. David had the greatest mansion in all the land. He no longer had enemies breathing down his neck and trying to kill him every day. So, David let up and began to coast. He stopped seeking God with the same intensity.

That's what caused him to commit this major moral failure. This wasn't just a mistake—an accidental, unintentional minor failure. This was a major departure from God, and it came as a result of choices. This sin was conceived over a period of time.

YOU CANNOT COAST!

This sin didn't really begin on the night David committed adultery with Bathsheba. It began months—possibly even years—before, when David started being so blessed and prosperous that he didn't think he had to seek the Lord with the same intensity as before. He let his spiritual life slide. David probably became so occupied with the affairs of being king that before he knew it, a long time had passed since he was intimately relating to God the way he had before. That's likely what caused this moral failure.

This is a warning to those of us who haven't had a moral failure like David's. David was a man after God's own heart, yet look what he did! He committed adultery and even murdered the woman's husband, trying to cover it up. How far can you go? David loved God with all his heart, but here he was, living in a way that even Saul never did. Many people in the Word of God who aren't considered as "great" examples didn't live as bad a life as David did. How can someone do something like this? It just goes to show that the flesh is capable of doing anything that anybody has ever done—if someone let's it go. We cannot coast!

When you're flying in an airplane, it seems so effortless. But if you turn off those motors, I can guarantee you that gravity is still pulling. You might think that because you've flown so long without any effort, and everything is working fine, that you can just do anything you want. However, I dare you to turn off those engines and see what happens. That's right—it's inevitable—you're going down!

It's the same thing in the Christian life. You always have to keep the engines running of seeking God and depending on Him. You can never get to a place where you don't have to want a better relationship with the Lord, wait on Him, and look to Him for everything. If you ever think you've arrived at such a place, you'll start to coast. If you ever become so prosperous and secure that you aren't seeking God and depending on Him, you're putting yourself in the most dangerous situation ever. Since your flesh is still capable of doing anything it ever could, it's just a matter of time before you fall. This ought to be a warning to you!

So, instead of waiting until you have this great temptation, or until some crisis hits, you need to learn to seek the Lord and keep your heart sensitive to Him right now! If you do that, you'll discover that you cannot wickedly depart from God unless you first of all departed from depending on Him. Even if you are prospering more than ever before, keep yourself aware of and acknowledging the truth that "Without You, God, I can do nothing. I need You every day of my life, not only when a crisis hits, but when everything is going good. Lord, I depend on You! I need You now just as much as ever before!" If you maintain this attitude, it'll keep you from great transgression.

SINS OF ARROGANCE

David himself wrote,

Keep back thy servant also from presumptuous sins.

PSALM 19:13A

The Hebrew word translated *"presumptuous"* literally speaks of sins of pride and arrogance. Pride is not just arrogance; it's self-sufficiency. When a person sins presumptuously, they no longer humbly recognize their dependence on God. When everything is going good, they think, *I've done all these things by my might and power*. They aren't recognizing their human frailty and need for God at all times. David essentialy wrote, "Keep us back from sins of arrogance and operating independent of You, Lord!"

Let them not have dominion over me: then shall I be upright, and I shall be innocent from the great transgression.

PSALM 19:13B

In this psalm, David was saying, "If You'll keep me from these sins of arrogance, God—thinking I can make it independent of You—it will keep me from a big fall. If You keep me in a situation where I recognize and acknowledge my dependence on You, that will keep me from the great transgression."

In other words, you have to sin in these small areas of not seeking the Lord and being dependent on Him before a big downfall. You have to sin in becoming arrogant, self-sufficient, and not being intimate with Him before you can enter into a great transgression.

These sins of adultery and murder didn't just jump on David; they had been coming on for months—perhaps even years—as he began to be so prosperous that he thought he didn't have to depend on the Lord. He didn't think he had to seek God the way he once did. That's where his sin was conceived. The adultery with Bathsheba and the murder of Uriah just happened to be the way it manifested itself.

LOOKING FOR TROUBLE

David was so blessed and prosperous that he didn't think he had to do what the Lord had told him to do. He wasn't obeying God. He was at home sleeping during the day, goofing off, and being aimless and purposeless. David was looking for trouble—and he found it!

If you sleep all day and carouse at night, you're going to run into trouble!

ANDREW'S RECOMMENDATIONS FOR FURTHER STUDY

My teaching entitled *How to Prepare Your Heart* explains why people do evil and that it doesn't just happen. I share how you can keep yourself from entering this process, simply by keeping yourself dependent on God. Humble dependence on the Lord makes all the difference!

Outline

I. You can learn many lessons from the negative aspects of David's life.
   A. You see how God dealt with him and was able to continue using him.
   B. You can receive instruction through David's life regarding how much his sin cost him and damaged those around him.
      i. It will definitely inspire you not to go that route.
   C. So, whether you've been through a major moral failure in your life or not, there are lessons God wants you to learn from David.

II. David didn't have a major departure from God "accidentally."

But every man is tempted, when he is drawn away of his own lust, and enticed. [15] Then when lust hath conceived, it bringeth forth sin: and sin, when it is finished, bringeth forth death.
JAMES 1:14-15

   A. Sin must be conceived.
   B. This episode with Bathsheba was an anomaly—totally contrary to how his heart was most of his life.
   C. But when he should have been out with his armies running the battles, he had delegated this role to Joab:

And it came to pass, after the year was expired, at the time when kings go forth to battle, that David sent Joab, and his servants with him, and all Israel; and they destroyed the children of Ammon, and besieged Rabbah. But David tarried still at Jerusalem.
2 SAMUEL 11:1

   D. This is our first clue as to why David had this major moral failure: He wasn't doing what the Lord had called him to do—he had lost his vision.
   E. One of the things that had made David such a great man was that he saw himself as God's appointed minister and kept that goal out in front of him.
   F. But David had won many victories, and the kingdom was now established—he was at the top of his game.
   G. Now that the pressure was off, David quit seeking the Lord with the same intensity.
   H. He basically became bored.

III. Temptation is worse in times of prosperity.
    A. In hardship, you know you need the Lord.
        i. Even someone with a low commitment to God will run to Him in hardship and ask Him for help, because it's easy to seek the Lord and be God dependent in a time of need.
    B. But what happens when the pressure is removed?
    C. David's major moral failure wasn't an accidental, unintentional minor failure; it was a major departure from God, and it came as a result of choices.

IV. What likely caused this moral failure was that he had become so occupied with the affairs of being king that before he knew it, a long time had passed since he was intimately relating to God the way he had before.
    A. This is a warning to those of us who haven't had a moral failure like David's.
    B. David was a man after God's own heart, yet he committed adultery and even murdered the woman's husband, trying to cover it up.
    C. David was living in a way that even Saul never did.
        i. It just goes to show that the flesh is capable of doing anything that anybody has ever done.
    D. We can never get to a place where we don't have to want a better relationship with the Lord, wait on Him, and look to Him for everything.
    E. If we ever think we've arrived at such a place, it's just a matter of time before we fall.
    F. If we learn to seek the Lord and keep our hearts sensitive to Him, we'll discover that we cannot wickedly depart from God unless we first of all departed from depending on Him.
    G. If we maintain an attitude of dependency on Him, it'll keep us from great transgression.

V. David himself wrote,

Keep back thy servant also from presumptuous sins.

PSALM 19:13A

   A. The Hebrew word translated *"presumptuous"* literally speaks of sins of pride and arrogance, which are self-sufficiency.
   B. The next part of the verse says,

Let them not have dominion over me: then shall I be upright, and I shall be innocent from the great transgression.

PSALM 19:13B

   C. In other words, you have to sin in these small areas of not seeking the Lord and being dependent on Him before a big downfall.

THE DANGER OF PROSPERITY

D. David had become so prosperous that he thought he didn't have to depend on the Lord the way he once did.
E. That's where his sin was conceived—the adultery with Bathsheba and the murder of Uriah just happened to be the way it manifested itself.
F. David wasn't obeying God; he was at home sleeping during the day, goofing off, and being aimless and purposeless.
   i. If you sleep all day and carouse at night, you're going to run into trouble!

ANDREW'S RECOMMENDATIONS FOR FURTHER STUDY

My teaching entitled *How to Prepare Your Heart* explains why people do evil and that it doesn't just happen. I share how you can keep yourself from entering this process, simply by keeping yourself dependent on God. Humble dependence on the Lord makes all the difference!

Teacher's Guide

1. We can learn many lessons from the negative aspects of David's life. We can see how God dealt with him and was able to continue using him. We can receive instruction through David's life regarding how much his sin cost him and damaged those around him. It will definitely inspire us not to go that route. So, whether we've been through a major moral failure in our lives or not, there are lessons God wants us to learn from David.

1a. *Discussion question:* Why do you think God wants you to learn from David?
<u>Discussion question</u>

2. David didn't have a major departure from God "accidentally":

> *But every man is tempted, when he is drawn away of his own lust, and enticed. [15] Then when lust hath conceived, it bringeth forth sin: and sin, when it is finished, bringeth forth death.*
>
> JAMES 1:14-15

Sin must be conceived. This episode with Bathsheba was an anomaly—totally contrary to how his heart was most of his life. But when he should have been out with his armies running the battles, he had delegated this role to Joab:

> *And it came to pass, after the year was expired, at the time when kings go forth to battle, that David sent Joab, and his servants with him, and all Israel; and they destroyed the children of Ammon, and besieged Rabbah. But David tarried still at Jerusalem.*
>
> 2 SAMUEL 11:1

This is our first clue as to why David had this major moral failure: He wasn't doing what the Lord had called him to do—he had lost his vision. One of the things that had made David such a great man was that he saw himself as God's appointed minister and kept that goal out in front of him. But David had won many victories, and the kingdom was now established—he was at the top of his game. Now that the pressure was off, David quit seeking the Lord with the same intensity. He basically became bored.

2a. Read James 1:14-15. Sin _____ be conceived.
   Must
2b. What is the first clue as to why David had this major moral failure?
   He wasn't doing what the Lord had called him to do—he had lost his vision
2c. David was at the top of his game, so he _____.
   A. Could relax and drink wine
   B. Felt he deserved a break
   C. Became bored and did not seek the Lord with his usual intensity
   D. All of the above
   E. None of the above
   C. Became bored and did not seek the Lord with his usual intensity
2d. *Discussion question:* What are some aspects of everyday life that you have seen distract you from seeking the Lord with intensity?
   Discussion question

3. Temptation is worse in times of prosperity. In hardship, we know we need the Lord. Even someone with a low commitment to God will run to Him in hardship and ask Him for help, because it's easy to seek the Lord and be God dependent in a time of need. But what happens when the pressure is removed? David's major moral failure wasn't an accidental, unintentional minor failure; it was a major departure from God, and it came as a result of choices.

3a. *True or false:* Temptation is not as bad in times of prosperity.
   False
3b. *Discussion question:* David's failure was a major departure from God, and it came as a result of choices. What do you think you can do specifically to safeguard against such a departure?
   Discussion question

4. What likely caused this moral failure was that he had become so occupied with the affairs of being king that before he knew it, a long time had passed since he was intimately relating to God the way he had before. This is a warning to those of us who haven't had a moral failure like David's. David was a man after God's own heart, yet he committed adultery and even murdered the woman's husband, trying to cover it up. David was living in a way that even Saul never did. It just goes to show that the flesh is capable of doing anything that anybody has ever done. We can never get to a place where we don't have to want a better relationship with the Lord, wait on Him, and look to Him for everything. If we ever think we've arrived at such a place, it's just a matter of time before we fall. If we learn to seek the Lord and keep our hearts sensitive to Him, we'll discover that we cannot wickedly depart from God unless we first of all departed from depending on Him. If we maintain an attitude of dependency on Him, it'll keep us from great transgression.

4a. David was living in a way that even Saul never did. What does this show?
   A. The flesh is capable of leading you in the right direction
   B. You can become preoccupied with eating cake
   C. You can never allow yourself to get to a place where you don't want a better relationship with the Lord
   D. No one can be trusted
   E. David really wasn't a good example
   C. You can never allow yourself to get to a place where you don't want a better relationship with the Lord
4b. You cannot wickedly depart from God unless _____.
   A. You watch too much TV
   B. You first depart from depending on Him
   C. You become rich and lazy
   D. You have lost everything
   E. You accidentally stumble into it
   B. You first depart from depending on Him

5. David himself wrote,

> *Keep back thy servant also from presumptuous sins.*
>
> **PSALM 19:13A**

The Hebrew word translated *"presumptuous"* literally speaks of sins of pride and arrogance, which are self-sufficiency. The next part of the verse says,

> *Let them not have dominion over me: then shall I be upright, and I shall be innocent from the great transgression.*
>
> **PSALM 19:13B**

In other words, we have to sin in these small areas of not seeking the Lord and being dependent on Him before a big downfall. David had become so prosperous that he thought he didn't have to depend on the Lord the way he once did. That's where his sin was conceived—the adultery with Bathsheba and the murder of Uriah just happened to be the way it manifested itself. David wasn't obeying God; he was at home sleeping during the day, goofing off, and being aimless and purposeless. If we sleep all day and carouse at night, we're going to run into trouble!

5a. Read Psalm 19:13a. The word *"presumptuous"* refers to what?
   A. Presuming in advance that God will forgive you
   B. Assuming that you are strong enough to handle all that comes
   C. Pride and arrogance, which are self-sufficiency
   D. All of the above
   E. None of the above
   C. Pride and arrogance, which are self-sufficiency

5b. True or false: You have to sin in small areas of not seeking the Lord and being dependent on Him before a big downfall.
   True

5c. If you sleep all day and carouse at night, you're going to run into _____.
   A. Red eyes and a sore throat
   B. Opportunity
   C. Criminals
   D. Trouble
   E. A friendly face
   D. Trouble

Discipleship Questions

1. *Discussion question:* Why do you think God wants you to learn from David?
   _____
   _____
   _____

2. Read James 1:14-15. Sin _____ be conceived.

3. What is the first clue as to why David had this major moral failure?
   _____
   _____
   _____

4. David was at the top of his game, so he _____.
   A. Could relax and drink wine
   B. Felt he deserved a break
   C. Became bored and did not seek the Lord with his usual intensity
   D. All of the above
   E. None of the above

5. *Discussion question:* What are some aspects of everyday life that you have seen distract you from seeking the Lord with intensity?
   _____
   _____
   _____

6. True or false: Temptation is not as bad in times of prosperity.

7. *Discussion question:* David's failure was a major departure from God, and it came as a result of choices. What do you think you can do specifically to safeguard against such a departure?
   _____
   _____
   _____

THE DANGER OF PROSPERITY

8. David was living in a way that even Saul never did. What does this show?
   A. The flesh is capable of leading you in the right direction
   B. You can become preoccupied with eating cake
   C. You can never allow yourself to get to a place where you don't want a better relationship with the Lord
   D. No one can be trusted
   E. David really wasn't a good example

9. You cannot wickedly depart from God unless _____.
   A. You watch too much TV
   B. You first depart from depending on Him
   C. You become rich and lazy
   D. You have lost everything
   E. You accidentally stumble into it

10. Read Psalm 19:13a. The word *"presumptuous"* refers to what?
    A. Presuming in advance that God will forgive you
    B. Assuming that you are strong enough to handle all that comes
    C. Pride and arrogance, which are self-sufficiency
    D. All of the above
    E. None of the above

11. True or false: You have to sin in small areas of not seeking the Lord and being dependent on Him before a big downfall.

12. If you sleep all day and carouse at night, you're going to run into _____.
    A. Red eyes and a sore throat
    B. Opportunity
    C. Criminals
    D. Trouble
    E. A friendly face

1. *Discussion question*
2. Must
3. He wasn't doing what the Lord had called him to do—he had lost his vision
4. C. Became bored and did not seek the Lord with his usual intensity
5. *Discussion question*
6. False
7. *Discussion question*
8. C. You can never allow yourself to get to a place where you don't want a better relationship with the Lord
9. B. You first depart from depending on Him
10. C. Pride and arrogance, which are self-sufficiency
11. True
12. D. Trouble

Scriptures

JAMES 1:14-15
But every man is tempted, when he is drawn away of his own lust, and enticed. [15] Then when lust hath conceived, it bringeth forth sin: and sin, when it is finished, bringeth forth death.

2 SAMUEL 11:1-2
And it came to pass, after the year was expired, at the time when kings go forth to battle, that David sent Joab, and his servants with him, and all Israel; and they destroyed the children of Ammon, and besieged Rabbah. But David tarried still at Jerusalem. [2] And it came to pass in an eveningtide, that David arose from off his bed, and walked upon the roof of the king's house: and from the roof he saw a woman washing herself; and the woman was very beautiful to look upon.

PSALM 19:13
Keep back thy servant also from presumptuous sins. Let them not have dominion over me: then shall I be upright, and I shall be innocent from the great transgression.

"You Are the Man!"

David saw a beautiful woman washing herself, so he…

…sent and enquired after the woman. And one said, Is not this Bathsheba, the daughter of Eliam, the wife of Uriah the Hittite? [4] And David sent messengers, and took her; and she came in unto him, and he lay with her; for she was purified from her uncleanness: and she returned unto her house. [5] And the woman conceived, and sent and told David, and said, I am with child.

2 SAMUEL 11:3-5

When David found out Bathsheba was pregnant, he knew it was going to look really bad for him. His sin would be found out. But rather than humbling himself and dealing with it, he tried to cover it up. This reveals how hard David's heart had become toward God.

SLEEPING ON THE STEPS

I can't imagine doing what David did! If I could, I think that by the time I found out the woman was pregnant, I'd repent and deal with it right then. I'd say, "O Lord, I can't go any further. Forgive me!"

David didn't miss a beat. He called for Bathsheba's husband, Uriah, to come back home. He was one of David's soldiers out fighting in the battles that David himself should have been fighting. David acted interested in the battle and what was going on with the troops out in the field. After Uriah gave him a report, David released him expecting that he would go home and have sexual relations with his wife. He even sent some food with him to bless him.

It turned out that Uriah didn't go home. Instead, he stayed on the steps of the king's house. David was told about it the next morning. So, he called Uriah in and asked, "Why didn't you go home last night?"

Uriah answered, "What am I going to do—go home and have relations with my wife while my comrades are out there sleeping on the ground and putting their lives on the line in battle? I will not do it!"

David saw that his plan didn't work, so he had Uriah stay over some more. He had a feast and called Uriah to join him. David made Uriah drunk, thinking, *Surely this man's resolve will crack when he's drunk!*

However, once the feast was over, Uriah decided to stay there again at the steps of David's palace. Even though he was drunk, he refused to go home.

SIN ALWAYS AFFECTS OTHERS

David finally realized that it wasn't going to work to get Uriah and Bathsheba together. So, he wrote a letter commanding his top general, Joab, to put Uriah in a place where he knew it was dangerous and then withdraw from Uriah so that he would be killed. David even sent this letter by Uriah's own hand! I'm sure the letter had some kind of seal on it for protection, but the king had seen that Uriah was a man of high standards and integrity—David probably had no doubt that the letter would be safely delivered. He sent Uriah's death sentence by Uriah's own hand!

The irony, hypocrisy, and evilness of this is just amazing! It's incredible to think that David could stoop so low.

But David didn't do all this by himself. He had servants go out and bring Bathsheba to him. He had Joab comply with this plan. David involved other people in his sin.

Many people say, "I'm not hurting anybody but myself by the things I do!" That's just never true. Somebody else is always hurt by our sin.

Once Joab executed David's order, he sent word back to the king. When David heard that Uriah was dead, he sent for Bathsheba and made her his wife.

> *And when the mourning was past, David sent and fetched her to his house, and she became his wife, and bare him a son. But the thing that David had done displeased the LORD.*
> 2 SAMUEL 11:27

What an understatement!

THE PARABLE

Nathan—David's longtime friend, advisor, and prophet—came to the king and gave him this parable:

> *And the LORD sent Nathan unto David. And he came unto him, and said unto him, There were two men in one city; the one rich, and the other poor. [2] The rich man had exceeding many flocks and herds: [3] But the poor man had nothing, save one little ewe lamb, which he*

"YOU ARE THE MAN!"

had bought and nourished up: and it grew up together with him, and with his children; it did eat of his own meat, and drank of his own cup, and lay in his bosom, and was unto him as a daughter. [4] And there came a traveller unto the rich man, and he spared to take of his own flock and of his own herd, to dress for the wayfaring man that was come unto him; but took the poor man's lamb, and dressed it for the man that was come to him.

2 SAMUEL 12:1-4

Of course, this was a parable that Nathan was giving. It didn't really happen but was symbolic of what David had done.

David was like the rich man. God had blessed him and given him everything. Yet when he had a need, he didn't go to the Lord—and what He had already provided—to meet it. David had multiple wives. Second Samuel 3:2-5 lists six of them. In addition to these six and Michal (2 Sam. 3:14), he also apparently had some concubines (2 Sam. 16:21-22). Therefore, David had at least seven wives who could satisfy his sexual desires. But instead of choosing one of them, which were all legal by law and given to him by God, David took another man's wife while the man was away serving his king and fighting the king's battle. Then he killed that man in an effort to cover up his sin. That's what this parable was all about.

MERCY OR JUDGMENT?

And David's anger was greatly kindled against the man; and he said to Nathan, As the LORD liveth, the man that hath done this thing shall surely die: [6] And he shall restore the lamb fourfold, because he did this thing, and because he had no pity.

2 SAMUEL 12:5-6

David didn't realize the parable was about him. He became furious and declared, "The man who has done this thing shall die! And he must also make fourfold restitution—give the poor man four lambs—for the one he took!"

In light of David's reaction, let's consider this scripture:

So speak ye, and so do, as they that shall be judged by the law of liberty. [13] For he shall have judgment without mercy, that hath shewed no mercy; and mercy rejoiceth against judgment.

JAMES 2:12-13

The Lord delights in showing mercy to people who have shown mercy. But to those who have shown no mercy—and been critical and judgmental instead—they reap what they sow!

David understood this principle. Although it's listed later in the chronology of the Bible, the psalm contained in 2 Samuel 22 was spoken by David on the day the Lord delivered him from his enemies, including Saul (2 Sam. 22:1). Therefore, this was before David became king and long before his sin with Bathsheba. Notice what he said:

With the merciful thou wilt shew thyself merciful, and with the upright man thou wilt shew thyself upright.

2 SAMUEL 22:26

In this passage, David basically said the same thing that is said in James 2: "Lord, with the merciful, You show Yourself merciful, and with the upright, You show Yourself upright." This shows that at one time, David had this principle revealed to him (see also 2 Samuel 22:27-28). He knew that if he wanted mercy, he had to show mercy. But if he didn't show mercy to other people, he himself would receive no mercy.

DAVID DETERMINED HIS JUDGMENT

Yet David had stopped seeking the Lord and had departed from Him. He had allowed himself to be drawn into adultery, and while trying to cover up that adultery, he committed murder. However, he was just going on as if nothing had happened.

David's heart had become so hardened that he had quit being responsive to the things God had shown him before. So, when he heard this parable, he responded in judgment to a much lesser transgression than he himself had just committed. Taking another man's lamb and feeding it to a guest is nowhere near as great a transgression as taking another man's wife and murdering him to cover it up. David was the one in greater transgression.

David basically determined his own judgment. The Lord gave him this parable through Nathan the prophet. David could have said, "This man did wrong, but I'm going to show him mercy. Instead of giving him all that he deserves, I'm just going to have him make restitution. Maybe his heart was right somehow." However, without asking for any further information or finding out any additional details, David jumped right into judgment, declaring, "This man shall die! He's going to suffer four times the punishment for the suffering he's caused." Mercy rejoices against judgment, but if you don't show mercy, you won't reap it!

God gave this parable to David to see how he would respond. Would he be merciful? If he had, I believe the Lord would have been merciful toward him in the way He dealt with his transgression. But when David showed no mercy, he didn't reap any either. God responded to David the way he was responding to other people. He himself determined the harshness of his judgment.

"YOU ARE THE MAN!"

If we would be merciful to other people, we would receive mercy ourselves. I've done some stupid things, but since I've been merciful to others, I've been able to reap mercy. God has been gracious to me when I've said and done things that hurt other people's feelings, because I've been merciful to those who have hurt mine.

Outline

I. David saw a beautiful woman washing herself, so he…

…sent and enquired after the woman. And one said, Is not this Bathsheba, the daughter of Eliam, the wife of Uriah the Hittite? [4] And David sent messengers, and took her; and she came in unto him, and he lay with her; for she was purified from her uncleanness: and she returned unto her house. [5] And the woman conceived, and sent and told David, and said, I am with child.

2 SAMUEL 11:3-5

    A. When David found out Bathsheba was pregnant, he knew it was going to look really bad for him.
    B. But rather than humbling himself and dealing with it, he tried to cover it up.
    C. This reveals how hard David's heart had become toward God.

II. If I could imagine doing what David, I think that by the time I found out the woman was pregnant, I'd repent and deal with it right then, but David didn't miss a beat.
    A. He called for Bathsheba's husband, Uriah, who was out fighting in the battles that David himself should have been fighting.
    B. David expected that Uriah would go home and have sexual relations with his wife, but he stayed on the steps of the king's house.
    C. David finally realized that it wasn't going to work to get Uriah and Bathsheba together, so he wrote a letter to his general, Joab, to have Uriah put in a place where he knew it was dangerous and then withdraw from Uriah so that he would be killed.
        i. David even sent this letter by Uriah's own hand!
    D. When David heard that Uriah was dead, he sent for Bathsheba and made her his wife:

And when the mourning was past, David sent and fetched her to his house, and she became his wife, and bare him a son. But the thing that David had done displeased the LORD.

2 SAMUEL 11:27

    E. What an understatement!

III. Nathan—David's longtime friend, advisor, and prophet—came to the king and gave him this parable:

"YOU ARE THE MAN!"

And the LORD sent Nathan unto David. And he came unto him, and said unto him, There were two men in one city; the one rich, and the other poor. [2] The rich man had exceeding many flocks and herds: [3] But the poor man had nothing, save one little ewe lamb, which he had bought and nourished up: and it grew up together with him, and with his children; it did eat of his own meat, and drank of his own cup, and lay in his bosom, and was unto him as a daughter. [4] And there came a traveller unto the rich man, and he spared to take of his own flock and of his own herd, to dress for the wayfaring man that was come unto him; but took the poor man's lamb, and dressed it for the man that was come to him.

2 SAMUEL 12:1-4

    A. This parable was symbolic of what David had done—he was like the rich man.
        i. When he had a need, he didn't go to the Lord—and what He had already provided—to meet it.
    B. Instead of choosing one of his own wives or concubines, which were given to him by God, he took another man's wife.
    C. Then he killed that man in an effort to cover up his sin.

IV.   David didn't realize the parable was about him:

And David's anger was greatly kindled against the man; and he said to Nathan, As the LORD liveth, the man that hath done this thing shall surely die: [6] And he shall restore the lamb fourfold, because he did this thing, and because he had no pity.

2 SAMUEL 12:5-6

    A. In light of his reaction, let's consider this scripture:

So speak ye, and so do, as they that shall be judged by the law of liberty. [13] For he shall have judgment without mercy, that hath shewed no mercy; and mercy rejoiceth against judgment.

JAMES 2:12-13

    B. The Lord delights in showing mercy to people who have shown mercy, but to those who have shown no mercy, they reap what they sow!
    C. Although it's listed later in the chronology of the Bible, David spoke this before he became king, showing he understood this principle:

With the merciful thou wilt shew thyself merciful, and with the upright man thou wilt shew thyself upright.

2 SAMUEL 22:26

LESSONS FROM DAVID

V. David's heart had become so hardened that he had quit being responsive to the things God had shown him before.
   A. So, when he heard this parable, he responded in judgment to a much lesser transgression than he himself had just committed.
   B. He basically determined his own judgment.
      i. David could have said, "This man did wrong, but I'm going to show him mercy. Instead of giving him all that he deserves, I'm just going to have him make restitution. Maybe his heart was right somehow."
      ii. However, without asking for any further information or finding out any additional details, David jumped right into judgment, declaring, "This man shall die! He's going to suffer four times the punishment for the suffering he's caused."
   C. God gave this parable to David because if he would have been merciful, I believe the Lord would have been merciful toward him.
   D. God responded to David the way he was responding to other people.

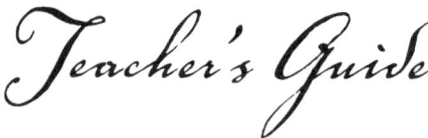

Teacher's Guide

1. David saw a beautiful woman washing herself, so he…

   …sent and enquired after the woman. And one said, Is not this Bathsheba, the daughter of Eliam, the wife of Uriah the Hittite? [4] And David sent messengers, and took her; and she came in unto him, and he lay with her; for she was purified from her uncleanness: and she returned unto her house. [5] And the woman conceived, and sent and told David, and said, I am with child.

   2 SAMUEL 11:3-5

When David found out Bathsheba was pregnant, he knew it was going to look really bad for him. But rather than humbling himself and dealing with it, he tried to cover it up. This reveals how hard David's heart had become toward God.

1a. True or false: David didn't know that Bathsheba was married when he sent for her.
   False
1b. What was the outcome of David's relations with Bathsheba?
   She became pregnant
1c. When David found out that Bathsheba was pregnant, what did he do?
   A. He humbled himself and dealt with it
   B. He thought it would make her look really bad
   C. He sent for the priest to confess his sins
   D. He tried to cover it up
   E. He fled Jerusalem
   D. He tried to cover it up
1d. *Discussion question:* How does David's reaction to finding out that Bathsheba was pregnant show that his heart had become hard toward God?
   Discussion question

LESSONS FROM DAVID

2. If Andrew could imagine doing what David, he thinks that by the time he found out the woman was pregnant, he'd repent and deal with it right then, but David didn't miss a beat. He called for Bathsheba's husband, Uriah, who was out fighting in the battles that David himself should have been fighting. David expected that Uriah would go home and have sexual relations with his wife, but he stayed on the steps of the king's house. David finally realized that it wasn't going to work to get Uriah and Bathsheba together, so he wrote a letter to his general, Joab, to have Uriah put in a place where he knew it was dangerous and then withdraw from Uriah so that he would be killed. David even sent this letter by Uriah's own hand! When David heard that Uriah was dead, he sent for Bathsheba and made her his wife:

> *And when the mourning was past, David sent and fetched her to his house, and she became his wife, and bare him a son. But the thing that David had done displeased the LORD.*
> 2 SAMUEL 11:27

What an understatement!

2a. Whom did David call for once he found out that Bathsheba was pregnant?
Her husband, Uriah

2b. What did David expect Uriah to do that would help him cover up his own sin?
   A. Sleep on the steps of the palace
   B. Go home and have sexual relations with his wife
   C. Discover his wife was pregnant
   D. Go back to battle
   E. Throw a party
B. Go home and have sexual relations with his wife

2c. Uriah did not help David's plan when he slept on the _____ of the king's house, instead of going home to his wife.
Steps

2d. True or false: Uriah carried the letter back to the battlefront that gave orders to orchestrate his own death.
True

2e. What did David do after Uriah was dead for a reasonable amount of time?
He married Bathsheba

2f. *Discussion question:* Andrew says that it is an understatement to say, *"But the thing that David had done displeased the LORD"* (2 Sam. 11:27b). Why?
Discussion question

3. Nathan—David's longtime friend, advisor, and prophet—came to the king and gave him this parable:

> *And the L<small>ORD</small> sent Nathan unto David. And he came unto him, and said unto him, There were two men in one city; the one rich, and the other poor. [2] The rich man had exceeding many flocks and herds: [3] But the poor man had nothing, save one little ewe lamb, which he had bought and nourished up: and it grew up together with him, and with his children; it did eat of his own meat, and drank of his own cup, and lay in his bosom, and was unto him as a daughter. [4] And there came a traveller unto the rich man, and he spared to take of his own flock and of his own herd, to dress for the wayfaring man that was come unto him; but took the poor man's lamb, and dressed it for the man that was come to him.*
>
> 2 SAMUEL 12:1-4

This parable was symbolic of what David had done—he was like the rich man. When he had a need, he didn't go to the Lord—and what He had already provided—to meet it. Instead of choosing one of his own wives or concubines, which were given to him by God, he took another man's wife. Then he killed that man in an effort to cover up his sin.

3a. Who was Nathan to David?
   A. Advisor
   B. Prophet
   C. Longtime friend
   D. All of the above
   E. None of the above
   D. All of the above
3b. True or false: The Lord's purpose in sending Nathan to King David was to tell him an entertaining story.
   False
3c. In the parable, the _____ represented David.
   Rich man
3d. *Discussion question:* How does the parable relate to David's sin of murdering Uriah?
   Discussion question

LESSONS FROM DAVID

4. David didn't realize the parable was about him:

> *And David's anger was greatly kindled against the man; and he said to Nathan, As the LORD liveth, the man that hath done this thing shall surely die: [6] And he shall restore the lamb fourfold, because he did this thing, and because he had no pity.*
>
> 2 SAMUEL 12:5-6

In light of his reaction, let's consider this scripture:

> *So speak ye, and so do, as they that shall be judged by the law of liberty. [13] For he shall have judgment without mercy, that hath shewed no mercy; and mercy rejoiceth against judgment.*
>
> JAMES 2:12-13

The Lord delights in showing mercy to people who have shown mercy, but to those who have shown no mercy, they reap what they sow! Although it's listed later in the chronology of the Bible, David spoke this before he became king, showing he understood this principle:

> *With the merciful thou wilt shew thyself merciful, and with the upright man thou wilt shew thyself upright.*
>
> 2 SAMUEL 22:26

4a. True or false: David didn't realize the parable was about him.
   True
4b. David's _____ was kindled against the rich man in the story (2 Sam. 12:5).
   Anger
4c. *Discussion question*: Why did David say the man who did this should be put to death and have to restore the lamb fourfold?
   Discussion question
4d. David had no _____ for the man in the story.
   A. Wisdom
   B. Tolerance
   C. Mercy
   D. Judgment
   E. Money
   C. Mercy

5. David's heart had become so hardened that he had quit being responsive to the things God had shown him before. So, when he heard this parable, he responded in judgment to a much lesser transgression than he himself had just committed. He basically determined his own judgment. David could have said, "This man did wrong, but I'm going to show him mercy. Instead of giving him all that he deserves, I'm just going to have him make restitution. Maybe his heart was right somehow." However, without asking for any further information or finding out any additional details, David jumped right into judgment, declaring, "This man shall die! He's going to suffer four times the punishment for the suffering he's caused." God gave this parable to David because if he would have been merciful, Andrew believes the Lord would have been merciful toward him. God responded to David the way he was responding to other people.

5a. True or false: Even after killing Uriah, David remained responsive and tenderhearted toward God.
 False
5b. Why did David respond in judgment against someone who had done something less sinful than he had done?
 His heart had become hardened
5c. In pronouncing judgment on the rich man in the story, who was David really pronouncing judgment on?
 Himself
5d. *Discussion question:* Share what you have learned from God giving David this parable to reveal to him his own heart.
 Discussion question

LESSONS FROM DAVID

Discipleship Questions

1. True or false: David didn't know that Bathsheba was married when he sent for her.

2. What was the outcome of David's relations with Bathsheba?
   _____
   _____
   _____

3. When David found out that Bathsheba was pregnant, what did he do?
   A. He humbled himself and dealt with it
   B. He thought it would make her look really bad
   C. He sent for the priest to confess his sins
   D. He tried to cover it up
   E. He fled Jerusalem

4. *Discussion question:* How does David's reaction to finding out that Bathsheba was pregnant show that his heart had become hard toward God?
   _____
   _____
   _____

5. Whom did David call for once he found out that Bathsheba was pregnant?
   _____
   _____
   _____

6. What did David expect Uriah to do that would help him cover up his own sin?
   A. Sleep on the steps of the palace
   B. Go home and have sexual relations with his wife
   C. Discover his wife was pregnant
   D. Go back to battle
   E. Throw a party

7. Uriah did not help David's plan when he slept on the _____ of the king's house, instead of going home to his wife.

"YOU ARE THE MAN!"

8. True or false: Uriah carried the letter back to the battlefront that gave orders to orchestrate his own death.

9. What did David do after Uriah was dead for a reasonable amount of time?
   _____
   _____
   _____

10. *Discussion question:* Andrew says that it is an understatement to say, *"But the thing that David had done displeased the LORD" (2 Sam. 11:27b).* Why?
    _____
    _____
    _____

11. Who was Nathan to David?
    A. Advisor
    B. Prophet
    C. Longtime friend
    D. All of the above
    E. None of the above

12. True or false: The Lord's purpose in sending Nathan to King David was to tell him an entertaining story.

13. In the parable, the _____ represented the David.

14. *Discussion question:* How does the parable relate to David's sin of murdering Uriah?
    _____
    _____
    _____

15. True or false: David didn't realize the parable was about him.

16. David's _____ was kindled against the man in the story (2 Sam. 12:5).

17. *Discussion question:* Why did David say the man who did this should be put to death and should have to restore the lamb fourfold?
_____
_____
_____

18. David had no _____ for the rich man in the story.
    A. Wisdom
    B. Tolerance
    C. Mercy
    D. Judgment
    E. Money

19. True or false: Even after killing Uriah, David remained responsive and tenderhearted toward God.

20. Why did David respond in judgment against someone who had done something less sinful than he had done?
_____
_____
_____

21. In pronouncing judgment on the rich man in the story, who was David really pronouncing judgment on?
_____
_____
_____

22. *Discussion question:* Share what you have learned from God giving David this parable to reveal to him his own heart.
_____
_____
_____

"YOU ARE THE MAN!"

Answer Key

1. False
2. She became pregnant
3. D. He tried to cover it up
4. *Discussion question*
5. Her husband, Uriah
6. B. Go home and have sexual relations with his wife
7. Steps
8. True
9. He married Bathsheba
10. *Discussion question*
11. D. All of the above
12. False
13. Rich man
14. *Discussion question*
15. True
16. Anger
17. *Discussion question*
18. C. Mercy
19. False
20. His heart had become hardened
21. Himself
22. *Discussion question*

Scriptures

2 SAMUEL 11:3-5

And David sent and enquired after the woman. And one said, Is not this Bathsheba, the daughter of Eliam, the wife of Uriah the Hittite? [4] And David sent messengers, and took her; and she came in unto him, and he lay with her; for she was purified from her uncleanness: and she returned unto her house. [5] And the woman conceived, and sent and told David, and said, I am with child.

2 SAMUEL 11:27

And when the mourning was past, David sent and fetched her to his house, and she became his wife, and bare him a son. But the thing that David had done displeased the LORD.

2 SAMUEL 12:1-6

And the LORD sent Nathan unto David. And he came unto him, and said unto him, There were two men in one city; the one rich, and the other poor. [2] The rich man had exceeding many flocks and herds: [3] But the poor man had nothing, save one little ewe lamb, which he had bought and nourished up: and it grew up together with him, and with his children; it did eat of his own meat, and drank of his own cup, and lay in his bosom, and was unto him as a daughter. [4] And there came a traveller unto the rich man, and he spared to take of his own flock and of his own herd, to dress for the wayfaring man that was come unto him; but took the poor man's lamb, and dressed it for the man that was come to him. [5] And David's anger was greatly kindled against the man; and he said to Nathan, As the LORD liveth, the man that hath done this thing shall surely die: [6] And he shall restore the lamb fourfold, because he did this thing, and because he had no pity.

2 SAMUEL 3:2-5

And unto David were sons born in Hebron: and his firstborn was Amnon, of Ahinoam the Jezreelitess; [3] And his second, Chileab, of Abigail the wife of Nabal the Carmelite; and the third, Absalom the son of Maacah the daughter of Talmai king of Geshur; [4] And the fourth, Adonijah the son of Haggith; and the fifth, Shephatiah the son of Abital; [5] And the sixth, Ithream, by Eglah David's wife. These were born to David in Hebron.

2 SAMUEL 3:14

And David sent messengers to Ishbosheth Saul's son, saying, Deliver me my wife Michal, which I espoused to me for an hundred foreskins of the Philistines.

"YOU ARE THE MAN!"

2 SAMUEL 16:21-22

And Ahithophel said unto Absalom, Go in unto thy father's concubines, which he hath left to keep the house; and all Israel shall hear that thou art abhorred of thy father: then shall the hands of all that are with thee be strong. [22] So they spread Absalom a tent upon the top of the house; and Absalom went in unto his father's concubines in the sight of all Israel.

JAMES 2:12-13

So speak ye, and so do, as they that shall be judged by the law of liberty. [13] For he shall have judgment without mercy, that hath shewed no mercy; and mercy rejoiceth against judgment.

2 SAMUEL 22:1

And David spake unto the LORD the words of this song in the day that the LORD had delivered him out of the hand of all his enemies, and out of the hand of Saul.

2 SAMUEL 22:26-28

With the merciful thou wilt shew thyself merciful, and with the upright man thou wilt shew thyself upright. [27] With the pure thou wilt shew thyself pure; and with the froward thou wilt shew thyself unsavoury. [28] And the afflicted people thou wilt save: but thine eyes are upon the haughty, that thou mayest bring them down.

"You Are the Man!"

I remember a certain media minister who was vicious and condemning toward anyone and everyone. When he fell, he received fourfold the judgment he had put on other people. People were merciless with him, and it's destroyed his ministry. If he would have shown more compassion toward others, he himself would have reaped more in his time of need.

You need to learn this. If you want God to be merciful to you, you need to be merciful to others. If you rail on people when they make a mistake, you can expect to be railed on when you make a mistake. Is that really what you want?

I'm sure you've seen someone who thought they were Mr. or Ms. Perfect. They tried to make everyone else "perfect" like them, but if they weren't, they judged and criticized them. When this "perfect" person made a mistake and stumbled, you got this feeling of justice by saying, "It's payback time. They've condemned me—and everyone else. Now it's time they tasted some of what they've been dishing out!" You just love to see a person like that receive what they deserve. But when someone has been merciful, you want to extend them mercy. That's just how things work!

David brought judgment upon himself by being so strict in his criticism of the man in the parable.

And Nathan said to David, Thou art the man.

2 SAMUEL 12:7A

This parable wasn't really about a rich man taking his poor neighbor's lamb; it was about David, Bathsheba, and Uriah. So, Nathan declared to David, "You are the man!"

GOD IS YOUR SOURCE!

Thus saith the Lord God of Israel, I anointed thee king over Israel, and I delivered thee out of the hand of Saul; [8] And I gave thee thy master's house, and thy master's wives into thy bosom, and gave thee the house of Israel and of Judah; and if that had been too little, I would moreover have given unto thee such and such things.

2 SAMUEL 12:7B-8

LESSONS FROM DAVID

The Lord was saying, "David, look what you've done! I've blessed you, prospered you, and done all these things for you. And if that wasn't enough, I would have given you more!" In other words, "If you weren't satisfied, I'm not against you having more—more wives, more money, more fame, anything."

The real sin here wasn't adultery or murder, but the fact that David quit trusting in the Lord. He had stopped looking to God as his source.

At one time, David couldn't do anything. He was a poor-and-despised nobody, so he knew he had to be God-dependent. However, once he became king, he was powerful. He was the head of one of the most powerful nations on the face of the earth at that moment. David could do anything he wanted, so he quit trusting God as his supply. He started doing things just because as king, he wanted to and could.

This is a real danger for us too. When we prosper to such a degree that we no longer have to pray and trust God to provide things for us but, instead, can just go out and get anything we need or want on our own, we need to beware! The danger is that we will quit depending on God as our source. That's really the transgression the Lord was bringing out here. He was saying, "David, I would have given you more, if you had asked Me!"

"YOU DESPISED ME!"

Then Nathan continued, saying,

> *Wherefore hast thou despised the commandment of the LORD, to do evil in his sight? thou hast killed Uriah the Hittite with the sword, and hast taken his wife to be thy wife, and hast slain him with the sword of the children of Ammon. [10] Now therefore the sword shall never depart from thine house; because thou hast despised me, and hast taken the wife of Uriah the Hittite to be thy wife.*
>
> 2 SAMUEL 12:9-10

Notice how the Lord reproved David. He didn't say, "David, look what you've done to Bathsheba—how you've defiled her. Look what you've done to Uriah—how you murdered him. Look at all of the people you've offended." No, that's not what the Lord said. It all came down to "David, look what I've done for you. If you had trusted Me, I would have given you even more. But all of these things are going to happen now because you have despised Me!" God said, "You despised Me!" This was all about David's personal relationship with God!

"YOU ARE THE MAN!"

THE HEART OF SIN

Most people think of sin in terms of the damage they do to others. Most people believe stealing is wrong because it violates and hurts the person they have stolen from. Since they look at it only in these external terms, many folks justify certain types of theft. Take, for instance, stealing from your employer. Many people—even Christians—take pens and other small things from work. They'll steal a little bit of time, thinking, *My employer has this big business; they can afford it!* So, they doctor their time sheets and allow for a little bit of extra time. But they don't feel bad about it, because they're not thinking of it as sin and stealing. To them, it's a relatively small amount of damage that they're doing.

Some big corporations allow for a certain amount of thievery. They have insurance to cover fraud and things like that, or they just write it off. So, there's a bunch of people involved in what's called "white-collar crime" and who think, *I'm not doing anybody any damage. This corporation won't even miss $100,000. They have insurance to cover it.* So, they think about it in those terms.

The issue isn't whether the company will miss it, has insurance to cover it, or has made allowances for a certain amount of shoplifting. It isn't even about whether you can get by with it. The issue is you're sinning against God! You are despising the Lord! Instead of trusting God and letting Him supply you with things in an honest way—a way of integrity—you're going against Him and doing it your way. Not trusting God—unbelief—is the heart of sin.

ANDREW'S RECOMMENDATIONS FOR FURTHER STUDY

My teaching entitled *The Positive Ministry of the Holy Spirit* is taken from John 16:8-11. In verse 8, Jesus said that the Holy Spirit would reprove us of sin, righteousness, and judgment. Most people interpret this as saying, "The Spirit reproves us of sins like adultery, lying, stealing, dope addiction, etc. Then, He tells us we're unrighteous because of what we did and—if we don't repent—we're going to be judged." That's not at all what Jesus was saying here. As a matter of fact, the Lord knew this verse would be misinterpreted, so He explained Himself in verses 9-11. Not believing on Jesus is the sin the Holy Spirit reproves us of (a.k.a. unbelief, verse 9). Also, He doesn't convict us of "unrighteousness," but that we are righteous in Christ (verse 10). Verse 11 doesn't say that the Holy Spirit would convict us that we would be judged, but rather that He would talk to us about the judgment of the devil. Religion has really twisted these verses up. Therefore, I strongly recommend this teaching. It'll be a blessing!

Outline

VI. If you want God to be merciful to you, you need to be merciful to others.
   A. If you rail on people when they make a mistake, you can expect to be railed on when you make a mistake.
      i. Is that really what you want?
   B. You just love to see a person who thinks they're perfect and criticizes others receive what they deserve.
   C. But when someone has been merciful, you want to extend them mercy—that's just how things work!

VII. The real sin here wasn't adultery or murder, but the fact that David quit trusting in the Lord:

And Nathan said to Daivd, Thou art the man. Thus saith the Lord God of Israel, I anointed thee king over Israel, and I delivered thee out of the hand of Saul; [8] And I gave thee thy master's house, and thy master's wives into thy bosom, and gave thee the house of Israel and of Judah; and if that had been too little, I would moreover have given unto thee such and such things.

2 SAMUEL 12:7-8

   A. David had stopped looking to God as his source.
      i. At one time, he knew he had to be God-dependent; however, once he became king, he quit trusting God and started doing things because he wanted to and could.
   B. When we prosper to such a degree that we no longer have to pray and trust God to provide things for us, we need to beware!
   C. The danger is that we will quit depending on God as our source.

VIII. Then Nathan continued, saying,

Wherefore hast thou despised the commandment of the Lord, to do evil in his sight? thou hast killed Uriah the Hittite with the sword, and hast taken his wife to be thy wife, and hast slain him with the sword of the children of Ammon. [10] Now therefore the sword shall never depart from thine house; because thou hast despised me, and hast taken the wife of Uriah the Hittite to be thy wife.

2 SAMUEL 12:9-10

"YOU ARE THE MAN!"

A. The Lord didn't say, "David, look what you've done to Bathsheba—how you've defiled her. Look what you've done to Uriah—how you murdered him. Look at all of the people you've offended."
B. It all came down to "David, look what I've done for you. If you had trusted Me, I would have given you even more. But all of these things are going to happen now because you have despised Me!"
C. This was all about David's personal relationship with God!

IX. Most people think of sin in terms of the damage they do to others.
A. But the issue is they're sinning against God!
B. They are despising the Lord!
C. Instead of trusting God and letting Him supply them with things in an honest way—a way of integrity—they're going against Him and doing it their way.
D. Not trusting God—unbelief—is the heart of sin.

ANDREW'S RECOMMENDATIONS FOR FURTHER STUDY

My teaching entitled *The Positive Ministry of the Holy Spirit* is taken from John 16:8-11. In verse 8, Jesus said that the Holy Spirit would reprove us of sin, righteousness, and judgment. Most people interpret this as saying, "The Spirit reproves us of sins like adultery, lying, stealing, dope addiction, etc. Then, He tells us we're unrighteous because of what we did and—if we don't repent—we're going to be judged." That's not at all what Jesus was saying here. As a matter of fact, the Lord knew this verse would be misinterpreted, so He explained Himself in verses 9-11. Not believing on Jesus is the sin the Holy Spirit reproves us of (a.k.a. unbelief, verse 9). Also, He doesn't convict us of "unrighteousness," but that we are righteous in Christ (verse 10). Verse 11 doesn't say that the Holy Spirit would convict us that we would be judged, but rather that He would talk to us about the judgment of the devil. Religion has really twisted these verses up. Therefore, I strongly recommend this teaching. It'll be a blessing!

6. If we want God to be merciful to us, we need to be merciful to others. If we rail on people when they make a mistake, we can expect to be railed on when we make mistakes. Is that really what we want? Many people just love to see a person who thinks they're perfect and criticizes others receive what they deserve. But when someone has been merciful, people want to extend them mercy—that's just how things work!

6a. True or false: Being merciful causes others to be merciful to you.
True

6b. People who rail on others for their mistakes inspire others to do what?
   A. Be merciful
   B. Make mistakes
   C. Hold them to their mistakes
   D. Play a game of cards
   C. Hold them to their mistakes

6c. If you have been merciful, people will want to _____ mercy to you.
Extend

"YOU ARE THE MAN!"

7. The real sin here wasn't adultery or murder, but the fact that David quit trusting in the Lord:

   And Nathan said to David, Thou art the man. Thus saith the LORD God of Israel, I anointed thee king over Israel, and I delivered thee out of the hand of Saul; [8] And I gave thee thy master's house, and thy master's wives into thy bosom, and gave thee the house of Israel and of Judah; and if that had been too little, I would moreover have given unto thee such and such things.

   2 SAMUEL 12:7-8

David had stopped looking to God as his source. At one time, he knew he had to be God-dependent; however, once he became king, he quit trusting God and started doing things because he wanted to and could. When we prosper to such a degree that we no longer have to pray and trust God to provide things for us, we need to beware! The danger is that we will quit depending on God as our source.

7a. What was David's real sin?
   A. Murder
   B. Not trusting God
   C. Adultery
   D. Lying
   E. Dancing
   B. Not trusting God

7b. David had stopped _____ to God as his _____.
   Looking / source

7c. Who or what did David depend on before he was king?
   God

7d. True or false: God prospers you so that you no longer have to bother Him to provide for you.
   False

7e. *Discussion question:* Prosperity is not the real danger—what must you beware of as you prosper?
   Discussion question

8. Then Nathan continued, saying,

> *Wherefore hast thou despised the commandment of the Lord, to do evil in his sight? thou hast killed Uriah the Hittite with the sword, and hast taken his wife to be thy wife, and hast slain him with the sword of the children of Ammon. [10] Now therefore the sword shall never depart from thine house; because thou hast despised me, and hast taken the wife of Uriah the Hittite to be thy wife.*
>
> 2 SAMUEL 12:9-10

The Lord didn't say, "David, look what you've done to Bathsheba—how you've defiled her. Look what you've done to Uriah—how you murdered him. Look at all of the people you've offended." It all came down to "David, look what I've done for you. If you had trusted Me, I would have given you even more. But all of these things are going to happen now because you have despised Me!" This was all about David's personal relationship with God!

8a. Which of the following sins did God emphasize when He corrected David?
   A. Despising God
   B. Killing Uriah
   C. Taking Uriah's wife
   D. Using the sword of Ammon to kill Uriah
   E. Eating the shewbread
   A. Despising God

8b. True or false: God cared most how David's sin hurt and offended other people.
   False

8c. If David had turned to God, God would have _____ him even _____ than He already had.
   Given / more

"YOU ARE THE MAN!"

9. Most people think of sin in terms of the damage they do to others. But the issue is they're sinning against God! They are despising the Lord! Instead of trusting God and letting Him supply them with things in an honest way—a way of integrity—they're going against Him and doing it their way. Not trusting God—unbelief—is the heart of sin.

9a. True or false: People usually only think about their sin and its damage to others.
True
9b. When people sin, what are they really doing?
   A. Not trusting God
   B. Despising the Lord
   C. Sinning against God
   D. All of the above
   E. None of the above
   D. All of the above
9c. When you sin, you are _____ _____ God and doing it _____ _____.
Going against / your way
9d. *Discussion question:* Share how you understand that not trusting God, unbelief, and sin are all connected.
Discussion question

Discipleship Questions

23. True or false: Being merciful causes others to be merciful to you.

24. People who rail on others for their mistakes inspire others to do what?
    A. Be merciful
    B. Make mistakes
    C. Hold them to their mistakes
    D. Play a game of cards

25. If you have been merciful, people will want to _____ mercy to you.

26. What was David's real sin?
    A. Murder
    B. Not trusting God
    C. Adultery
    D. Lying
    E. Dancing

27. David had stopped _____ to God as his _____.

28. Who or what did David depend on before he was king?
    _____
    _____
    _____

29. True or false: God prospers you so that you no longer have to bother Him to provide for you.

30. *Discussion question:* Prosperity is not the real danger—what must you beware of as you prosper?
    _____
    _____
    _____

"YOU ARE THE MAN!"

31. Which of the following sins did God emphasize when He corrected David?
    A. Despising God
    B. Killing Uriah
    C. Taking Uriah's wife
    D. Using the sword of Ammon to kill Uriah
    E. Eating the shewbread

32. True or false: God cared most how David's sin hurt and offended other people.

33. If David had turned to God, God would have _____ him even _____ than He already had.

34. True or false: People usually only think about their sin and its damage to others.

35. When people sin, what are they really doing?
    A. Not trusting God
    B. Despising the Lord
    C. Sinning against God
    D. All of the above
    E. None of the above

36. When you sin, you are _____ _____ God and doing it _____ _____.

37. *Discussion question:* Share how you understand that not trusting God, unbelief, and sin are all connected.
_____
_____
_____

LESSONS FROM DAVID

Answer Key

23. True
24. C. Hold them to their mistakes
25. Extend
26. B. Not trusting God
27. Looking / source
28. God
29. False
30. *Discussion question*
31. A. Despising God
32. False
33. Given / more
34. True
35. D. All of the above
36. Going against / your way
37. *Discussion question*

"YOU ARE THE MAN!"

Scriptures

2 SAMUEL 12:7-10

And Nathan said to David, Thou art the man. Thus saith the Lord God of Israel, I anointed thee king over Israel, and I delivered thee out of the hand of Saul; [8] And I gave thee thy master's house, and thy master's wives into thy bosom, and gave thee the house of Israel and of Judah; and if that had been too little, I would moreover have given unto thee such and such things. [9] Wherefore hast thou despised the commandment of the Lord, to do evil in his sight? thou hast killed Uriah the Hittite with the sword, and hast taken his wife to be thy wife, and hast slain him with the sword of the children of Ammon. [10] Now therefore the sword shall never depart from thine house; because thou hast despised me, and hast taken the wife of Uriah the Hittite to be thy wife.

JOHN 16:8-11

And when he is come, he will reprove the world of sin, and of righteousness, and of judgment: [9] Of sin, because they believe not on me; [10] Of righteousness, because I go to my Father, and ye see me no more; [11] Of judgment, because the prince of this world is judged.

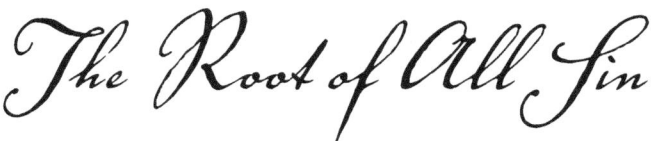

The Root of All Sin

The root of all sin is the fact that you aren't trusting God. That's really what's wrong with stealing. You aren't trusting God. It doesn't matter if a person or a corporation ever misses it or not—God is missing you depending on Him. You are going about obtaining your needs in an ungodly manner, contrary to His instruction. That's the transgression against God.

That's what's really wrong with sexual immorality and adultery. Even the church has fallen to this place where people reason against sin based on the physical consequences. They say, "If you sin sexually, you're exposing yourself to sexually transmitted diseases. And with today's AIDS epidemic, etc., you're just playing Russian roulette!" They try to argue for sexual purity on the basis of just the possible physical consequences that could result. Those things exist, and if that's all the reasoning you had, it would be good enough to remain sexually pure. It's just stupid to go out and do things like that. But at its core, this is really the wrong reasoning.

What would happen if medicine somehow came up with a cure for all sexually transmitted diseases? What if AIDS was obliterated? Would that all of a sudden make sexual promiscuity okay? Of course not! But if you use this kind of logic to reason with people why they shouldn't live in sexual immorality, then they'll be able to excuse it by saying, "I'm using protection. I'm having protected sex." They will just explain it away. However, the real root of sin is that you aren't trusting God!

MARRIAGE IS HONORABLE

If you're married, the Lord gave you that mate.

> *Let thy fountain be blessed: and rejoice with the wife of thy youth. [19] Let her be as the loving hind and pleasant roe; let her breasts satisfy thee at all times; and be thou ravished always with her love.*
>
> PROVERBS 5:18-19

> *Marriage is honourable in all, and the bed undefiled.*
>
> HEBREWS 13:4A

In other words, God has purposed for you to satisfy your sexual desires with the marriage partner He gave you. Even from the very beginning, the Lord ordained that there should be one woman for one man for life. Due to certain things, there are exceptions. But this was God's original plan. It's revealed in the fact that He made Adam and Eve—not Adam and Eve, Sue, Peggy, and all these others. God didn't give Adam multiple wives. It was one woman for one man.

That's what is wrong with homosexuality: People say, "You could get all of these diseases and the suicide rate among homosexuals is the highest of any segment of society." You could reason from all of these consequences and try to get people against it, but the real root of what's wrong with homosexuality is that a person is rejecting God's design. He made them Adam and Eve—not Adam and Steve. Homosexuals say, "I don't care what God did. I don't care what He says or what His will is. This is just the way I am!" No, it's not! They are rejecting and rebelling against God.

What would happen if a man's wife went out and committed adultery? What's really wrong with that? Well, you could talk about sexually transmitted diseases and ask, "What if she gets pregnant? What would happen to the child?" You could reason from all of these things, which are legitimate problems. But what if she did this and there was no sexually transmitted disease and no pregnancy that came of it. Just because there was an absence of physical consequences, would the husband say, "It's okay, honey. You didn't pick up a sexually transmitted disease or become pregnant, so don't worry about it." Of course not! The real issue is that she broke her covenant with her husband. He would be grieved and have to deal with it.

It's the same way with God. Whether you get caught in sin or experience any consequences in the natural isn't the issue; God knows that you aren't trusting in Him and looking to Him to meet your needs.

BROKEN TRUST

That's what the Lord was telling David. He didn't say, "Look what you did to Bathsheba! Look what you did to Uriah! Look what it's going to cost you and the nation!" Instead, He asked, "How could you have despised Me?"

When I first let my boys start taking the car to go on a date or some other outing, I'd tell them, "Be in by 11:00." They would arrive at 11:10, 11:15, or whatever. So, when they came in the house, I'd ask them, "Why are you late?"

They would answer, "It's only ten or fifteen minutes. It's not a big deal."

Like most parents, I didn't always communicate things right. I remember saying, "It's late at night. What would have happened if you had a flat, run out of gas, gotten stuck, or something? Nighttime is when all the weirdos are out and about. It's dangerous. You could have been hurt. Something could have happened!" Kids don't believe they're going to run out of gas, have a flat, or whatever. They look at the consequences and wonder, *What's the big deal between 11:00 and 11:15?* They just don't understand.

I might not have made this clear to my own children—it took me a while to figure it out myself—but the real issue was a violation of my trust. It's not that in those fifteen minutes, the whole world turns bad and the car converts back into a pumpkin. The issue to address with them is, "I don't owe you this. It's not a God-given right that you drive the family car and stay out as late as you want. It's a privilege. I've extended grace to you and trusted you, but you didn't honor me. You've offended me because you didn't honor my trust. If I say 11:00 and you're going to push it to 11:15, the real issue is that you've broken my trust—not these other things. How could you have done this to me?"

Many times, kids just think, *What's the difference between 11:00 and 11:15? That's no big deal!*

The big deal is that they were trusted. By not honoring that trust, they've shown that they can't be trusted. They've proven that they don't really respect their parents; they're going to do whatever they want. And if their parents say eleven, they're going to push it fifteen minutes or so.

That's the way it is with God. This is what's really wrong with sin.

IT'S PERSONAL!

You could argue that substance abuse is wrong because of its consequences: "Drugs and alcohol will damage your brain and your body. They'll cost you money and maybe even your job. You'll be shamed and rejected." In reality, a substance abuser is miserable and looking for an escape, willing to waste money and put their health on the line. They're saying, "I'm so miserable that I'm willing to run all of these risks just for a few moments of being high, numb, and euphoric so I don't feel my problems." In other words, they're turning to a pill, a needle, or a bottle to alleviate their problems instead of turning to God. They're using this substance as a substitute for the Lord. That's what is offensive to Him! It's not just the health risk or the fact that they could have a car accident and kill someone. These things are factors, but the root issue is that they aren't letting God meet their needs. They're trying to get them met some other way—and that's what grieves Him!

When you start looking at sin this way, it totally changes your perspective. The consequences wouldn't matter to you. Whether you could get by with something or not wouldn't matter. It wouldn't matter if anyone else was around or not. You would have a personal standard on the inside of you that would hold you up in any circumstance because it's a personal deal between you and God.

That's how it was with Joseph. He was sold into slavery, bought by Potiphar in Egypt, and worked as a slave in his house. But because he was faithful to the Lord, God gave him favor. Joseph was promoted, but he caught the attention of his master's wife. She came and repeatedly tried to entice Joseph into committing adultery with her. Even though she pressed him, he wouldn't do it. Finally, one day Joseph declared,

How then can I do this great wickedness, and sin against God?

GENESIS 39:9B

If Joseph had been looking at it only from a situational ethics perspective—through the eyes of "relative morality"—he could have reasoned, *I'm a slave. I was forsaken and sold into slavery. God hasn't done me any good!* In bitterness, he could have decided, *I'll just indulge myself. How could I ever get caught? Mrs. Potiphar certainly isn't going to tell her husband. That would put her own head on the line.* If Joseph had only been looking at *Can I get by with this?* he probably would have indulged himself.

STAND UP OR STAND DOWN?

But Joseph said,

How then can I do this great wickedness, and sin against God?

GENESIS 39:9B

Although he knew it was a sin against Potiphar, the main issue was that it was against God. This same logic kept me pure as a young American soldier in Vietnam while most of the other people I knew just lived like animals. I was in a company of two hundred guys, and about once every six weeks, we had what was called "stand down." They would take all of the frontline troops and bring them to the rear for all of the booze and sex they wanted. They'd bring in Asian showgirls, who were nothing but glorified prostitutes. After the "show," they would give them several bunkers so the men could have all the sex they wanted. Out of the two hundred guys in my company, I'm the only one I'm aware of who didn't participate!

One of the guys was a fellow I had grown up with back home. We had even gone to the same church together. He wasn't a bad kid or anything like that. But when I talked to him about this, he just gave me the logic most guys used: "I'm probably going to get killed next week anyway. What does it matter? I'm on the other side of the world and these are prostitutes. Nobody will ever know what I've done. Besides, everybody else is doing it!" Due to this reasoning, the vast majority of my fellow soldiers did things they wouldn't have done if they had been back home in the United States.

THE ROOT OF ALL SIN

It didn't matter to me whether anybody else ever knew what I did or not, because God was there. I had a personal relationship with the Lord, and I couldn't just sin against Him that way. That's what kept me from giving in.

That's how God reproved David. He said, "David, how could you have done these things and despised Me?" And that's what brought David back. The Lord didn't rebuke him based on just consequences; it was all about, "David, at one time, you loved Me!" The New Testament terminology for this is "David, you've left your first love!" (Rev. 2:4). God basically told David, "At one time, you used to adore Me. I satisfied you and gave you all these things. But now, you've moved away from Me and you're satisfying your desires through lust, instead of love." That's the reasoning God used—and David got the message!

THE HEART OF THE MATTER

David repented of his sin with Bathsheba, as recorded in Psalm 51:

Have mercy upon me, O God, according to thy lovingkindness: according unto the multitude of thy tender mercies blot out my transgressions. [2] Wash me thoroughly from mine iniquity, and cleanse me from my sin. [3] For I acknowledge my transgressions: and my sin is ever before me. [4] Against thee, thee only, have I sinned, and done this evil in thy sight: that thou mightest be justified when thou speakest, and be clear when thou judgest.

PSALM 51:1-4

Notice how David said, "Against You, and You only, have I sinned!" In one sense, that's not right. He sinned against Bathsheba. He sinned against Uriah. He opened a door for sexual sin and murder to work in his family. David caused a lot of trouble for many people. But these consequences were really only side issues. The heart of the matter was David repenting and coming back into proper relationship with God.

Outline

I. The root of all sin is the fact that you aren't trusting God.
   A. He is missing you depending on Him.
   B. You are going about obtaining your needs in an ungodly manner, contrary to His instruction.
   C. That's what's really wrong with sexual immorality and adultery.

II. God has purposed for you to satisfy your sexual desires with the marriage partner He gave you:

   Let thy fountain be blessed: and rejoice with the wife of thy youth. [19] Let her be as the loving hind and pleasant roe; let her breasts satisfy thee at all times; and be thou ravished always with her love.
   PROVERBS 5:18-19

   Marriage is honourable in all, and the bed undefiled.
   HEBREWS 13:4A

   A. Even from the very beginning, the Lord ordained that there should be one woman for one man for life.
   B. That's what is wrong with homosexuality: The real root is that a person is rejecting God's design.
   C. A man whose wife had committed adultery but didn't get a sexually transmitted disease or become pregnant would never say, "It's okay, honey. Don't worry about it."
      i. The real issue is that she broke her covenant with her husband.
   D. In the same way, whether you get caught in sin or experience any consequences in the natural isn't the issue; God knows that you aren't trusting in Him and looking to Him to meet your needs.

III. God didn't say, "Look what you did to Bathsheba! Look what you did to Uriah! Look what it's going to cost you and the nation"; instead, He asked, "How could you have despised Me?"
   A. That's what's wrong when children break their parents' trust.
      i. They've shown that they can't be trusted.
      ii. They've proven that they don't really respect their parents.
      iii. They're going to do whatever they want.
   B. That's the way it is with God.
   C. This is what's really wrong with sin.

IV. When you substitute anything for the Lord, that's offensive to Him!
   A. You aren't letting Him meet your needs.
   B. The fact that you're trying to get them met some other way is what grieves Him!
   C. When you start looking at sin the right way, it totally changes your perspective.
      i. The consequences wouldn't matter to you.
      ii. Whether you could get by with something or not wouldn't matter.
      iii. You would have a personal standard on the inside of you that would hold you up in any circumstance because it's a personal deal between you and God.

V. Look at what Joseph said to Potiphar's wife, who tried to entice him to commit adultery with her:

How then can I do this great wickedness, and sin against God?

GENESIS 39:9B

   A. If Joseph had only been looking at *Can I get by with this?* he probably would have indulged himself.
   B. The main issue is that he would have sinned against God.
   C. This same logic kept me pure as a young American soldier in Vietnam while most of the other people I knew just lived like animals.
   D. It didn't matter to me whether anybody else ever knew what I did or not, because God was there.
   E. I had a personal relationship with the Lord, and I couldn't just sin against Him that way.

VI. God's reproof is what brought David back.
   A. The Lord didn't rebuke him based on just consequences; it was all about, "David, you've left your first love!" (Rev. 2:4).
   B. The reasoning God used with David was, "At one time, you used to adore Me. I satisfied you and gave you all these things. But now, you've moved away from Me and you're satisfying your desires through lust, instead of love."
   C. David got the message!

VII. David repented of his sin with Bathsheba, as recorded in Psalm 51:

Have mercy upon me, O God, according to thy lovingkindness: according unto the multitude of thy tender mercies blot out my transgressions. [2] Wash me thoroughly from mine iniquity, and cleanse me from my sin. [3] For I acknowledge my transgressions: and my sin is ever before me. [4] Against thee, thee only, have I sinned, and done this evil in thy sight: that thou mightest be justified when thou speakest, and be clear when thou judgest.

PSALM 51:1-4

A. Notice how David said, "Against You, and You only, have I sinned!"
B. In one sense, that's not right.
    i. He sinned against Bathsheba.
    ii. He sinned against Uriah.
    iii. He opened a door for sexual sin and murder to work in his family.
C. But the heart of the matter was David repenting and coming back into proper relationship with God.

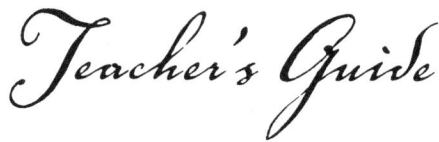

Teacher's Guide

1. The root of all sin is the fact that we aren't trusting God. He is missing us depending on Him. We are going about obtaining our needs in an ungodly manner, contrary to His instruction. That's what's really wrong with sexual immorality and adultery.

1a. The root of all sin is what?
   A. God misses you
   B. You are trying to obtain your needs through immorality
   C. The fact that you are not trusting God
   D. All of the above
   E. None of the above
   C. The fact that you are not trusting God

1b. *Discussion question:* What are some of the ways you can identify that you are not trusting God?
   Discussion question

2. God has purposed for us to satisfy our sexual desires with the marriage partners He gave us:

Let thy fountain be blessed: and rejoice with the wife of thy youth. [19] Let her be as the loving hind and pleasant roe; let her breasts satisfy thee at all times; and be thou ravished always with her love.

PROVERBS 5:18-19

Marriage is honourable in all, and the bed undefiled.

HEBREWS 13:4A

Even from the very beginning, the Lord ordained that there should be one woman for one man for life. That's what is wrong with homosexuality: The real root is that a person is rejecting God's design. A man whose wife had committed adultery but didn't get a sexually transmitted disease or become pregnant would never say, "It's okay, honey. Don't worry about it." The real issue is that she broke her covenant with her husband. In the same way, whether we get caught in sin or experience any consequences in the natural isn't the issue; God knows that we aren't trusting in Him and looking to Him to meet our needs.

2a. *Discussion question:* Why do you think God chose marriage as the place to satisfy your sexual desires?
<u>Discussion question</u>

2b. Why is homosexuality inherently wrong?
It rejects God's design

2c. A man whose wife committed adultery but had no physical consequences would not tell her "That's okay," because of what?
   A. She didn't confess instead of waiting to get caught
   B. She broke covenant with him
   C. She only did it once
   D. He's partially at fault
   E. It was understandable
   B. She broke covenant with him

3. God didn't say, "Look what you did to Bathsheba! Look what you did to Uriah! Look what it's going to cost you and the nation"; instead, He asked, "How could you have despised Me?" That's what's wrong when children break their parents' trust. They've shown that they can't be trusted. They've proven that they don't really respect their parents. They're going to do whatever they want. That's the way it is with God. This is what's really wrong with sin.

3a. What did God ask David?
    A. "Were you drinking too much?"
    B. "Do you realize what you've done to Bathsheba and Uriah?"
    C. "How can I help you out of this?"
    D. "How could you have despised Me?"
    E. "Do you have a good reason for your sin?"
    D. "How could you have despised Me?"

3b. *Discussion question:* Does God consider everyone trustworthy? Why or why not?
Discussion question

4. When we substitute anything for the Lord, that's offensive to Him! We aren't letting Him meet our needs. The fact that we're trying to get them met some other way is what grieves Him! When we start looking at sin the right way, it totally changes our perspective. The consequences wouldn't matter to us. Whether we could get by with something or not wouldn't matter. We would have a personal standard on the inside of us that would hold you up in any circumstance because it's a personal deal between us and God.

4a. It is offensive to God when _____.
    A. You do rude things in public
    B. You take a shortcut to His destiny for you
    C. You don't let Him provide for you
    D. You substitute anything for the Lord
    E. You get defensive
    D. You substitute anything for the Lord

4b. *Discussion question:* Do you have a personal standard in your relationship with God that you think would hold you up in any circumstance?
Discussion question

5. Let's look at what Joseph said to Potiphar's wife, who tried to entice him to commit adultery with her:

   How then can I do this great wickedness, and sin against God?

   GENESIS 39:9B

If Joseph had only been looking at *Can I get by with this?* he probably would have indulged himself. The main issue is that he would have sinned against God. This same logic kept Andrew pure as a young American soldier in Vietnam while most of the other people he knew just lived like animals. It didn't matter to him whether anybody else ever knew what he did or not, because God was there. He had a personal relationship with the Lord, and he couldn't just sin against Him that way.

5a. What would have happened if Joseph had thought, *Can I get by with this?*
   A. He would have refused to sin
   B. God would have sent lightning to strike him
   C. He probably would have indulged
   D. He would have asked God about it
   E. He would have challenged Potiphar to a duel
   C. He probably would have indulged

5b. When Andrew was in Vietnam, it didn't matter to him whether anybody else knew what he did or not, because:
   A. God was there
   B. He had a personal relationship with the Lord
   C. He couldn't just sin against Him that way
   D. All of the above
   E. None of the above
   D. All of the above

6. God's reproof is what brought David back. The Lord didn't rebuke him based on just consequences; it was all about, "David, you've left your first love!" (Rev. 2:4). The reasoning God used with David was, "At one time, you used to adore Me. I satisfied you and gave you all these things. But now, you've moved away from Me and you're satisfying your desires through lust, instead of love." David got the message!

6a. God's reproof is what brought David _____.
   A. A crushed spirit
   B. Back
   C. Mentally to the breaking point
   D. Joy
   E. A new psalm
   B. Back

6b. The Lord didn't rebuke David based on just consequences, because:
   A. David still wore his promise ring
   B. He moved to another city
   C. David left his first love
   D. David used to adore the Lord
   E. C and D
   E. C and D

6c. *Discussion question:* Do you suppose it took David very long to "get the message" from the Lord? How quick are you to hear God's correction?
   Discussion question

LESSONS FROM DAVID

7. David repented of his sin with Bathsheba, as recorded in Psalm 51:

> *Have mercy upon me, O God, according to thy lovingkindness: according unto the multitude of thy tender mercies blot out my transgressions. [2] Wash me thoroughly from mine iniquity, and cleanse me from my sin. [3] For I acknowledge my transgressions: and my sin is ever before me. [4] Against thee, thee only, have I sinned, and done this evil in thy sight: that thou mightest be justified when thou speakest, and be clear when thou judgest.*
>
> **PSALM 51:1-4**

David said, "Against You, and You only, have I sinned!" In one sense, that's not right. He sinned against Bathsheba. He sinned against Uriah. He opened a door for sexual sin and murder to work in his family. But the heart of the matter was David repenting and coming back into proper relationship with God.

7a. Even though David sinned against Bathsheba and Uriah, he said _____.
  A. "My sin was mostly against Uriah"
  B. "God will spare the child"
  C. "Against you, God, and You only, have I sinned"
  D. "It'll be all right"
  E. "I'll pay them back and make it good"
  C. "Against You, God, and You only, have I sinned"

Discipleship Questions

1. The root of all sin is what?
   A. God misses you
   B. You are trying to obtain your needs through immorality
   C. The fact that you are not trusting God
   D. All of the above
   E. None of the above

2. *Discussion question:* What are some of the ways you can identify that you are not trusting God?
   _____
   _____
   _____

3. *Discussion question:* Why do you think God chose marriage as the place to satisfy your sexual desires?
   _____
   _____
   _____

4. Why is homosexuality inherently wrong?
   _____
   _____
   _____

5. A man whose wife committed adultery but had no physical consequences would not tell her, "That's okay," because of what?
   A. She didn't confess instead of waiting to get caught
   B. She broke covenant with him
   C. She only did it once
   D. He's partially at fault
   E. It was understandable

6. What did God ask David?
   A. "Were you drinking too much?"
   B. "Do you realize what you've done to Bathsheba and Uriah?"
   C. "How can I help you out of this?"
   D. "How could you have despised Me?"
   E. "Do you have a good reason for your sin?"

7. *Discussion question:* Does God consider everyone trustworthy? Why or Why not?
   _____
   _____
   _____

8. It is offensive to God when _____.
   A. You do rude things in public
   B. You take a shortcut to His destiny for you
   C. You don't let Him provide for you
   D. You substitute anything for the Lord
   E. You get defensive

9. *Discussion question:* Do you have a personal standard in your relationship with God that you think would hold you up in any circumstance?
   _____
   _____
   _____

10. What would have happened if Joseph had thought, *Can I get by with this?*
    A. He would have refused to sin
    B. God would have sent lightning to strike him
    C. He probably would have indulged
    D. He would have asked God about it
    E. He would have challenged Potiphar to a duel

11. When Andrew was in Vietnam, it didn't matter to him whether anybody else knew what he did or not, because:
    A. God was there
    B. He had a personal relationship with the Lord
    C. He couldn't just sin against Him that way
    D. All of the above
    E. None of the above

12. God's reproof is what brought David _____.
    A. A crushed spirit
    B. Back
    C. Mentally to the breaking point
    D. Joy
    E. A new psalm

13. The Lord didn't rebuke David based on just consequences, because:
    A. David still wore his promise ring
    B. He moved to another city
    C. David left his first love
    D. David used to adore the Lord
    E. C and D

14. *Discussion question:* Do you suppose it took David very long to "get the message" from the Lord? How quick are you to hear God's correction?
_____
_____
_____

15. Even though David sinned against Bathsheba and Uriah, he said_____.
    A. "My sin was mostly against Uriah"
    B. "God will spare the child"
    C. "Against you, God, and You only, have I sinned"
    D. "It'll be all right"
    E. "I'll pay them back and make it good"

1. C. The fact that you are not trusting God
2. *Discussion question*
3. *Discussion question*
4. C. It rejects God's design
5. B. She broke covenant with him
6. D. "How could you have despised Me?"
7. *Discussion question*
8. D. You substitute anything for the Lord
9. *Discussion question*
10. C. He probably would have indulged
11. D. All of the above
12. B. Back
13. E. C and D
14. *Discussion question*
15. C. "Against You, God, and You only, have I sinned"

Scriptures

PROVERBS 5:18-19
Let thy fountain be blessed: and rejoice with the wife of thy youth. [**19**] Let her be as the loving hind and pleasant roe; let her breasts satisfy thee at all times; and be thou ravished always with her love.

HEBREWS 13:4
Marriage is honourable in all, and the bed undefiled: but whoremongers and adulterers God will judge.

GENESIS 39:9
There is none greater in this house than I; neither hath he kept back any thing from me but thee, because thou art his wife: how then can I do this great wickedness, and sin against God?

PSALM 51:1-4
Have mercy upon me, O God, according to thy lovingkindness: according unto the multitude of thy tender mercies blot out my transgressions. [**2**] Wash me thoroughly from mine iniquity, and cleanse me from my sin. [**3**] For I acknowledge my transgressions: and my sin is ever before me. [**4**] Against thee, thee only, have I sinned, and done this evil in thy sight: that thou mightest be justified when thou speakest, and be clear when thou judgest.

Consequences

Although consequences aren't the main issue, they do exist. David's sin unleashed a barrage of negative consequences, and we would do well to learn from them.

Since David let sexual immorality into his life, I believe it gave it access—through him—into his entire family. His firstborn son, Amnon, lusted after and raped his half-sister Tamar (2 Sam. 13:1-20). Due to this, Absalom—David's third oldest son and Tamar's full brother—became incensed at Amnon. It took him two years, but eventually, he brought vengeance upon Amnon and killed him (2 Sam. 13:28-29). So, David opened a door that allowed sexual sin—and then murder—to influence his own children.

Absalom fled Jerusalem and lived in self-imposed exile for three years due to the fear of what his father, David, might do (2 Sam. 13:38). When he finally came back, David still wouldn't talk to him for another two years (2 Sam. 14:21-24 and 28). Absalom became upset and finally got an audience with his father, the king. David kissed him and hugged him, but apparently there wasn't total reconciliation (2 Sam. 14:33). So, after David didn't respond to him the way he wanted, Absalom began the process of stealing the people's hearts away from him (2 Sam. 15:6). David allowed this treason to go on unchallenged. Finally, Absalom tried to kill David and take over the kingdom. In the ensuing civil war, thousands and thousands of people died (2 Sam. 15-17).

When David fled Jerusalem as Absalom and his forces approached, he left some of his concubines behind to guard his house. Absalom set up a tent on the roof of the house, went in, and had sexual relations with his father's concubines in the sight of all the people (2 Sam. 16:22).

Although the main issue was David's relationship with God, his sin caused some major consequences! It opened up his son to lust and, therefore, one of his daughters to being raped. It opened up another son to murder. It also caused a civil war and his own concubines to be defiled in the sight of all the people. On and on it goes!

DEFILED & DESTROYED

Ahithophel, the Gilonite, David's counselor, was the one who counseled Absalom to have sexual relations with his father's concubines (2 Sam. 16:20-21). Back then, when a new king took over a kingdom from another, it was customary for him to take the wives and/or concubines of the previous king and have sexual relations with them. The logic behind it was, "If the previous king could have done anything about it, he would have." This signaled the fact that the previous king was out and the new king was in. It was a symbolic gesture demonstrating the total impotence of the previous king. It proved that the new king was now fully in power.

Although this was often customary, perhaps Absalom could have done something else to have solidified the people behind him. Surely there was something else he could have done to communicate that this was a fight to the death with no chance of reconciliation. Why would Ahithophel—who was reputedly always right and never missed it—counsel Absalom to publicly defile David's concubines?

In 2 Samuel 23:34, the Bible reveals that Eliam was the son of Ahithophel. Over in 2 Samuel 11:3—where David's adultery is chronicled—Bathsheba was listed as *"the daughter of Eliam."*

This would make Ahithophel Bathsheba's grandfather! From the very day when Ahithophel first saw that David had defiled his granddaughter and killed Uriah, he nurtured bitterness and un-forgiveness in his heart toward the king. While brooding over this for years and years, Ahithophel had been waiting for an opportunity to get even with David. I'm sure this contributed to his motivation for counseling Absalom in this way.

David's sin was costly! It let lust into Amnon and cost him his life. It cost Tamar her virginity. Absalom became bitter and caused a civil war. Ahithophel was polluted with un-forgiveness. These concubines were defiled and their lives destroyed. All of these things were consequences of David's sin.

MAN CONSCIOUS!

Just because I'm emphasizing that the root of David's sin was his personal rebellion toward and lack of dependence upon God, it doesn't mean that sin doesn't have consequences. Sin will take you further than you want to go, keep you longer than you want to stay, and cost you more than you want to pay! You don't want to sin, just from the consequence level. But you need to recognize and understand that sin is a transgression against the Lord. You aren't trusting and believing God!

It doesn't matter if the people you steal from can afford it, are rich, and have insurance. The issue is that you aren't trusting God as your Source. You're doing it your way instead of trusting God. You're imposing your wisdom above God's wisdom. It doesn't matter if you can commit sexual immorality without contracting a sexually transmitted disease, becoming pregnant, or getting caught. The issue is that you would be sinning against God.

This understanding will make a huge difference in your level of integrity. You'll get to where you operate in integrity whether anyone is watching, checking, or holding you accountable or not. Sad to say, most people don't live this way.

I actually read an article where they put some money in a wallet and laid it on the sidewalk. In the wallet was a name and address—all the information needed to return it to its original owner. They laid it on the sidewalk and then watched to see what people would do. Only about 40 percent of the people actually operated in integrity and turned the wallet in. All the others just took it. When they did, the authors stopped them and quizzed them about why they didn't turn it in. Most people answered, "If I had known someone was watching, I would have turned it in." In other words—situational ethics. "Am I going to get caught? Will there be any consequences?" It's not because they are God conscious. It's because they are man conscious.

SERVE THE LORD!

A person who is only doing what's right because it's expected of them and they're being held accountable for it doesn't have a heart after God. True morality and integrity operate that way whether people see it or not. God's Word says we are to serve…

> *In singleness of your heart, as unto Christ; [6] Not with eyeservice, as menpleasers; but as the servants of Christ, doing the will of God from the heart; [7] With good will doing service, as to the Lord, and not to men.*
> EPHESIANS 6:5B-7

> *And whatsoever ye do, do it heartily, as to the Lord, and not unto men; [24] Knowing that of the Lord ye shall receive the reward of the inheritance: for ye serve the Lord Christ.*
> COLOSSIANS 3:23-24

In other words, it doesn't matter whether your employer knows that you are cutting your break short and working an extra five minutes. It doesn't matter whether you ever get rewarded from people or not. You need to boil everything down to doing it as unto the Lord, and not unto people.

My personal relationship with God is what kept me pure as a young soldier in the midst of many temptations in Vietnam. It didn't matter to me if my family or anybody else I looked up to knew what I was doing or not—God knew! And my relationship with Him caused me to have a level of integrity that most of the people over there at that time didn't have. What a powerful truth!

A NEW COVENANT

There were reasons David sinned. He quit having this intimacy with God. It stopped being a personal relationship. He became so prosperous that he didn't think he had to seek God the way he did before. So, he turned off his engines and began to coast. Without realizing it, he started sinking at that very moment. It was just a matter of time before some form of sin manifested. He committed adultery and then murder in an effort to cover up his adultery. Then David displayed a harsh judgment, and because of that, God gave him the same judgment that he meted out.

Praise God for the New Covenant! All the judgment we deserved for our sins was placed upon Jesus 2,000 years ago at the cross of Calvary. Now we have a better covenant, based on better promises, that was ratified through the shed blood of our Lord. Looking forward to this New Covenant, David himself exclaimed,

> *Blessed is the man unto whom the Lord imputeth not iniquity, and in whose spirit there is no guile.*
>
> PSALM 32:2

Paul even quoted this passage in Romans 4:8:

> *Blessed is the man to whom the Lord will not impute sin.*

Under the Old Covenant, David had his sin imputed unto him. But you and I live in a covenant today where our sin has been imputed to Jesus. We aren't going to suffer judgment from God, but there is still much we can learn from God's judgment on David. Even though Jesus has borne our punishment, we should still abhor sin and walk in integrity, knowing that it cost our beloved Savior His life. He suffered. Every time we commit a sin, Jesus suffered that sin. I don't want to add to what the Lord has already borne. I want to live a life that glorifies God.

GOD'S GRACE IS EVIDENT

David suffered the consequences for his sin. God forgave him, but the child born to Bathsheba died (2 Sam. 12:18). David interceded, thinking that maybe God would have mercy. But since David had shown no mercy, he got no mercy. And the child died.

But after this judgment was done, you can still see the forgiveness and grace of God in David's life. He had sexual relations with Bathsheba again, this time as her lawfully wedded husband. Even though their whole relationship had been conceived in lust and sin, that was over and repented of. God blessed their union, and she conceived a second son, who lived. David called him Solomon. But God sent Nathan the prophet and renamed him Jedidiah, which means beloved of the Lord (2 Sam. 12:24-25). God put His stamp of approval upon that marriage.

Now, that's a powerful lesson. I've met many people who were married completely out of the will of God. The initial situation was totally ungodly, yet they find themselves in that marriage. What should they do now that they have turned their lives over to the Lord? Should they divorce, cause a break, go find someone else, and complicate this thing? Well, here's a scriptural precedent. If you become born again while in a totally ungodly marriage relationship, you—through your repentance—become a brand-new person. God sanctifies you. Just like David and Bathsheba, the Lord can make that relationship that was conceived in sin turn out to be godly. In fact, Solomon was chosen to be the next king. God's grace is evident throughout the entire life of David.

I encourage you to learn these life lessons at David's expense, rather than through your own hard knocks. May these truths take root in your life so that you, too, would walk like David—a man after God's own heart!

Outline

I. Although the main issue was David's relationship with God, his sin unleashed a barrage of negative consequences, and we would do well to learn from them.
   A. It opened up his son to lust and, therefore, one of his daughters to rape.
   B. It opened up another son to murder.
   C. It caused a civil war and his own concubines to be defiled in the sight of all the people.

II. Sin will take you further than you want to go, keep you longer than you want to stay, and cost you more than you want to pay!
   A. But you need to recognize and understand that sin is a transgression against the Lord—you aren't trusting and believing God!
   B. This understanding will make a huge difference in your level of integrity.
      i. You'll get to where you operate in integrity whether anyone is watching, checking, or holding you accountable or not.
   C. You need to be God conscious, not man conscious.

III. A person who is only doing what's right because it's expected of them and they're being held accountable for it doesn't have a heart after God.
   A. God's Word says we are to serve…

In singleness of your heart, as unto Christ; [6] Not with eyeservice, as menpleasers; but as the servants of Christ, doing the will of God from the heart; [7] With good will doing service, as to the Lord, and not to men.

EPHESIANS 6:5B-7

And whatsoever ye do, do it heartily, as to the Lord, and not unto men; [24] Knowing that of the Lord ye shall receive the reward of the inheritance: for ye serve the Lord Christ.

COLOSSIANS 3:23-24

   B. It doesn't matter whether you ever get rewarded from people or not; you need to boil everything down to doing it as unto the Lord, and not unto people.
   C. What a powerful truth!

IV. The reason David sinned is because he quit having this intimacy with God.
   A. It was just a matter of time before some form of sin manifested.

B. Then David displayed a harsh judgment, and because of that, God gave him the same judgment that he meted out.
C. Looking forward to the New Covenant, David himself exclaimed,

Blessed is the man unto whom the Lord imputeth not iniquity, and in whose spirit there is no guile.

PSALM 32:2

D. Under the Old Covenant, David had his sin imputed unto him, but you and I live in a covenant today where our sin has been imputed to Jesus.
E. However, there is still much we can learn from God's judgment on David.
   i. Even though Jesus has borne our punishment, we should still abhor sin and walk in integrity, knowing that it cost our beloved Savior His life.
   ii. Every time we commit a sin, Jesus suffered that sin.
F. We should want to live lives that glorify God.

V. After God judged David, you can still see the forgiveness and grace of God in his life.
   A. God blessed his and Bathsheba's union, and she conceived a second son, who lived.
   B. God sent Nathan the prophet and renamed the son Jedidiah, which means beloved of the Lord (2 Sam. 12:24-25).
   C. If you become born again while in a totally ungodly marriage relationship, the Lord can make that relationship that was conceived in sin turn out to be godly, just like He did for David and Bathsheba.
   D. I encourage you to learn these life lessons at David's expense, rather than through your own hard knocks.
   E. May these truths take root in your life so that you, too, would walk like David—a man after God's own heart!

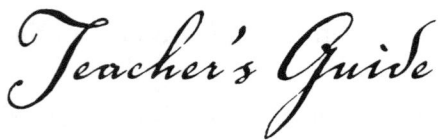

1. Although the main issue was David's relationship with God, his sin unleashed a barrage of negative consequences, and we would do well to learn from them. It opened up his son to lust and, therefore, one of his daughters to rape. It opened up another son to murder. It caused a civil war and his own concubines to be defiled in the sight of all the people.

1a. David's sin unleashed a barrage of _____ _____.
   Negative consequences
1b. What were some of the results of sin for David's immediate family?
   A. One of his daughters was raped
   B. One of his sons was murdered
   C. One of his sons killed his mother
   D. A and B
   E. A and C
   D. A and B
1c. What consequence did David's sin have on his own nation?
   Civil war
1d. What consequence did David's sin have for his concubines?
   They were defiled in front of all the people

CONSEQUENCES

2. Sin will take us further than we want to go, keep us longer than we want to stay, and cost us more than we want to pay! But we need to recognize and understand that sin is a transgression against the Lord—we aren't trusting and believing God! This understanding will make a huge difference in our level of integrity. We'll get to where we operate in integrity whether anyone is watching, checking, or holding us accountable or not. We need to be God conscious, not man conscious.

2a. What will sin always do to you?
    A. Cost you more than you want to pay
    B. Put you in jail
    C. Take you further than you want to go
    D. A and B
    E. A and C
    E. A and C

2b. True or false: When you sin, you are sinning against the people you hurt even more than God.
False

2c. Sin always means that you aren't _____ and _____ God.
Trusting / believing

2d. True or false: Integrity is doing what's right whether anyone is watching or checking or not.
True

2e. *Discussion question:* What do you think it means to be God conscious instead of man conscious?
Discussion question

3. A person who is only doing what's right because it's expected of them and they're being held accountable for it doesn't have a heart after God. God's Word says we are to serve…

> *In singleness of your heart, as unto Christ; [6] Not with eyeservice, as menpleasers; but as the servants of Christ, doing the will of God from the heart; [7] With good will doing service, as to the Lord, and not to men.*
>
> EPHESIANS 6:5B-7

> *And whatsoever ye do, do it heartily, as to the Lord, and not unto men; [24] Knowing that of the Lord ye shall receive the reward of the inheritance: for ye serve the Lord Christ.*
>
> COLOSSIANS 3:23-24

It doesn't matter whether we ever get rewarded from people or not; we need to boil everything down to doing it as unto the Lord, and not unto people. What a powerful truth!

3a. True or false: If you do what's right because you're being held accountable, then you have a heart for God.
False

3b. According to Colossians 3:24, whom should you expect your reward from?
From the Lord

3c. It doesn't matter if you ever get _____ from people or not.
Rewarded

3d. *Discussion question*: What powerful truth should you boil everything down to and why?
Discussion question

4. The reason David sinned is because he quit having this intimacy with God. It was just a matter of time before some form of sin manifested. Then David displayed a harsh judgment, and because of that, God gave him the same judgment that he meted out. Looking forward to the New Covenant, David himself exclaimed,

> *Blessed is the man unto whom the Lord imputeth not iniquity, and in whose spirit there is no guile.*
>
> PSALM 32:2

Under the Old Covenant, David had his sin imputed unto him, but you and I live in a covenant today where our sin has been imputed to Jesus. However, there is still much we can learn from God's judgment on David. Even though Jesus has borne our punishment, we should still abhor sin and walk in integrity, knowing that it cost our beloved Savior His life. Every time we commit a sin, Jesus suffered that sin. We should want to live lives that glorify God.

4a. What did David quit doing that caused him to sin?
Having intimacy with God

4b. True or false: When you stop being intimate with God, it's only a matter of time before some sin manifests.
True

4c. Why did David receive a harsh judgment?
   A. He committed adultery and murder
   B. He judged another harshly
   C. His sin had consequences
   D. God felt like punishing him
   E. So he would learn his lesson well
B. He judged another harshly

4d. Under the Old Covenant, David's sins were imputed to him, but under the New Covenant, your sins have been imputed to _____.
Jesus

4e. *Discussion question*: Knowing that Jesus suffered the sins you commit, how does that change your desire to sin or not sin?
Discussion question

5. After God judged David, we can still see the forgiveness and grace of God in his life. God blessed his and Bathsheba's union, and she conceived a second son, who lived. God sent Nathan the prophet and renamed the son Jedidiah, which means beloved of the Lord (2 Sam. 12:24-25). If we become born again while in totally ungodly marriage relationships, the Lord can make that relationship that was conceived in sin turn out to be godly, just like He did for David and Bathsheba. We should learn these life lessons at David's expense, rather than through our own hard knocks. May these truths take root in our lives so that we, too, would walk like David—a man after God's own heart!

5a. True or false: Even though David's sin was judged, you can still see the grace and forgiveness upon his life.
True

5b. What are some of the ways that God showed His grace to David?
   A. God made him even wealthier
   B. God blessed David's union with Bathsheba, and she conceived a second son
   C. All of David's children were blessed and lived in peace
   D. All of the above
   E. None of the above
   B. God blessed David's union with Bathsheba, and she conceived a second son

5c. God sent Nathan to rename his son Jedidiah, which means what?
Beloved of the Lord

5d. *Discussion question:* How does Nathan renaming David's son show God's forgiveness and grace on David?
Discussion question

5e. True or false: If a relationship is conceived in sin, it can never turn out to be godly.
False

Discipleship Questions

1. David's sin unleashed a barrage of _____ _____.

2. What were some of the results of sin for David's immediate family?
   A. One of his daughters was raped
   B. One of his sons was murdered
   C. One of his sons killed his mother
   D. A and B
   E. A and C

3. What consequence did David's sin have on his own nation?
   _____
   _____
   _____

4. What consequence did David's sin have for his concubines?
   _____
   _____
   _____

5. What will sin always do to you?
   A. Cost you more than you want to pay
   B. Put you in jail
   C. Take you further than you want to go
   D. A and B
   E. A and C

6. True or false: When you sin, you are sinning against the people you hurt even more than God.

7. Sin always means that you aren't _____ and _____ God.

8. True or false: Integrity is doing what's right whether anyone is watching or checking or not.

9. *Discussion question:* What do you think it means to be God conscious instead of man conscious?
   _____
   _____
   _____

10. True or false: If you do what's right because you're being held accountable, then you have a heart for God.

11. According to Colossians 3:24, whom should you expect your reward from?
    _____
    _____
    _____

12. It doesn't matter if you ever get _____ from people or not.

13. *Discussion question:* What powerful truth should you boil everything down to and why?
    _____
    _____
    _____

14. What did David quit doing that caused him to sin?
    _____
    _____
    _____

15. True or false: When you stop being intimate with God, it's only a matter of time before some sin manifests.

16. Why did David receive a harsh judgment?
    A. He committed adultery and murder
    B. He judged another harshly
    C. His sin had consequences
    D. God felt like punishing him
    E. So he would learn his lesson well

17. Under the Old Covenant, David's sins were imputed to him, but under the New Covenant, your sins have been imputed to _____.

18. *Discussion question:* Knowing that Jesus suffered the sins you commit, how does that change your desire to sin or not sin?
   _____
   _____
   _____

19. True or false: Even though David's sin was judged, you can still see the grace and forgiveness upon his life.

20. What are some of the ways that God showed His grace to David?
    A. God made him even wealthier
    B. God blessed David's union with Bathsheba, and she conceived a second son
    C. All of David's children were blessed and lived in peace
    D. All of the above
    E. None of the above

21. God sent Nathan to rename his son Jedidiah, which means what?
   _____
   _____
   _____

22. *Discussion question:* How does Nathan renaming David's son show God's forgiveness and grace on David?
   _____
   _____
   _____

23. True or false: If a relationship is conceived in sin, it can never turn out to be godly.

Answer Key

1. Negative consequences
2. D. A and B
3. Civil war
4. They were defiled in front of all the people
5. E. A and C
6. False
7. Trusting / believing
8. True
9. *Discussion question*
10. False
11. From the Lord
12. Rewarded
13. *Discussion question*
14. Having intimacy with God
15. True
16. B. He judged another harshly
17. Jesus
18. *Discussion question*
19. True
20. B. God blessed David's union with Bathsheba, and she conceived a second son
21. Beloved of the Lord
22. *Discussion question*
23. False

Scriptures

2 SAMUEL 13:1-20

And it came to pass after this, that Absalom the son of David had a fair sister, whose name was Tamar; and Amnon the son of David loved her. [2] And Amnon was so vexed, that he fell sick for his sister Tamar; for she was a virgin; and Amnon thought it hard for him to do any thing to her. [3] But Amnon had a friend, whose name was Jonadab, the son of Shimeah David's brother: and Jonadab was a very subtil man. [4] And he said unto him, Why art thou, being the king's son, lean from day to day? wilt thou not tell me? And Amnon said unto him, I love Tamar, my brother Absalom's sister. [5] And Jonadab said unto him, Lay thee down on thy bed, and make thyself sick: and when thy father cometh to see thee, say unto him, I pray thee, let my sister Tamar come, and give me meat, and dress the meat in my sight, that I may see it, and eat it at her hand. [6] So Amnon lay down, and made himself sick: and when the king was come to see him, Amnon said unto the king, I pray thee, let Tamar my sister come, and make me a couple of cakes in my sight, that I may eat at her hand. [7] Then David sent home to Tamar, saying, Go now to thy brother Amnon's house, and dress him meat. [8] So Tamar went to her brother Amnon's house; and he was laid down. And she took flour, and kneaded it, and made cakes in his sight, and did bake the cakes. [9] And she took a pan, and poured them out before him; but he refused to eat. And Amnon said, Have out all men from me. And they went out every man from him. [10] And Amnon said unto Tamar, Bring the meat into the chamber, that I may eat of thine hand. And Tamar took the cakes which she had made, and brought them into the chamber to Amnon her brother. [11] And when she had brought them unto him to eat, he took hold of her, and said unto her, Come lie with me, my sister. [12] And she answered him, Nay, my brother, do not force me; for no such thing ought to be done in Israel: do not thou this folly. [13] And I, whither shall I cause my shame to go? and as for thee, thou shalt be as one of the fools in Israel. Now therefore, I pray thee, speak unto the king; for he will not withhold me from thee. [14] Howbeit he would not hearken unto her voice: but, being stronger than she, forced her, and lay with her. [15] Then Amnon hated her exceedingly; so that the hatred wherewith he hated her was greater than the love wherewith he had loved her. And Amnon said unto her, Arise, be gone. [16] And she said unto him, There is no cause: this evil in sending me away is greater than the other that thou didst unto me. But he would not hearken unto her. [17] Then he called his servant that ministered unto him, and said, Put now this woman out from me, and bolt the door after her. [18] And she had a garment of divers colours upon her: for with such robes were the king's daughters that were virgins apparelled. Then his servant brought her out, and bolted the door after her. [19] And Tamar put ashes on her head, and rent her garment of divers colours that was on her, and laid her hand on her head, and went on crying. [20] And Absalom her brother said unto her, Hath Amnon thy brother been with thee? but hold now thy peace, my sister: he is thy brother; regard not this thing. So Tamar remained desolate in her brother Absalom's house.

2 SAMUEL 13:28-29

Now Absalom had commanded his servants, saying, Mark ye now when Amnon's heart is merry with wine, and when I say unto you, Smite Amnon; then kill him, fear not: have not I commanded you? be courageous, and be valiant. [29] And the servants of Absalom did unto Amnon as Absalom had commanded. Then all the king's sons arose, and every man gat him up upon his mule, and fled.

2 SAMUEL 13:38

So Absalom fled, and went to Geshur, and was there three years.

2 SAMUEL 14:21-24

And the king said unto Joab, Behold now, I have done this thing: go therefore, bring the young man Absalom again. [22] And Joab fell to the ground on his face, and bowed himself, and thanked the king: and Joab said, To day thy servant knoweth that I have found grace in thy sight, my lord, O king, in that the king hath fulfilled the request of his servant. [23] So Joab arose and went to Geshur, and brought Absalom to Jerusalem. [24] And the king said, Let him turn to his own house, and let him not see my face. So Absalom returned to his own house, and saw not the king's face.

2 SAMUEL 14:28

So Absalom dwelt two full years in Jerusalem, and saw not the king's face.

2 SAMUEL 14:33

So Joab came to the king, and told him: and when he had called for Absalom, he came to the king, and bowed himself on his face to the ground before the king: and the king kissed Absalom.

2 SAMUEL 15:6

And on this manner did Absalom to all Israel that came to the king for judgment: so Absalom stole the hearts of the men of Israel.

2 SAMUEL 16:20-22

Then said Absalom to Ahithophel, Give counsel among you what we shall do. [21] And Ahithophel said unto Absalom, Go in unto thy father's concubines, which he hath left to keep the house; and all Israel shall hear that thou art abhorred of thy father: then shall the hands of all that are with thee be strong. [22] So they spread Absalom a tent upon the top of the house; and Absalom went in unto his father's concubines in the sight of all Israel.

2 SAMUEL 23:34

Eliphelet the son of Ahasbai, the son of the Maachathite, Eliam the son of Ahithophel the Gilonite.

CONSEQUENCES

2 SAMUEL 11:3

And David sent and enquired after the woman. And one said, Is not this Bathsheba, the daughter of Eliam, the wife of Uriah the Hittite?

EPHESIANS 6:5-7

Servants, be obedient to them that are your masters according to the flesh, with fear and trembling, in singleness of your heart, as unto Christ; [6] Not with eyeservice, as menpleasers; but as the servants of Christ, doing the will of God from the heart; [7] With good will doing service, as to the Lord, and not to men.

COLOSSIANS 3:23-24

And whatsoever ye do, do it heartily, as to the Lord, and not unto men; [24] Knowing that of the Lord ye shall receive the reward of the inheritance: for ye serve the Lord Christ.

PSALM 32:2

Blessed is the man unto whom the Lord imputeth not iniquity, and in whose spirit there is no guile.

ROMANS 4:8

Blessed is the man to whom the Lord will not impute sin.

2 SAMUEL 12:18

And it came to pass on the seventh day, that the child died. And the servants of David feared to tell him that the child was dead: for they said, Behold, while the child was yet alive, we spake unto him, and he would not hearken unto our voice: how will he then vex himself, if we tell him that the child is dead?

2 SAMUEL 12:24-25

And David comforted Bathsheba his wife, and went in unto her, and lay with her: and she bare a son, and he called his name Solomon: and the Lord loved him. [25] And he sent by the hand of Nathan the prophet; and he called his name Jedidiah, because of the Lord.

Conclusion

Remember that all the things recorded in Scripture about David were to serve as examples for us (1 Corinthians 10:6 and 11). Here is a brief summary of some of the lessons I've shared in this study guide.

1. David wasn't God's first choice, yet God used him powerfully. We are still being inspired by him over 4,000 years later.
2. David's own family didn't see his potential, but God did and exalted him over those who were older and stronger. God saw his heart.
3. David didn't let the persecution of others get him off the track and up into the grandstands, arguing with the spectators.
4. David based his ability to succeed on God's covenant, not himself.
5. David had confidence to fight Goliath because he had been faithful in smaller things.
6. David fought until his enemy was dead, not just down.
7. David was humble and depended on God instead of himself.
8. David was able to encourage himself in the Lord.
9. David's great failures came because of his prosperity. Success is a greater temptation than hardship.
10. David didn't receive mercy, because he showed no mercy.
11. David truly humbled himself and repented of his sins and continued to be used of the Lord.
12. Although God totally forgave David, there were consequences to his sins that cost him and his family dearly.

These lessons I've learned through David encouraged me to continue on in hard times and have saved me much heartache. I'm better off because of what I've learned through the good and bad experiences of David. I'm so thankful to the Lord for recording all of these things for my instruction. And I pray that you, too, will benefit greatly from the truths revealed in this study guide.

Everyone can learn through their own mistakes. I certainly have. But I've discovered a better way. That is to learn through someone else's mistakes. I pray the Lord will use these truths to enrich your life and cause you to prosper in the Lord as never before.

Receive Jesus as Your Savior

Choosing to receive Jesus Christ as your Lord and Savior is the most important decision you'll ever make!

God's Word promises *"that if thou shalt confess with thy mouth the Lord Jesus, and shalt believe in thine heart that God hath raised him from the dead, thou shalt be saved. [10] For with the heart man believeth unto righteousness; and with the mouth confession is made unto salvation"* (Rom. 10:9-10). *"For whosoever shall call upon the name of the Lord shall be saved"* (Rom. 10:13).

By His grace, God has already done everything to provide salvation. Your part is simply to believe and receive.

Pray out loud, "Jesus, I confess that You are my Lord and Savior. I believe in my heart that God raised You from the dead. By faith in Your Word, I receive salvation now. Thank You for saving me!"

The very moment you commit your life to Jesus Christ, the truth of His Word instantly comes to pass in your spirit. Now that you're born again, there's a brand-new you!

It doesn't really matter whether you felt anything or not when you prayed to receive the Lord and His Spirit. If you believed in your heart that you received, then God's Word promises that you did. *"Therefore I say unto you, What things soever ye desire, when ye pray, believe that ye receive them, and ye shall have them"* (Mark 11:24). God always honors His Word. Believe it!

Please contact me and let me know that you've prayed to receive Jesus as your Savior or be filled with the Holy Spirit. I would like to rejoice with you and help you understand more fully what has taken place in your life. *Welcome to your new life!*

Receive the Holy Spirit

As His child, your loving heavenly Father wants to give you the supernatural power you need to live this new life.

"For every one that asketh receiveth; and he that seeketh findeth; and to him that knocketh it shall be opened...how much more shall your heavenly Father give the Holy Spirit to them that ask him?" (Luke 11:10 and 13).

All you have to do is ask, believe, and receive!

Pray, "Father, I recognize my need for Your power to live this new life. Please fill me with Your Holy Spirit. By faith, I receive it right now! Thank You for baptizing me! Holy Spirit, You are welcome in my life!"

Congratulations—now you're filled with God's supernatural power!

Some syllables from a language you don't recognize will rise up from your heart to your mouth (1 Cor. 14:14). As you speak them out loud by faith, you're releasing God's power from within and building yourself up in the spirit (1 Cor. 14:4). You can do this whenever and wherever you like!

It doesn't really matter whether you felt anything or not when you prayed to receive the Lord and His Spirit. If you believed in your heart that you received, then God's Word promises that you did. *"Therefore I say unto you, What things soever ye desire, when ye pray, believe that ye receive them, and ye shall have them"* (Mark 11:24). God always honors His Word. Believe it!

Please contact me and let me know that you've prayed to receive Jesus as your Savior or be filled with the Holy Spirit. I would like to rejoice with you and help you understand more fully what has taken place in your life. *Welcome to your new life!*

Andrew's Recommendations for Further Study in This Study Guide

THE SOVEREIGNTY OF GOD - LESSON 1.2

Item Code: L03-C   Single CD

THE TRUE NATURE OF GOD - LESSON 3.1

"I've tried to be the perfect person God expects me to be, but I just can't. I give up." "I know God loves me, but it seems like He never answers my prayers." "I do everything the Bible says I should, so why hasn't God blessed me like He promised?" "Is God schizophrenic? The Bible is full of nothing but contradictions." Questions and comments like these compelled Andrew to introduce the profoundly simple concepts found in this teaching. Often, human perspective and the mechanics of Christianity eclipse the true nature of God - the God who wants nothing more than to share an intimate friendship with His children. If you're wondering who God is, or if He cares, let Andrew show you The True Nature of God.

Item Code: 1002-C   5-CD series
Item Code: 318   Paperback

SELFISHNESS, THE BEACHHEAD OF SATAN - LESSON 3.1

Item Code: HT16-C   Single CD from the *How to Deal with Temptation* series

THE END OF SELF IS THE BEGINNING OF GOD - LESSON 3.1

Item Code: A22-C   Single CD from the *Faith Builders* series

UNGODLY ANGER'S SOURCE - LESSON 3.1

Item Code: K118-C   Single CD from the *Anger Management* series

SELF-CENTEREDNESS: THE SOURCE OF ALL GRIEF - LESSONS 3.1 & 14

Difficult situations have a way of revealing the heart. Extreme financial pressure, a broken family relationship, or the death of a loved one may be a crisis to one person, while to another, an opportunity to prove the power of God's Word. What's the difference? That's the question Andrew will answer in this book. He speaks straight to the heart of the matter and clearly teaches how two people facing the same set of pressing circumstances can respond very differently. You'll learn what the Bible means when it says "I am crucified with Christ: nevertheless I live; yet not I, but Christ liveth in me"? and how that knowledge can change the way you respond in a crisis. Love, joy, and peace can be yours, even in the worst of situations.

Item Code: 315   Booklet
Item Code: 3503-D   2 DVDs

WHO YOU ARE IN THE SPIRIT - LESSON 5

Item Code: E09-C   Single CD

SPIRIT, SOUL & BODY - LESSON 5

This teaching is a foundational truth that is essential for understanding how much God loves you and believing what He says about you in His Word. Each person is made up of three different parts: spirit, soul, and body. Learn how these three parts relate to God and to each other. At salvation your spirit is totally changed, but your soul and body is not yet redeemed. This series will teach you how to release the life that is already in your spirit, into your physical body and emotions.

Item Code: 1027-C 4-CD series   Item Code: 1027-D DVD series
Item Code: 318 Paperback   Item Code: 418 Companion study guide
Item Code: 701 Spanish paperback

HARNESSING YOUR EMOTIONS - LESSON 12

We all have emotions, but do they rule us or do we rule them? Psychologists and Christians alike agree that actions are the result of inner thoughts and feelings, emotions. But that is where the agreement ends. The Word says that sin is conceived in our emotions. If that is true, then the Word must also give us a way to harness our emotions. Andrew's teaching will present you with a new perspective on emotions.

Item Code: 1005-C   4-CD series
Item Code: 1005-D   DVD series
Item Code: 313   Paperback

CHRISTIAN SURVIVAL KIT - LESSON 12

This series is a verse-by-verse teaching from John, chapters 14, 15, and 16. These are Jesus' instructions to His disciples the night before His crucifixion. He knew what they would go through, and He told them what they needed to know to keep them from being overcome with grief during this trying time. The same things He spoke to them will work for us in our crisis situations. This series is a must for all Christians.

Item Code: 1001-C   16-CD series

HARDNESS OF HEART - LESSON 14

The Hardness of Heart series deals with the crisis, the cause, and the cure for a hardened heart. A hard heart is simply a heart that is more sensitive to other things than to God. It is caused by what we focus our attention on, and it dictates the level of unbelief in our lives.

Item Code: 1003-C   4-CD series
Item Code: 1003-D   DVD series
Item Code: 303   Paperback

HOW TO PREPARE YOUR HEART - LESSON 16

Item Code: 1010-C   3-CD series

THE POSITIVE MINISTRY OF THE HOLY SPIRIT - LESSON 17.2

On the night before His crucifixion, Jesus spoke to His disciples and told them that He would send them the Holy Spirit: the Comforter. The ministry of the Holy Spirit is a comforting ministry, not a ministry of condemnation. Discern the difference between your conscience and the Holy Spirit. Another function of the Holy Spirit is to convince believers of their right standing in Jesus Christ and their authority over the devil. Once you receive this positive ministry, you will praise God for your imputed righteousness and the devil's defeat.

Item Code: 1020-C   5-CD series
Item Code: 3214-D   DVD series